AF716840

CARBON FINANCE

A RISK MANAGEMENT VIEW

CARBON FINANCE
A RISK MANAGEMENT VIEW

MARTIN HELLMICH
Deloitte Audit Analytics, Germany

RÜDIGER KIESEL
University Duisburg-Essen, Germany

World Scientific

NEW JERSEY • LONDON • SINGAPORE • BEIJING • SHANGHAI • HONG KONG • TAIPEI • CHENNAI • TOKYO

Published by

World Scientific Publishing Europe Ltd.

57 Shelton Street, Covent Garden, London WC2H 9HE

Head office: 5 Toh Tuck Link, Singapore 596224

USA office: 27 Warren Street, Suite 401-402, Hackensack, NJ 07601

Library of Congress Cataloging-in-Publication Data
Names: Hellmich, Martin, author. | Kiesel, Rüdiger, 1962– author.
Title: Carbon finance : a risk management view / Martin Hellmich, Deloitte Audit Analytics, Germany, Rüdiger Kiesel, University Duisburg-Essen, Germany.
Description: Hackensack, NJ : World Scientific, [2022] | Includes bibliographical references and index.
Identifiers: LCCN 2021035089 | ISBN 9781800611016 (hardcover) | ISBN 9781800611023 (ebook) | ISBN 9781800611030 (ebook other)
Subjects: LCSH: Emissions trading. | Climate change mitigation--Economic aspects | Risk management--Mathematical models. | Finance--Mathematical models. | Federated database systems.
Classification: LCC HC79.P55 H45 2022 | DDC 363.738/746--dc23
LC record available at https://lccn.loc.gov/2021035089

British Library Cataloguing-in-Publication Data
A catalogue record for this book is available from the British Library.

Cover design by Andrea Wöhr, Erwinstraße 5c, 79102 Freiburg; layout inspired by the artwork *Prometheus Bound* by Barnett Newman.

Copyright © 2022 by World Scientific Publishing Europe Ltd.

All rights reserved. This book, or parts thereof, may not be reproduced in any form or by any means, electronic or mechanical, including photocopying, recording or any information storage and retrieval system now known or to be invented, without written permission from the Publisher.

For photocopying of material in this volume, please pay a copying fee through the Copyright Clearance Center, Inc., 222 Rosewood Drive, Danvers, MA 01923, USA. In this case permission to photocopy is not required from the publisher.

For any available supplementary material, please visit
https://www.worldscientific.com/worldscibooks/10.1142/Q0325#t=suppl

Desk Editors: Nimal Koliyat/Michael Beale/Shi Ying Koe

Typeset by Stallion Press
Email: enquiries@stallionpress.com

To my parents, Marieluise and Peter Hellmich
Martin Hellmich

To my parents, Lydia and Siegfried Kiesel
Rüdiger Kiesel

Prometheus Bound, 1952, Barnett Newman.

Copyrights: © Museum Folkwang Essen — ARTOTHEK;
© Barnett Newman Foundation/VG Bild-Kunst, Bonn 2021.

Prometheus Bound

The 3.35 m high work by the American painter Barnett Newman (1905–1970) towers above every observer. Both the subject of Prometheus, the 'forethought' (from the Ancient Greek: Προμηθεύς), and the context of the work's genesis build a bridge to the narrative of the presented book.

In his book *Against the Gods: The Remarkable Story of Risk* (1996), Peter L. Bernstein expressed the idea that humanity is not at the mercy of nature but can actively position itself by anticipating risks.

The Titan Prometheus taught mankind and gave them fire by means of a ruse. He is considered the creator of human civilisation. For his trickery and deception of Zeus, Prometheus was punished with bondage and torture. The ancient tragedy of Aeschylus describes this punishment in *Prometheus Bound.* The motif has been reproduced many times in art history, mostly depicting the moment the defenceless Prometheus pays for his transgression under the torment of the eagle forever pecking at his liver.

Barnett Newman's interpretation of the theme illuminates the aspect of the end of passive suffering.

In 1952, Barnett Newman created *Prometheus Bound* as a sombre self-representation of an artist at the mercy of critics. A year earlier, Newman's second solo exhibition in New York had been torn apart by the critics, and many companions turned their backs on him. A severe heart attack also weakened him physically and Newman considered giving up his artistic career. It was not until 1958, with the landmark exhibition at the Museum of Modern Art, that he received recognition for his works, with which he went down in art history as the leading representative of Abstract Expressionism.

In his work *Prometheus Bound*, the painter depicts the exact moment when the crushing stasis of the status quo ends. The burden still seems overwhelming, but a new beginning is already announced. It is the awareness of being able to act in the face of overwhelming circumstances.

Dr. Caroline Li-Li Yi
Art Historian

Preface

Man vergißt, das frühere Bildung des Menschengeschlechts die Waldungen verdrängt und daß der umschaffende Geist der Nationen der Erde allmählich den Schmuck raubt.[1]

— Alexander von Humboldt, 1849

Climate change and the transition to a low-carbon economy create both risks and opportunities for the financial sector.[2]

— Governor Lael Brainard, Fed, 2021

In his book *Against The Gods — The Remarkable Story of Risk*,[3] Peter L. Bernstein states as follows: 'What is it that distinguishes the thousands of years of history from what we think of as modern times? The revolutionary idea that defines the boundary between modern times and the past is the mastery of risk: the notion that the future is more than a whim of the gods and that men and women are not passive before nature.'

Currently, humanity faces the greatest risk of all times — Climate Change — but until recently we have seen only a few meaningful attempts to manage this risk. Have we gone passive on risk management? Are we thrown back to the whim of the gods facing extreme weather we cannot handle? Snowstorms, floods, droughts that stretch and even outlast vital parts of our infrastructure have hit humanity

[1] Ansichten 1849, Bd. 2.
[2] Speech at the 2021 IIF U.S. Climate Finance Summit, February. 18, 2021.
[3] John Wiley & Sons, 1996.

as never before — humanity is not able to implement a proper strategy to handle these risks.

We face a risk-management problem with many features of deep uncertainty. But as for all stochastic problems, we should develop a risk-management strategy with meaningful hedges. This is in contrast to a deterministic problem, for which we develop a strategy and suffer through unforeseen events. The purpose of this book is to present and discuss risk-management strategies for climate change.

We use *Carbon Finance* as a collective term for all forms of financial activities directed at limiting climate change and adapting to its likely consequences. Developing strategies and preparing actions that serve this purpose requires in-depth knowledge of the complex interactions between human actions and the state of the natural environment, the dynamic interlinkages between economic activities in individual sectors and regions, and the opportunities and challenges brought about by technological change.

The data that confer this information often do not come in a standardised form that easily lends itself to economic and statistical analysis. Rather, they arrive in huge quantities in a large variety of formats and often at an enormous speed. This calls for the application of state-of-the-art techniques for storing data, establishing the connectivity of mutually related items, and preprocessing data for analytical purposes.

So, this text offers a unique blend of economic modelling, statistical analysis, data handling, and financial analysis in the handling of carbon finance and the associated carbon risks. We try to think of these problems from a risk-management point of view as the *rote Faden* of our book. Typically, risk managers see challenges as opportunities, and we will approach our analysis in this spirit.

The book has arisen out of our professional work and academic teaching. R. K. has given courses on topics from *Carbon Finance* at the University Duisburg-Essen, NTNU Trondheim, Oslo University, and Mysore University, and always benefited from discussions with students. Many colleagues discussed the topics with us, in particular Andrej Bajic, Frank Bauer, Richard Biegler-König, Reik Börger, T. S. Devaraja, Stein-Erik Fleten, Sikandar Siddiqui, and Sunil D. Sousa.

R. K. spent many joyful hours with Fred-Espen Benth, Florentina Paraschiv, and Luca Taschini in vivid conversations, not always only on carbon finance.

The book would not have been possible without the help of the Python wizards Andrej Bajic and Alex Blasberg, who always produced any analysis we could think of. Kateryna Chekriy was very helpful in generating the LaTeX files, and Ulrike Keller provided many of the graphs and figures.

N. H. Bingham has given the manuscript the final touches in terms of proper use of the English language.

R. K. is very grateful to Una and Roman for spending a social–medicine–climate science lockdown with him. Una also read parts of the manuscript and made inspiring comments.

R. K. thanks Li-Li for giving him so much inspiration, support, and love.

M. H. wants to express his profound gratitude to Gabriele for providing unfailing support throughout the process of researching and writing this book. The double challenge of doing in-depth research and managing his daily professional workload would not have been possible without her.

About the Authors

Martin Hellmich is Deloitte-Partner and Co-Leader of the Deloitte FSI Audit Garage. His key responsibilities encompass IT and risk management services for central banks, financial institutions, auditors and regulatory authorities with focus on Big Data infrastructures and AI solutions. Since 2013, he has been Advisor and Project Manager for the Common European Pricing Hub (CEPH), which is responsible for the valuation of all eligible non-ABS securities in the Eurosystem. Since 2018, he has been working on the Financial Big Data Cluster, a decentralized European data and infrastructure ecosystem for financial market data in accordance with GAIA-X principles. His focus is on the application of privacy-enhancing techniques, such as federated learning and multi-party computation-enabling institutions to collaboratively gain insights from data or to share data while enhancing data security. Another one of his main activities is the development of data-centered approaches for the integration of ESG and carbon risk in risk management decisions and the development of trading infrastructures to ensure transparency and market integrity in the developing carbon credit markets.

From 2012 to 2017, Martin was a Full-Time Professor for Risk Management and Regulation at the Frankfurt School of Finance and Management. His lectures and research cover risk management and regulation, quantitative finance and financial mathematics, financial markets and products. He has publications in several leading quantitative journals on Credit Risk Modelling, Portfolio Management, Strategic Asset Allocation, and Derivative Products.

For more than 15 years, he has been working in a variety of roles in risk management, portfolio management, and derivatives trading and sales for investment banking companies, such as Allianz Group, Barclays, and Cantor Fitzgerald Europe.

Rüdiger Kiesel heads the Chair for 'Energy Trading and Financial Services' and is Executive Director of the 'House of Energy Markets and Finance' at the University Duisburg-Essen. Previously, he has been Director of the Institute for Mathematical Finance at the University of Ulm. He also held positions for actuarial science and financial mathematics at Birkbeck College, University of London, the London School of Economics (full-time and visiting), and the Department of Mathematics at the University of Oslo (as a Visiting Professor). He has served as a member on the boards of several academic associations.

His main research areas are quantitative climate finance, modelling of electricity markets, valuation and hedging of derivatives (interest rate, credit- and energy-related), risk management for financial and energy-related institutions, and methods of risk transfer and structuring of risk (securitisation).

He is co-author of the Springer Finance monograph *Risk-Neutral Valuation* (now in its second edition) and has authored more than 70 published research papers. He is a frequent speaker at international conferences and has also organised several conferences, summer schools, and practitioner seminars. Professor Kiesel also consults financial institutions, utilities, and regulators on (credit- and energy-) risk management, derivative pricing models, and asset allocation.

Contents

Part I

Carbon Finance — Fundamentals

Part I discusses the physical effects of climate change and what the international community is doing about it. A particular emphasis in our exposition is on the role of uncertainty and, of course, its impact and how to manage it. We present the fundamental aspects of climate change and the contemporary response of the global community. We review the background on climate economics with market-based instruments as our main focus. Then we turn to the definition of climate risk and possible metrics to measure it. Finally, we provide the theoretical framework for the more empirical analysis in Part III.

Chapter 1

Climate Change

1.1 Climate Change Is Happening

1.1.1 *Physical Evidence*

The climate of the Earth is warming at an increasingly rapid rate and will, with a high probability, continue to do so for the next decades to come. The global temperature has risen, at a rate faster than any found in the past, by about 1.1°C on average since the pre-industrial levels. 2020 was Europe's hottest year on record, and globally, it tied with 2016 as the hottest year on record (see Hook (2020)). Datasets from National Oceanic and Atmospheric Administration and NASA show that the five (10, 20) warmest years on global record have all come since 2010 (1998, 1995). Even in comparison with a recent period (1981–2010), the global average temperature in 2020 was 0.6°C higher, with Europe even 1.6°C above the 1981–2010 average, according to the assessment by the Science Advisory Group of the UN Climate Action Summit 2019 (United in Science, 2020).

In addition, the year 2020 saw temperatures in parts of the Arctic and northern Siberia reach record levels — more than 6°C higher than their historic average. Extreme temperatures, such as 38°C in June, were recorded in northern Russia inside the Arctic Circle.

Thus, average changes come with more dramatic changes at the extremes. Temperature distributions are shifting to the right (medians are below the average) and showing heavy tails (increasing probabilities of extreme outcomes). As in financial markets, where modelling of returns can no longer (if ever) be done with

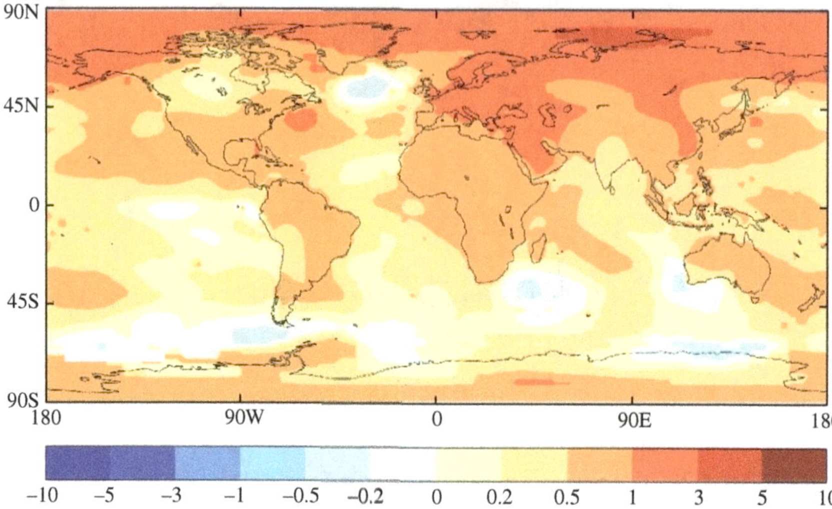

Fig. 1.1. 2016–2020 five-year average temperature anomalies relative to the 1981–2010 average (Data from NASA GISTEMP v4., up to July 2020).
Source: United in Science (2020).

the Normal (Gaussian) distribution, heavy-tailed distributions and extreme-value theory (as done for decades in assessing the height of dikes as protection against high tides and violent storms (Embrechts *et al.*, 1997) need to be used. The effect is that the average day is hotter (as the mean moves), and extremely hot days are becoming more likely (as the distributional tails become heavy).

Figure 1.1 demonstrates the shift in temperatures and United in Science (2020) data also indicate that the global sea level rise is accelerating from around 3 mm/year in 1990 to almost 5 mm/year in 2020. This is about 2.5 times the rate for the period 1901–1990. As a quadratic function fits the annual data quite well, the increase is linear. According to United in Science (2020), the increase is driven by a greater loss of the ice sheets, besides the expansion by ocean waters due to global warming.

The global average temperature increase will have an impact on the frequency and severity of climate hazards around the world. The most severe climate science scenario (RCP 8.5 scenario) implies already an average temperature increase with a local variability of 1.5–5°C, with a particular exposure of the arctic.

Extreme precipitation and hurricanes are expected to hit exposed areas around the world (Southeast US, parts of Southeast Asia) more often and harder. Lethal heat waves[1] will occur with substantial annual event probability above 60%. Droughts will extend spatially and in duration. Renewable freshwater supplies will be severely affected. South Africa, Australia, the Mediterranean, and parts of the United States and Mexico will suffer from a decrease in mean annual surface water supply.

So, the world is in the middle of a climate change process. According to the definition of the Intergovernmental Panel on Climate Change (IPCC) (2007), climate change 'refers to a change in the state of the climate that can be identified (e.g., by using statistical tests) by changes in the mean and/or the variability of its properties and that persists for an extended period, typically decades or longer.' A key additional observation is that not only the mean and variance of relevant distributions but also the heaviness is changing. This translates to an increase in frequency and severity of extreme observations. Attending to changes in the tails of distribution of relevant risks is the main topic in risk management. Thus, it is very natural to discuss climate change and its consequences from a risk-management point of view.

1.1.2 *Risk Perception*

Global warming has become a mainstream topic in public and academic discussions in the last few years. The Fridays for Future movement has taken off, and pre-COVID-19, its Friday and other events have attracted many students (and older ages). A flurry of books discuss all aspects of climate change and emphasise the need for action (to name a few, Gates (2021); Mann (2021); Helm (2020); Cullenward and Victor (2020), and ours, of course).

In the last two decades, climate change has become a steadily reported and a highly politicised media topic (see Engle *et al.* (2020) for the construction of a Wall Street Journal Climate Change News Index and Faccini and Matin (2021a) for a similar news index). Particularly on the risk of climate change, there is a strong

---

[1]Three-day events during which average daily maximum temperature exceeds the survivability threshold for a healthy human being resting in the shade.

interconnection of media, politics, and public opinion (see Boykoff (2013) for a comprehensive overview and the role of academia). As Barkemeyer *et al.* (2017) reports, a substantial increase in coverage of climate change could be identified in the last decades with clear differences between countries. Unfortunately, especially in the US, the media coverage of climate change was rather limited due to political, economical, and structural reasons. Also, the norm of balancing gave climate sceptics in the US a disproportional share of media coverage (see Boykoff (2013) and Park (2018)).

The World Economic Forum (WEF) 16th Global Risks Report World Economic Forum (2021) sees, for the first time in history, a domination of environmental risks. Environmental concerns dominate the long-term risks by likelihood for the WEF's multi-stakeholder community. Three of the top five risks by impact are environmental. Environmental risks are top in short- and long-term risks in the ranking of the Global Shapers Community (the WEF's younger constituents).

The WEF Risk Report Global Risk Landscape (World Economic Forum, 2021), illustrated in Figure 1.2, is dominated by climate risks. These risks also dominate by likelihood and in terms of impact.

Still, the risk that climate change constitutes is not fully perceived by the general public. Factors contributing to this may be a lack of perception of the danger, a lack of clarity of information, and high complexity. In addition, the temporal and geographical distances of the cause–effect mechanism contribute to the difficulty in appreciating climate risk.

1.1.3 *Scientific Evidence*

The scientific discussion of climate change is institutionalised by the IPCC, which is the international body for assessing the science related to climate change. The IPCC was set up in 1988 by the World Meteorological Organisation (WMO) and the United Nations Environment Programme (UNEP) to provide policymakers with regular assessments of the scientific basis of climate change, its impacts and future risks, and options for adaptation and mitigation. The IPCC is currently preparing its Sixth Assessment Report (AR6), which is due later in 2021. The Fifth Assessment Report (AR5) provided a review of the state of scientific knowledge relevant to climate change (see IPCC (2014)). It acknowledges clear evidence

Fig. 1.2. The WEF Global Risks Landscape.
Source: WEF Risk Report (2021).

of human influence in warming of the atmosphere and ocean, in changes in the global water cycle, in reductions in snow and ice, in global mean sea level rise, and in changes to the frequency and magnitude of climate extremes. In particular, the assessment report states as follows (AR5, p. 4):

'Anthropogenic greenhouse gas (GHG) emissions have increased since the pre-industrial era, driven largely by economic and population growth, and are now higher than ever. This has led to atmospheric concentrations of carbon dioxide, methane and nitrous oxide that are unprecedented in at least the last 800,000 years. Their effects, together with those of other anthropogenic drivers, have been detected throughout the climate system and are extremely likely to have been the dominant cause of the observed warming since the mid-20th century.'

CO_2[2] accounts for around 75% of human-generated global warming. Additionally, there are further significant contributions by methane (some being released now from former permafrost in Siberia), nitrous oxides, and hydrofluorocarbons (HFCs).

The steady rise of GHG emissions can be traced back to the start of the industrial revolution. Compared with pre-industrial times, the increase of these emissions is so significant that it is highly unlikely that it is happening as part of a natural process. A higher rate of emissions of GHG expands the concentration of GHG in the atmosphere, which allows more infrared radiation from the Earth to be reflected back to the surface of the Earth, which pushes the surface temperature upwards.

There is strong evidence that cumulative CO_2 emissions are directly linked (analysis shows an almost linear relationship) to global warming. As pointed out, the overall stock of CO_2 in the atmosphere is the relevant quantity.

The IPCC Report AR5 (IPCC, 2014) gives a wide range of temperature forecasts and provides further scientific evidence to better understand climate change and possible responses to climate change. Besides the detailed discussion of causes and consequences of global warming, the report also presents several reference scenarios linking CO_2 emission pathways to the rise of global temperatures.

[2]As CO_2 is the main source of GHGs, we will not distinguish in our notation between CO_2, GHG, and CO_2e (i.e., CO_2 equivalents).

Should current emission trends continue, global average temperature would likely rise to 3.5°C above pre-industrial levels by 2100. A temperature rise of this magnitude will push critical natural carbon sinks (including permafrost or the Amazon rainforest) beyond dangerous tipping points, initiating harmful feedback loops in the climate system (such as ice loss, rapid release of methane, and changes in ocean circulation). This will amplify the impacts of anthropogenic emissions. Physical impacts such as fires, flooding, and storms will continue to increase in frequency and intensity, leading to vast ecosystem and human impacts. From a socioeconomic perspective, the following five systems are directly affected by climate change: liability and workability, food, physical assets, infrastructure, and natural capital.

By now, it is already evident that the world is edging closer to several of these tipping points. A point in case is the weakening of the Gulf Stream system, for which new evidence was presented recently (RealClimate, 2015; Caesar *et al.*, 2021). Other climatic tipping points we are at risk of crossing are the destruction of the Amazon rainforest, the melting and breaking up of the Arctic and Antarctic sea ice, and the melting of the Siberian permafrost. A theoretical discussion of these tipping points (or thresholds) is given in Steffen (2018). We will discuss the need for including the possibility of crossing such thresholds in the economic analysis in Chapter 3.

Another disturbing fact is the loss of biodiversity. Biodiversity is traditionally defined as the variety of life on Earth in all its forms. It comprises the number of species, their genetic variation, and the interaction of these life forms within complex ecosystems. In a UN report published recently (IPBES, 2020), scientists warned that one million species — out of an estimated total of eight million — are threatened with extinction, many within decades. It takes millions of years for ecosystems to recover from such an event.

1.2 Global Risk Management

1.2.1 *International Climate Negotiations: Conference of the Parties (COP)*

The global community started formally in 1992 with the United Nations Framework Convention on Climate Change (UNFCCC) signed by 154 states at the United Nations Conference on Environment and Development (UNCED) in Rio 1992 (also known as Earth summit) to address climate change.[3] The UNFCCC is a framework for international cooperation to combat climate change by limiting average global temperature increases and the resulting climate change. It is left to the COP to develop a legal framework and set mandatory goals. By 1995, countries launched negotiations to strengthen the global response to climate change and, two years later, adopted the Kyoto Protocol. The Kyoto Protocol is the first implementation of measures to limit global warming and legally binds developed country parties to emission-reduction targets. It aimed to establish obligations for developed countries to reduce their greenhouse gas emissions during the time period 2008–2021 (first period) and then in a second period 2013–2020 under an amendment, which was agreed upon during the Doha conference in 2012. The targets of the Kyoto Protocol should be primarily met through national measures. Also, the carbon market started as the Kyoto Protocol introduced three market-based mechanisms, namely emission trading, clean development mechanism, and joint implementation. Unfortunately, there were no real sanctions for countries in case of a breach of obligations as many international flexibility options are allowed and future obligations as a compensation remained unspecified.

Already, during the 2010 conference in Cancún, an agreement on limiting future global warming at 2°C was established. This was formalised during the 2015 Paris conference, which established several new approaches (see Section 1.2.2). The 2015 Paris Agreement marks the latest step in the evolution of the UN climate change regime and builds on the work undertaken under the convention.

In the following, we present a timeline of COPs pointing out the most important decisions taken.

1.2.2 *The Paris Agreement*

The Paris Agreement was adopted by 196 parties at the COP21 in December 2015 in Paris as a legally binding treaty on measures to

[3]Scientific evidence about man-made causes for climate change was presented at the World Climate Conference, 1979, in Geneva.

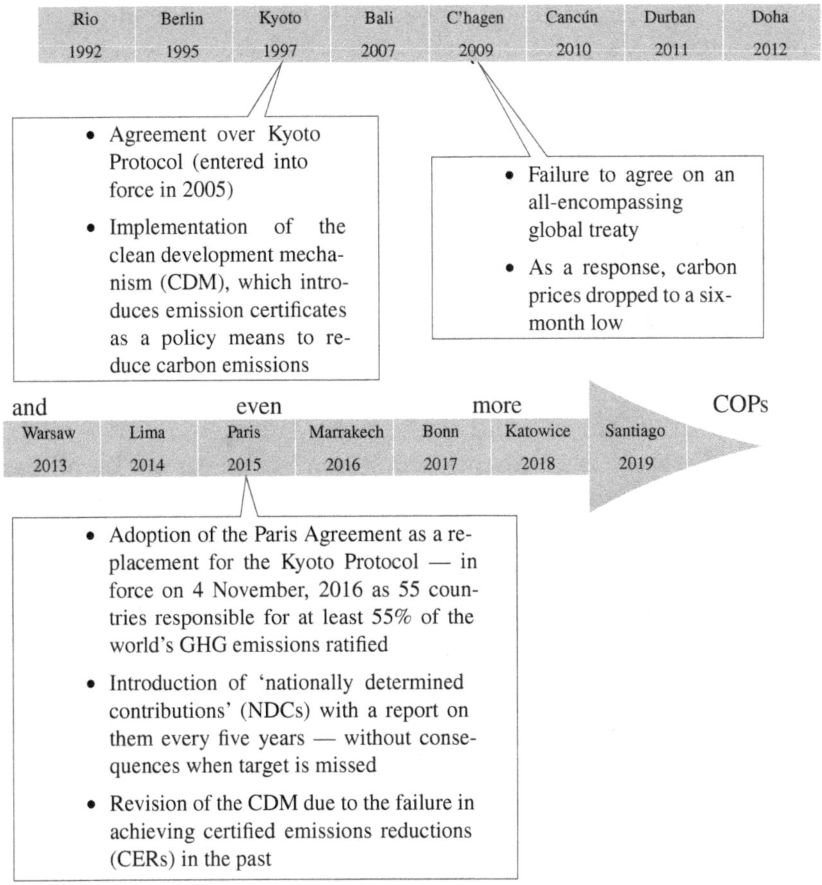

combat climate change. It went into force in November 2016 after 55 countries, which account for more than 55% of total GHG emissions, had ratified it. All nations commit to undertake ambitious efforts to combat climate change and adapt to its effects, with enhanced support to assist developing countries. The Paris Agreement requires all parties to put forward their best efforts through nationally determined contributions (NDCs) and to strengthen these efforts in the years ahead. With the NDCs, countries also communicate their adaption and mitigations actions.

The aim of the Paris Agreement is to keep the global temperature rise this century well below 2°C (preferably below 1.5°C) and to strengthen the ability of countries to deal with the impacts of climate change. The peak of global GHG emissions should occur as soon as possible, and a climate neutral world should be achieved by mid-century. In order to achieve its goals, the Paris Agreement also provides a framework for financial, technical, and capacity-building support among countries. This should support technology development and transfer for both improving resilience to climate change and reducing GHG emissions as well as capacity-building actions to deal with challenges brought by climate change. Developed countries provide financial assistance to countries less well endowed.

The Paris Agreement also implements a *global stocktake*, which will take place in 2023 for the first time and then every five years thereafter. Collective progress in the process of achieving the goals of the Paris Agreement will be assessed by using the best available scientific methods. Such a stocktaking then serves to inform all parties and enforce an updating and enhancing of methods and support measures. Its outcome will inform parties in updating and enhancing their actions and support international cooperation. The Paris Agreement also puts emphasis on public participation by increasing public awareness (a goal that has been achieved during the last couple of years), public participation, and public access to information. As in many recent regulatory efforts, the role of transparency has been strengthened.[4] The Paris Agreement requires that information on mitigation, adaption, and support reported is subject to international technical expert review.

In an updated special report on global warming (IPCC, 2019), several pathways to reaching the 1.5°C target are presented. Figure 1.3 shows illustrative pathways of the timing of net-zero CO_2 emissions. The report also discusses the range of potential mitigation strategies. It highlights the wide variety of projected energy use, population developments, economic growth, and consequences for financial markets. This variety is an important issue which we will focus on in more detail when discussing stress tests (see Chapter 12).

Any serious effort to achieve the goals of the Paris Agreement is bound to have significant economic side effects, and many of these effects are already measurable. The discussion of these, particularly towards the energy and finance sectors, will be the main focus in the chapters to come.

---

[4]See Hull (2018), Chapter 15 for transparency in Banking Basel regulation.

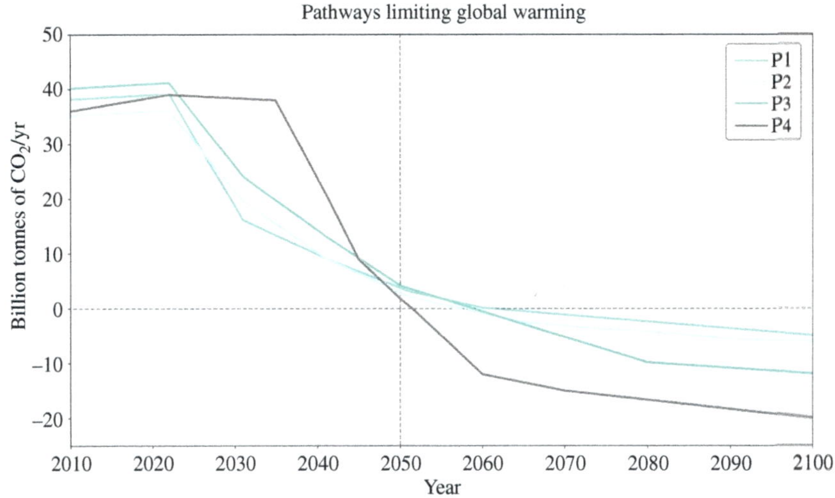

Fig. 1.3. Exemplary pathways for global net CO_2 emissions as in IPCC (2019).

1.2.3 *The Role of Finance*

The Paris Agreement emphasises the responsibility of developed countries to provide financial resources to assist developing countries in implementing the objectives of the agreement. It also asks developed countries to mobilise climate finance from a wide variety of sources, including public and private funds. The term *Climate Finance* is applied to local, national, or transnational financial flows from public, private, and alternative sources to support mitigation and adaptation actions that will address climate change. Mostly, these flows are (as before) from developed to less-developed countries. Climate finance is critical to addressing climate change because large-scale investments are required to significantly reduce emissions and put in place adaption measures.

To facilitate the provision of climate finance, the Paris Agreement established a financial mechanism for developed country parties (Annex II parties) to provide financial resources. The Global Environment Facility and the Green Climate Fund are the main operating entities of the financial mechanism. In addition, the Standing Committee on Finance (SCF) was established to, among other tasks, support the COP in the measurement, reporting, and verification of support provided to developing countries. It is important that transparency is established in how these financial resources are mobilised, transferred, and accessed. Thus, the SCF organises an annual forum on climate finance, provides a periodic review of the financial mechanism, and prepares a biennial assessment and overview of climate finance flows.[5]

At COP16, the Green Climate Fund (GCF) was established as the operating entity of the financial mechanism of the convention. The GCF will support projects, programmes, policies, and other activities in developing country parties. The governance of the GCF is in the hands of the GCF board, which was established by the 194 sovereign governments party of the UNFCCC. The board is independent and guided by the COP. It ensures a balanced governance between developed and developing countries and aims for consensus-based decisions.

Currently, the project portfolio of the GCF shows 158 approved projects in 117 developing countries with USD 7.2 billion financing from the GCF and USD 15.7 billion of co-financing. The funds are invested in adaption (24%), mitigation (44%), and cross cutting (32%). Cross-cutting projects refer to projects that both reduce future GHG emissions and improve the resilience of industries or communities.

1.3 Analysis

1.3.1 *Uncertainty*

Climate change is characterised by a multitude of risks and uncertainties. According to AR5 of the IPCC, *uncertainty* denotes a cognitive state of incomplete knowledge that results from a lack of information and/or from disagreement about what is known or even knowable. To represent uncertainty, probability distributions and confidence intervals may be used. *Risk* refers to the potential for adverse effects on lives, livelihoods, health status, economic, social and cultural assets, services (including environmental), and infrastructure due to uncertain states of the world. Experts will normally be in agreement regarding

[5]Updated information can be obtained from the climate finance data portal of the UNFCCC, https://unfccc.int/climatefinance?home.

estimates of the likelihood of its occurrence and its resulting consequences.

In the context of our discussion, we will be more specific and distinguish more precisely between several degrees of uncertainty. A *Risk* is a situation where we are able to specify a unique distribution (or probability $\mathbb{P}$) and face the outcome of random events drawn from that distribution. This is a situation we typically encounter for well-established and liquid financial markets (equity or fixed-income). In the case of *ambiguity*, we are facing several possible distributions (or probabilities $\mathbb{P}_1, \mathbb{P}_2, \ldots$), which may come from a parametric family. Typically, this is the situation for less liquid financial markets, such as credit markets, or the assessment of operational risk. Finally, in the case of (*Knightian*) *uncertainty*, we are not able to specify a precise distribution (or probability $\mathbb{P}$). In fact, we may not even be able to name all the possible outcomes.

Recently, concepts such as the black (Taleb, 2008) and green swan (Bolton *et al.*, 2020) have been developed. These concepts coincide in that (i) they are unexpected given past events, (ii) they have an extreme impact, and (iii) they can be rationalised by conceptional frameworks after the event. In addition, (iv) green swan events will almost certainly materialise, although it is not clear how, when, and where they will occur, and (v) green swan events may be irreversible and systemic. Although these are illustrative concepts for extreme events on financial markets and with regard to climate change, we will stay in our more precise quantitative setting outlined above.

For the sake of exposure, we will use the term *uncertainty* in a broader sense in the descriptive part and will be more precise when discussing specific frameworks. Still, the quantification of climate risks in probabilistic statements involves high uncertainties regarding the probabilities of future developments/scenarios (Smith and Stern, 2011) and the range of possible scenarios. Therefore, quantitative approaches in academic and especially public discussion are highly controversial. Systematic modelling of the various levels of uncertainty has been largely lacking (see, for example, the classifications in the IPCC report, Kunreuther *et al.* (2014)). An attempt to frame aspects of climate change in a risk-management approach is already outlined in Kunreuther *et al.* (2012).

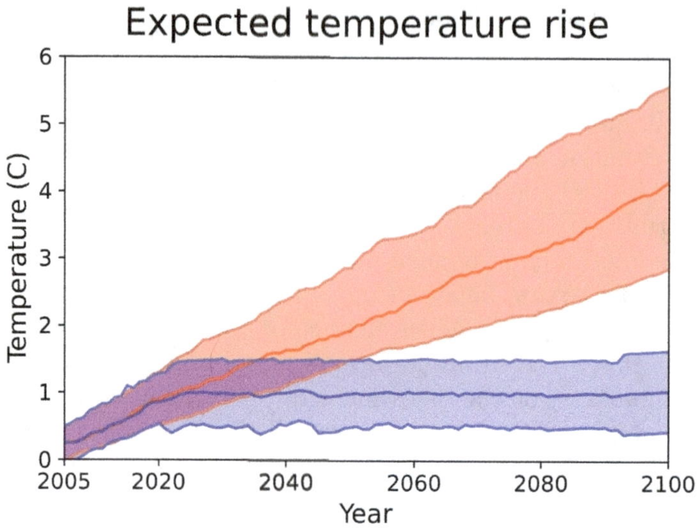

Fig. 1.4. Scenarios for temperature change as in IPCC (2014).

As an example for the profound uncertainties, let us have a further look at the AR5 report (IPCC, 2014). Figure 1.4 shows global average surface temperature change from 2000 to 2100 for two reference scenarios. It is evident that there is a wide variation in the temperature development within the scenarios. Thus, in the analysis of such scenarios, the size of the confidence intervals has to be taken into account.

The main challenges of a risk-management approach to climate change is the range and interaction of uncertainties involved and the dynamics of feedback effects. Through GHG emissions, global climate will vary, and the variation will translate into local effects. These effects may be specific hazards with physical damage, which may affect agriculture and infrastructure. Individual and societal financial harm will be done, which has direct and indirect socioeconomic impacts, and the socioeconomic response has to be taken into consideration. There is, however, widespread agreement that the impact of climate risk mitigation activities on key macroeconomic aggregates (e.g., GDP, inflation, and employment), and the sectoral composition/'industry mix' of the economies involved will be profound. Thus, climate policies can be viewed as risk-management tools and need to be evaluated as such.

1.3.2 *Probabilities of Temperature Increases*

For financial risk-management purposes, one is primarily concerned with containing the downside uncertainty, i.e., to place bounds on the potential losses or the amount by which the final value of a trading position falls short of the expected return. Thus, measures of risk that focus on the lower tail of the distribution of the random variable representing the final outcome are defined. Hence, mean and variance as measures of variability, which relate more to the centre of the distribution, are replaced by an assessment of the tails of the underlying distribution.

In a financial context, a well-known measure of tail risk is the value at risk (VaR) which quantifies a value that the potential future loss will not be exceeded with a defined confidence level α in a defined time period T. More formally, let X be a random variable that represents the change in value of some position during some trading period T. Then, we are looking for the largest number $q_{1-\alpha}$, such that the probability

$$\mathbb{P}(X \leq q_{1-\alpha}) = 1 - \alpha, \tag{1.1}$$

where $q_{1-\alpha}$ is the $(1 - \alpha)$-quantile of the distribution of X. Then, $-q_{1-\alpha}$ is the loss level that will not be exceeded with a probability of $\alpha\%$. We call

$$\mathrm{VaR}_\alpha(X) = -q_{1-\alpha}(X)$$

the VaR at confidence level α. For each risk type, VaR numbers are calculated with specific confidence levels and time periods, e.g., market risk of a liquid position may require a moderate confidence level and a short time period, while credit risk may have a high confidence level and a longer time horizon. Of course, these assessments are based on rich datasets and time horizons well short of the time horizon required to assess climate change (a fact that Mark Carney called the tragedy of the horizon (Carney, 2021)).

For illustration, let us apply a value-at-risk approach to limiting the increase of the global average temperature. For this purpose, we

Table 1.1. Probability of temperature increase higher than that in different scenarios (based on Table 6.3 in IPCC, 2014 WGIII).

CO_2e range in ppm	Temp. range	Prob. >1.5°C	Prob. >2°C	Prob. >3°C	Prob. >4°C
(RCP 2.6) 430–480	1.5–1.7	49–86	12–37	1–3	0–1
(RCP 4.5) 580–650	2.3–2.6	96–100	74–93	14–35	2–8
(RCP 6) 720–1000	3.1–3.7	100	97–100	55–83	14–39
(RCP 8.5) >1000	4.1–4.8	100	100	92–98	53–78

consider estimates of the full radiative forcing level in 2100, expressed in CO_2e[6] concentrations. Radiative-forcing levels are often used as goals in scenarios, and the RCPs have been formulated in terms of these indicators (Van Vuuren, 2011). The scenario categories were chosen to relate to the four RCPs, but the scenarios considered cover a substantial part of the literature (IPCC, 2014). Table 1.1 shows probabilities (in %) of temperature increase by 2100 relative to the average from 1850 to 1900. Stern (2010), Table 2.1, shows specific stabilisation levels, probabilities and likelihoods, which display comparable evidence.

One could use this table to ask the question 'What probability do I accept that the temperature by 2100 exceeds 4°C with all the consequences?' Given the effects of a global warming of this size, a 2% probability as in RCP 4.5 seems hardly acceptable. From a risk manager point of view, an immediate hedge is necessary. Unfortunately, the global community could not agree on a suitable hedging strategy so far.

1.3.3 *Reference Scenarios*

A widely used approach in risk management is to use scenario analysis. This is particularly the case for the analysis of unusual market conditions. As the value-at-risk concept relies on (estimated or empirical) distributions, it is a backward-looking approach and has to be accompanied by forward-looking assessments. Many of the most

[6] CO_2e refers to CO_2 equivalents and includes all GHG expressed in terms of CO_2 quantities.

severe financial disasters happened because of changing market conditions not seen before. Especially, after the financial crisis in 2009, stress tests have been employed. In addition, worst-case scenarios (extremely costly outcomes with a small but positive probability) need to be considered.

As climate risks are recognised as financial risks (at least within the finance community), it is natural to use the scenario approach in the context of climate change. These scenarios are based on a combination of integrated assessment models,[7] climate models, physical models, and global carbon cycles.

The most well-known of these models are the four representative concentration pathways (RCPs) defined for AR5 (WGI, see IPCC (2014)). They are defined in terms of their approximate total radiative forcing in 2100. They include one mitigation scenario with a low forcing level (RCP 2.6), two stabilisation scenarios (RCPs 4.5 and 6) and one with a high level (RCP 8.5), which has often been used to model a business-as-usual (BAU) GHG emission development.[8]

AR5 illustrates the consequences of the high-end scenarios in the report on physical effects as follows. For RCP 8.5, the situation looks dire — global temperatures could rise well above 4°C this century — substantially above the 1.5°C scientists regard as the safety limit. Sea level rises will overwhelm one to two billion people living in low-lying areas. Four billion people could be put at risk of water shortages. The surface of the Earth will change dramatically as the ice caps will melt entirely and the Amazon rainforest may die off. But even in RCP 2.6, the low-emission scenario, the hottest parts of the world will suffer serious declines in crop yields, but increases in fertility in other areas may offset this. We will see an increase in floods, droughts, and storms, but the damage remains manageable.

[7]Integrated Assessment Models (IAMs) simulate both future energy technologies and emissions. Their emission scenarios are subsequently used to run complex climate models that simulate how the climate might change in the future. The complexity of these models allows only a limited number of emission scenarios to be considered.

[8]RCP 8.5 was intended to represent the 90th percentile of no-mitigation scenarios available at around 2011.

For the upcoming IPCC AR6, additional forcing scenarios are being discussed. These scenarios are based on shared socioeconomic pathways (SSPs) (Riahi, 2017), which rely on assumptions on population, economic growth, and other socioeconomic factors. So, the SSPs cover differences, e.g., in technology development, access to education, urbanisation, resources availability, supply constraints, and drivers of demand, such as lifestyle changes. There are five narratives on socioeconomic trends that vary in the degree of global cooperation, sharing of resources, and energy use. SSP1 (sustainability-focused) and SSP5 (growth focused) envision optimistic trends with improving global education and health and a high-degree of cooperation. They separate themselves in their use of energy sources as SSP1 shifts towards sustainability, while SSP5 is based on an energy-driven fossil-fuel-based economy. SSP3 (resurgent nationalism) and SSP4 (increasing inequality) are more pessimistic in terms of global cooperation. There, besides a select few, fast-growing populations will have poor access to education and heath systems. SSP2 (continuation in historic patterns) relies on developments between the other groups. Each of the SSPs generates their own set of challenges towards mitigation and climate adaptation. To assess these, integrated assessment models (IAMs) are used to translate the socioeconomic conditions of the SSPs into estimates of future energy use and GHG emissions. Their scenarios show how GHG emissions vary in the SSPs based on how energy production, energy use, and economic activity vary and are changed to meet climate mitigation targets. By using shared policy assumptions, the scenarios also examine how quickly international collaboration on climate policy could occur within each SSP as well as respecting limitations imposed by the underlying assumptions around population growth, economic activity, and technological development in each pathway.

In our later analysis, we will refer to some of these scenarios when discussing the design of stress tests at systemic and individual firm levels.

1.3.4 *Resume*

As Tol (2019) puts it, 'International negotiations of climate policy confirm that it is difficult to agree on the provision on a global public good. After 20 years of trying, international climate policy has abandoned legally binding targets in favour of pledge and review centred on voluntary contributions.'

So, for various reasons discussed in several excellent texts on international cooperation and climate policy, we are still far away from a global risk-management process, or to quote Greta Thunberg, 'The house is on fire,'[9] but nobody is putting out the fire, at least not on a global level. In the following, we will turn to some of the burning rooms of the global house and discuss tools to manage the fire there.

[9]Speech at the World Economic Forum 2019.

Chapter 2

Climate Economics

2.1 Climate Change Policy

2.1.1 *Economic Tools*

GHG emissions are externalities in terms of climate economics and as such represent a market failure. An externality arises when the utility position of one entity (individual, household, firm, or state) depends on an activity performed by another entity. Any divergence between a market equilibrium and an optimum should be corrected by economic policy. In other words, the externalities should be internalised (see Endres (2011)). Of course, this aim is far too ambitious for most economic (and environmental) problems, but the analysis and attempt on correction will reveal structural causes for market failures, which could be resolved. In order to do so, the externality should be monetised, and the sum of private and external costs should be taken into account. The representation of an externality in terms of money is, as we will see, a highly complex question.

Climate change policy faces the serious complication that the accumulation of emissions in the atmosphere is relevant rather than the level of emissions in any time interval or the place of origin of emissions. Thus, the effects are governed by a flow-stock process on a long timescale. In addition, there is substantial uncertainty about the scale, interaction, and feedback of effects. The result of current emissions and policy measures will only be experienced in a distant future, which may also look very different due to irreversible consequences of crossing (unknown) tipping points (see Chapter 3).

So, climate policy faces a free-rider problem, and current generations are asked to make sacrifices to the benefit of — possibly richer — future generations.

A standard approach to pricing carbon as an externality is to use a Pigouvian tax and set the carbon price equal to the social cost of carbon (SCC), i.e., the expected present value of all utility loss from emitting one extra tonne of carbon today. However, key questions arise: What utility function and which social discount factor should be used?

The utility function needs to take environment, health, technological progress, and types of consumption into account. It also affects the intratemporal distribution of resources and efforts (between different people at the same time).

The choice of the social discount factor, however, affects the valuation of benefits accruing to different people at different times and addresses the intertemporal distribution (between generations). It is subject to a heated academic and public debate. Nordhaus (2007) describes the social discount factor as the most important decision variable in the context of climate policy proposals. Stern (2007b) uses a discount factor of 1.4% and receives a 10 times higher carbon price compared to that received by Nordhaus (2008), who proposes a discount factor of 5.5%. However, as Stern (2010) argues, social discount rates are endogenous and depend on ethical values, paths that result from climate change and investment choices. Market rates thus may not represent all aspects of importance for policies towards climate change.

In addition, an increase in temperature will affect productivity and thus the economic growth rate. Burke *et al.* (2020) show empirically that overall economic productivity is nonlinear in temperature, with productivity peaking at an annual average temperature of 13°C and declining strongly at higher temperatures. Their results suggest that expected global economic losses are approximately linear in global mean temperature. Depending on which damage ratio estimate is used, the optimal carbon price varies widely. A damage ratio as in Nordhaus (2017) allows temperatures to rise above the targets of the Paris Agreement. Using the Burke *et al.* (2020) results, temperatures need to stay below 2°C.

As we have seen, the optimal carbon price is driven by ethical considerations (the utility discount rate and intergenerational inequality aversion), geophysical considerations (the transient climate response to cumulative emissions), and economic considerations (the level of economic activity and its trend rate of growth) as well as by the marginal effect of temperature on the damage ratio. Therefore, various modelling assumptions and parametrisation approaches for models result in a wide range of estimates for the optimal carbon price.

Given all these uncertainties, the Pigouvian approach was abandoned in favour of the stabilisation target, which is easier to understand (and communicate) by the IPCC, governments, and regulators. The objective now is to choose a cost-minimising time path for the carbon price that keeps average temperature always below a given ceiling. Since average temperature is a function of cumulative emissions, this corresponds to a cap on cumulative emissions or a carbon budget. A cap on cumulative emissions is also easier to enforce, as temperatures may show stochastic variations around a trend. From the stabilisation target, subsequent measures such as permissible flow of emissions and emission-reduction targets are inferred. Of course, this approach carries significant uncertainties as well. The climate sensitivity, i.e., the relation between the stock of GHG in the atmosphere and the increase in temperatures, has to be considered. General circulation models (GCM) of climate science try to shed light on this quantity. Using computationally intensive simulations (Monte Carlo analysis), probability distributions of outcome are produced, which by design have a high sensitivity to parameter values. Cost estimates are obtained by comparing model evaluation with and without a climate policy. It is obvious that cost estimates are only as good as the models and the accuracy of parameters used.

In a deterministic world, a carbon price would be essentially equivalent to a quantity and could be inferred from a given cap. However, in a setting which features risk and uncertainty, prices are highly sensitive to structural assumptions and carry risks from realising higher stocks (quantities) than anticipated, which leads to tail risks. Given all these uncertainties, we may have taken 'The Big Green Bet' (Gollier, 2020): We do not know the safe carbon budget, the future growth in emissions, the future size of abatement cost, and the costs of mitigation measures. Countries may engage in international free riding, and we may see carbon leakage if carbon pricing in some countries is uncertain (political risk). Climate policy may be done with a disproportional burden on poorer and developing countries. Already, there is the issue of climate colonialism, 'the domination of less powerful countries and peoples by richer countries through initiatives meant to slow the pace of climate breakdown,' as it is cheaper to set up offsetting projects in the Global South at the cost of diminishing the rights of indigenous peoples. For example, Amnesty International reports that the Sengwer people of Embobut forest in Kenya were violently forced from their homes and dispossessed of their ancestral lands as part of a government plan to reduce deforestation. The Sengwer people were moved without being consulted and never consented to the plans for their removal — a violation of both Kenyan and international laws (see Greenpeace UK (2021)).

In the light of the discussion in previous paragraphs, we will now discuss carbon pricing with a quantity target (stock of GHG emissions related to a temperature target). In addition, there should be a credible commitment to a rising path of carbon prices with a transparent mechanism to achieve that.

Such an affirmative climate policy will produce various collateral benefits, such as an improvement of air quality in cities. Thus, the effects are locally visible and help increase the acceptance of climate policies.

As the Intergovernmental Panel on Climate Change pointed out in several documents, explicit carbon prices are needed to implement ambitious climate policies, and their robust price signals guide towards cost-effective decarbonisation pathways.

2.2 Putting a Price on Carbon

As we aim to achieve a cap on the average temperature increase (to cap the level of GHG in the atmosphere), we now need to consider the possible mechanisms to achieve this aim. Essentially, there are two ways to move forward as outlines in Figure 2.1.

Following the command-and-control approach requires legal limits on the amount of emissions an individual source is allowed to emit. This would, in theory, guarantee that the required level of emissions is achieved, but obviously, in practice, a huge organisational effort is required, and the costs of implementation would be far too high. Thus, market-based mechanisms seem to be more attractive. So, the choice is between imposing a tax to fix a carbon price directly or to fix

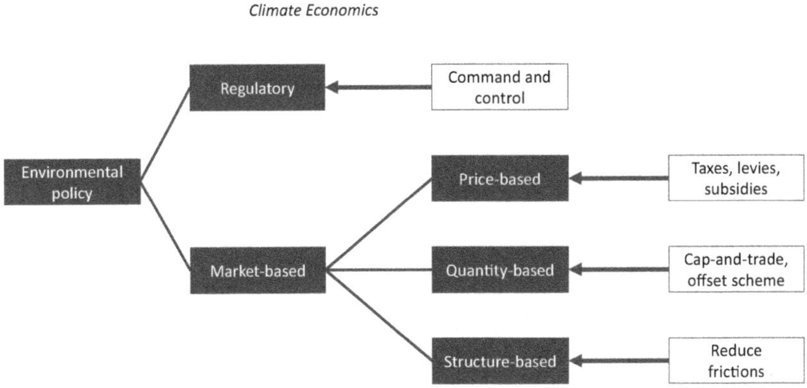

Fig. 2.1. Regulatory strategies.

quantities and implement a trading mechanism which will establish a price. As mentioned in the previous section, in a deterministic world, this would be equivalent, but in a stochastic setting, several effects need to be considered. So, let us compare a carbon tax and an emission trading scheme (ETS).

2.2.1 *Tax vs. Emission Trading*

A carbon tax stipulates the price of emissions but leaves the aggregate emissions level uncertain. The supply of allowances is infinitely elastic, as there are as many allowances as agents wish to buy at a fixed price (the tax rate). An ETS controls aggregate emissions, as the supply is completely inelastic, but the price is left uncertain. So, using a cap, an emission trading, in theory, establishes precisely the level of emissions which is desired (100% effectiveness). A tax system cannot guarantee an exact amount of emissions as an outcome, as the tax level is set under uncertainty about the marginal abatement costs.

However, in his seminal paper, Weitzman (1974) compares efficiency gains for price and quantity mechanisms under uncertainty and shows that the relative advantage depends on the slope of marginal environmental damages and costs as functions of emissions. Since compliance costs are uncertain, the choice of instrument depends on the relative curvatures of the marginal benefit curve and the marginal abatement cost curve. In the case of GHG, where damage does not depend on the flow of emissions but on their accumulation in the atmosphere, this result suggests that a carbon tax is more economically efficient under uncertainty than emission trading.

Studies applying the Weitzman approach to climate policy usually suggest that the marginal abatement cost function is steeper than the damage function and thus tend to support the carbon tax.

One may think of hybrid schemes that create a supply curve that is neither fully flat (a pure tax) nor fully vertical (pure cap and trade) but (stepwise) upward sloping. Hybrid systems use a price ceiling and a price floor to define a trade area. They will reach the target cap value as long as the system is in its trade area. As soon as the ceiling is reached, additional certificates are supplied (or participants are allowed to emit additionally for a fixed fee), and the ecological target becomes diluted. In case the floor is hit, the regulator buys allowances or a fee is applied that purchasers must pay in addition to the allowance price. Imposing a floor presents a potential liability on the public finances.

A price ceiling and floor provide significantly greater clarity to investors to deliver dynamic efficiency (in the form of optimal investment over longer time frames). The price floor would guarantee a certain minimum return on investment in low-carbon technologies, reducing the risk faced by innovating firms.

Hybrid systems have been widely discussed during the first phase of the European Union Emission Trading Scheme (EU ETS) (see Section 2.3). There, a severe permit price drop followed by a price hovering above zero for more than five months triggered a discussion among policymakers on whether the new cap-and-trade schemes would need additional safety-valve features. Several national governments subsequently introduced additional features nationally to establish *de facto* a hybrid system. For a discussion of these issues, see Hepburn (2009). We will only present a brief cost analysis based on option theory.

Assume a company with a permit shortage at compliance date faces a penalty P. If a company ends up with an excess of permits, it receives a subsidy S per unit of permit. Let $0 < S \leq P$, and let N be the initial amount of permits allocated to relevant companies. Then, $F(t,T) = P \cdot \mathbb{P}\left(q_{[0,T]} > N \mid \mathcal{F}_t\right)$ is the futures permit price in an ordinary system. We now compute the value of a put with strike S and maturity T (see Appendix A):

$$
\begin{aligned}
&\mathbb{E}\left[(S - F(T,T))^+ \mid \mathcal{F}_t\right] \\
&\quad = \mathbb{E}\left[\left(S - P\mathbf{1}_{\{q_{[0,T]}>N\}}\right)^+ \mid \mathcal{F}_t\right] \\
&\quad = (S-P)^+ \,\mathbb{P}\left(q_{[0,T]} > N \mid \mathcal{F}_t\right) + (S-0)^+ \,\mathbb{P}\left(q_{[0,T]} \le N \mid \mathcal{F}_t\right) \\
&\quad \overset{S\le P}{=} S \cdot \mathbb{P}\left(q_{[0,T]} \le N \mid \mathcal{F}_t\right).
\end{aligned}
$$

Let us now compute the futures price $\tilde{F}(t,T)$ of a permit in a hybrid system:

$$
\begin{aligned}
\tilde{F}(t,T) &= P \cdot \mathbb{P}\left(q_{[0,T]} > N \mid \mathcal{F}_t\right) + S \cdot \mathbb{P}\left(q_{[0,T]} \le N \mid \mathcal{F}_t\right) \\
&= P \cdot \mathbb{P}\left(q_{[0,T]} > N \mid \mathcal{F}_t\right) + S \cdot \left(1 - \mathbb{P}\left(q_{[0,T]} > N \mid \mathcal{F}_t\right)\right) \\
&= S + \frac{P-S}{P} \cdot P \cdot \mathbb{P}\left(q_{[0,T]} > N \mid \mathcal{F}_t\right) \\
&= S + \frac{P-S}{P} \cdot F(t,T) = \; F(t,T) + S\left(1 - \frac{F(t,T)}{P}\right).
\end{aligned}
$$

The first line immediately shows that the price of a futures in the hybrid scheme is the price of the futures in the ordinary scheme plus the value of a put option on the futures with strike S and maturity T. So, the implementation of such a hybrid system might result in a significant financial burden for the environmental policy regulator. The current magnitude of this burden can be obtained by calculating the price of the put option.

In addition, hybrid schemes resemble multi-policy strategies, which result in efficiency losses.

2.2.2 *Multiple Policy Instruments*

Current policies often involve multiple instruments, such as command-and-control regulation, subsidies, taxes, and trading schemes. Combinations of permit trading schemes, carbon taxes, technology-specific subsidies, and regulatory standards have been introduced, e.g., by Sweden, Norway, Denmark, and Ireland (taxes) and by Germany and Spain (subsidies for renewable energy).

However, these combinations may result in efficiency losses, which we now illustrate within a simple model (see Fankhauser (2011)).

Let us assume a tax and trade regulation with a carbon tax t (EUR per tonne) and a cap-and-trade scheme with price p. Any firm subject to the scheme pays the tax and is required to procure certificates for emissions. For e_0 the baseline emission and a the abatement, the emissions after abatement are $e = e_0 - a$. We assume that the firm optimises costs and faces convex abatement costs $c(a)$ (so, $c' > 0, c'' > 0$). Thus, it has to solve the optimisation problem

$$\min_e\{c(e_0 - e) + te + pe\} = \min_e\{f(e)\}. \tag{2.1}$$

Given convexity, it is easy to find the optimal abatement quantity as $e^* = e_0 - c'^{-1}(t+p) = e^*(t,p)$ to obtain minimum costs. Now, the sensitivities of the optimal quantity are obtained by calculating the partial derivatives[1]

$$e_t^* = e_p^* = -\frac{1}{c''} < 0. \tag{2.2}$$

Thus, increases in tax reduce emissions and vice versa.

Consider an economy with n identical firms, which face a cumulative cap c, so that aggregate emissions are $c = ne^*$. For fixed cap, we find from $ne_t^* dt + ne_p^* dp = 0$, so that

$$\frac{dp}{dt} = -\frac{e_t^*}{e_p^*} = -1. \tag{2.3}$$

That is, 'a small increase in tax results one-for-one in an equivalent reduction of the permit price.' So, an increase in tax reduces the permit price, and no additional abatement will be achieved. The average carbon price will be reduced, and the risk that the price system will collapse is increased.

Analogous calculations can be done for subsidy-and-trade and trade-and-trade regulations (see Fankhauser (2011)).

In a situation where additional regulation only affects a fraction of firms (as in the European Union for member states imposing individual regulation), a similar type of calculation shows that marginal costs for firms diverge and mitigation costs will increase.

---

[1] We denote the partial derivatives of $f(t,x)$ as $f_t(t,x)$ and $f_x(t,x)$.

In summary, the analysis of efficiency under uncertainty has had little influence on the choice of policy instruments. The preference for carbon trading over carbon taxes is driven largely by powerful political economy concerns. Trading systems are easier to implement and also sell better politically.

2.3 Emission Trading Schemes

2.3.1 *Design of an ETS*

As discussed in the previous sections, a cap is established on the total amount of emissions from the installations (firms) covered by the system. Firms receive (grandfathering), auction, or buy emission allowances and can trade them during a trading period. Within the trading period, firms must produce at the end of the years covered emission allowances to cover their emissions, otherwise they have to pay a fine. Firms can trade allowances, and in case banking is allowed, keep spare emission allowances for future needs. The idea is that trading brings flexibility that ensures emissions are cut where it is cost efficient.

In order for an ETS to run properly and produce credible price signals, the regulator must monitor emissions and establish a registry to record and track all physical transactions, i.e., changes of ownership. It also needs to provide essential information to enable the market to function properly. In its first decade, the EU ETS has seen several cases of value-added-tax (VAT) fraud and emission allowance thefts — see Nield and Pereira (2011) for a discussion. Since then, significant improvements to the framework for protecting the integrity of the system have been achieved. A major step forward in that regard was the qualification of emission allowances as financial instruments, which allowed the application of several regulatory standards. Also, the security of the registry has been significantly improved. By now, secondary markets for emission certificates are well established, so that transparency increased substantially.

For an emission market to work properly and produce price signals for investors to reduce carbon emissions, the potential cost benefits should be signalled through the prices of emission certificates. As the supply of emission allowances is perfectly inelastic as soon as allocations are completed, there is a possibility of high price volatility from spikes in demand. Thus, there should be some intertemporal flexibility in the scheme. This could be done by allowing the banking of certificates, as this effectively increases the depth and liquidity of the market. Thus, the current price is a function of a longer time span of activity, rather than being entirely determined by short-term developments. Additionally, banking creates an interest for firms with banked allowances in an increase of prices and the continuation (and success) of the system. A possible increase in prices also creates an incentive for firms to take early action to limit costs for allowances in later time periods.

Borrowing of allowances is not regarded as a useful feature of a trading scheme. Typically, the regulator is not suitably equipped to assess the creditworthiness and solvency of firms, which become debtors to the system when borrowing allowances. These firms will also delay action if they assume that targets will prove too onerous and will subsequently be softened. In addition, firms with borrowed allowances have an active interest to lobby for weaker targets or for abandoning emission trading altogether to have their debts cancelled.

Thus, trading schemes usually allow banking within and between periods (a notable example was the EU ETS in phase I), and there is typically no (or only very limited) borrowing allowed.

It is also important to set the length of commitment periods properly. Investments to reduce emissions require many years for investors to recover their costs. If commitment periods are too short, investors have to guess the emissions caps set by future governments and attempt to anticipate changes in the underlying structure of the carbon trading framework. A detailed discussion of conceptual dimensions of ETS is given in Frankhauser and Hepburn (2009).

Thus, transparency in the design of the scheme and a firm commitment to keep the scheme running are needed. It is important to generate a robust carbon price signal, so that investment in clean, low-carbon technologies is promoted.

2.3.2 *Current Emission Trading Schemes*

There are 21 systems covering 29 jurisdictions with an ETS in force worldwide. The number has more than tripled since 2012.

Several states in the USA already run schemes. The Regional Greenhouse Gas Initiative (RGGI), which was launched in 2009, was the first mandatory cap-and-trade program in the United States to limit carbon dioxide (CO_2) from the power sector. It consists of 11 eastern states. After going through a comprehensive program review in 2017, the RGGI states implemented a new cap reduction trajectory of 30% over the period 2020–2030. The RGGI CO_2 cap represents a regional budget for CO_2 emissions from the power sector. The Transportation and Climate Initiative (TCI) also released a draft framework outlining basic design features of a regional transport sector ETS, starting as early as 2022. California started an ETS in 2013, which applies to large electric power plants, industrial plants, and fuel distributors. California's cap-and-trade program is linked with the cap-and-trade system of Québec since 2014.

China's carbon trading markets started with the launch of its national ETS on 1st February, 2021, covering only a small fraction of emissions (from 2225 power generators). Eventually, it will cover the power sector and then expand gradually to seven other sectors, including petrochemical, building materials, and steel. Together, these sectors represent more than 50% of China's total energy consumption. However, the scheme has been criticised for possible flaws in its design as *The Economist* (2021b) points out. For instance, it does not use an absolute emission cap, but rates polluters on the basis of four benchmarks. Furthermore, the penalty for breaching the cap is rather low, as they are limited to 20% of the emission overflow.

An Australian ETS was supposed to start in 2014. There was a tax-based first phase. After a change of government, the tax was abolished and the plan of an ETS was shelved. New Zealand decided on further reforms to its system in 2019, including the phasing down of industrial free allocations starting in 2021 and the cancelling and replacing of units from the first commitment period of the Kyoto Protocol. It also introduced new accounting methods for the forestry sector and confirmed a new repayment penalty. Furthermore, an agreement was reached with the agricultural sector to foster on-farm emission reductions and to work towards implementing farm-level pricing by 2025.

The European Union set up the EU ETS as the world's first international trading scheme in 2005. It is now trading in its fourth phase. Germany will launch a national ETS for heating and transport fuels in 2021 complementing the EU ETS. Legislation was adopted in 2019 to implement the system gradually, first with a fixed annual price, increasing over the period 2021–2025. In 2026, auctions with minimum and maximum prices will be introduced.

2.3.3 *The EU ETS as an Example of Trading Schemes*

The EU ETS was the first international trading scheme at the time of its implementation in 2005. It is designed as a cap-and-trade scheme. Initially, it was split into three phases, covering the period 2005–2020. Phase I (2005–2007) was intended as a learning-by-doing period to prepare the scheme for subsequent phases with the Kyoto Protocol in place. During the first phase, it covered only CO_2 emissions from power generators and energy-intensive industries. Allowances were allocated by grandfathering (i.e., they where given for free) and could not be banked for use in later phases. The penalty for non-compliance was EUR 40 per tonne. As there was an overallocation of allowances, the total amount of allocated allowances was set on the basis of too high estimates, and the price for allowances fell to zero in 2007.

Phase II (2008–2012) coincided with commitment period of Kyoto Protocol. The proportion of free allowances fell to 90%, as some auctions were held. The cap on allowances was reduced, and the fine for each emitted tonne of CO_2 that is not covered by an allowance was increased to EUR 100. Furthermore, the allocation scheme was based on verified annual emissions from phase I. Each country had to submit a national allocation plan (NAP) to the European Commission (EC). The European Commission adjusted the NAPs, if necessary, and countries distributed allowances among regulated firms according to the final NAP, as approved by the European Commission. Still, as the economic crisis in 2008 led to a significant reduction of economic activities, emission reductions exceeded expectations. Thus, a large surplus on allowances was created, which subdued the price during the period (as banking was possible now the price remained positive).

Phase III (2013–2020) induced significant changes compared to the two previous periods. The scheme of national caps was replaced by a single EU-wide cap. From 2013 onwards, auctioning was the default method of initial allowance allocation (so NAPs were abolished). The initial auctioning share in the power sector was 100%. For all other sectors, the initial auction share was 20% and increased to 70% by 2020 (and to 100% by 2027). The distribution of non-auctioned allowances was harmonised and based on benchmarks. Furthermore, the amount of the excess emission penalty in the third phase was indexed to the annual inflation rate of the Eurozone. At the start of phase III in 2013, the surplus of allowances stood at almost two billion — double its level in early 2012. As a short-term measure, the Commission has postponed the auctioning of 900 million allowances until 2019–2020 to allow demand to pick up. As back-loading is only a temporary measure, the Commission proposes to establish a market stability reserve at the beginning of the next trading period in 2021.

In order for the EU to achieve its overall GHG emission-reduction target for 2030, it is necessary that emissions are reduced by 43% compared to 2005 levels for the sectors covered by the EU ETS. Thus, the overall number of emission allowances need to decline at an increased pace (at an annual rate of 2.2% compared to 1.74% in phase III).

In the current phase, benchmarking is divided into two distinct periods: 2021–2025 and 2026–2030. Benchmarks will be updated according to the level of technological progress within an industry. Along with updating a benchmark based on technological progress, an additional update will be done based on a predetermined decrease of annual reduction rate, which will be between 0.2% and 0.6%. This further decrease of a benchmark depends on the industry and the risks associated with it. If the risks such as leakage and abatement costs are high, a reduction of a benchmark from the lower end will be applied. Further adjustments of allocation are based on a change in production. A precondition for free allocation change based on a change in production is the increase/decrease of 15% or more based on a two-year moving average.

As economic recessions triggered severe demand shocks, and the general shift to a less carbon-intensive economy led to a diminished allowance demand, more flexibility in system responses is required. Thus, the market stability reserve (MSR) was substantially reinforced. Between 2019 and 2023, the amount of allowances put in the reserve is doubled to 24% of the allowances in circulation. It is envisaged to restore the regular feeding rate of 12% by 2024. See Kollenberg and Taschini (2019) for an analytic analysis of a supply management mechanism (SMM) similar to the market stability reserve. The authors show under which conditions an SMM (with implications for the MSR) affects optimal banking and emissions abatement. A first review of the MSR is currently underway, which discusses the overall design in detail. This includes an analysis of the efficiency of the current volume-based supply mechanism compared to a price-based adjustment (see Perino *et al.* (2021)).

As further policy measures are underway, most notably in terms of European Green Deal, effects on allowance prices are to be expected. The European Green Deal is a set of policy initiatives introduced by the President of the European Commission, Ursula von der Leyen, on 11 December, 2019 with the overarching aim to make Europe the world's first climate-neutral continent. It includes a review and possible revision of all relevant climate-related policy instruments, including the EU ETS. A revision of energy taxation directive will be considered, which will have effects on fossil fuel subsidies and tax exemptions (aviation, shipping) and knock-on effects on allowance prices.

The EU emphasises the importance of the effective functioning of the EU ETS scheme, as a robust carbon price is an increasingly pivotal aspect of investment appraisal. The revision has considerably reinforced the carbon price signal and strengthened the system in the long-term horizon, extending protection against the risk of carbon leakage and establishing instruments dedicated to fostering low-carbon investment. With climate change being one of the top priorities of the European Commission, the EU ETS will continue to play a critical role in delivering emission reductions and driving sectoral transformation. A strengthened EU ETS is central to the Commission's international engagement on climate change, with 2019 marking the official linking of the EU ETS and the Swiss ETS, and continued collaboration, including with California, China, and New Zealand. The experience of establishing, managing, and reinforcing a carbon pricing framework will prove invaluable in delivering a progressive transformation in line with the objectives of the European Green Deal.

The European market represents about 90% of the overall global compliance markets value for the year 2020. In the same year, 8.1 billion emission allowances, both regular and aviation EUAs, have been traded. Total market value increased to EUR 201 billion in comparison with EUR 169 billion for 2019. Market price closed at EUR 33.72/t at the end of December, and the positive trends continued in 2021, with the market price at the beginning of April 2021 at around EUR 43. Anticipation of the 'Fit for 55' package is the major price driver as it will compose legislative proposals for achieving the 55% target emission reduction in 2030 and is expected to be released by the European Commission in June 2021. Additionally, the scope of EU ETS is expected to further cover maritime, road transport, and building industry sectors.

2.3.4 *EUA Prices*

As we already indicated in the previous section, the EU allowance price was in earlier phases often driven by regulatory misconceptions (number of allowances in phase I) or regulatory announcements. Price movements can be traced back to discussions or decisions of the European Commission, the European Parliament, and even Committees of the Parliament. Figure 2.2 highlights a few in connection with back-loading, which was supposed to increase allowances prices. In particular, on 20th December, 2011, the European Parliament's Environmental Committee voted in favour of removing 1.4 billions of permits. Immediately, EUA prices rose by 40%. On 24th January, 2013, the European Parliament's industry committee rejected the idea of back-loading. After this, EUA prices dropped by 60%. Then, the narrow rejection of back-loading on 16th April, 2013 by the European

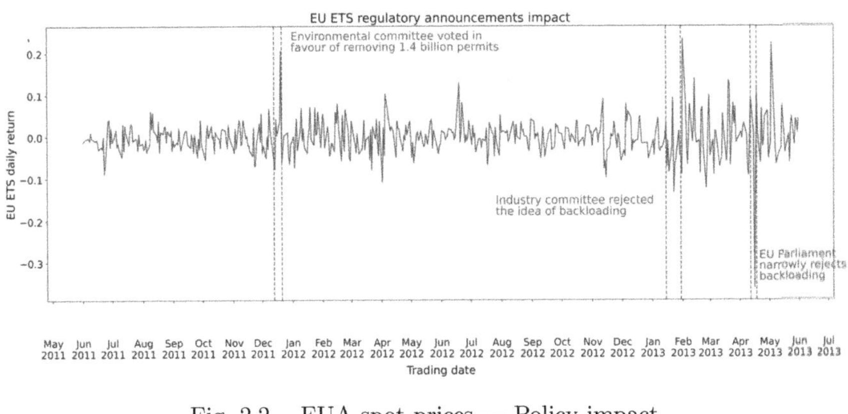

Fig. 2.2. EUA spot prices — Policy impact.

Fig. 2.3. Change points in EUA spot prices.

Parliament sent EU carbon prices down by another 40%. For additional analysis relating to further announcements, see Koch *et al.* (2016).

The time series of EUAs exhibits structural changes as identified by a change point analysis.[2] The different phases of the EU ETS are clearly visible. In addition, we can identify the change in investor attitude in Figure 2.3, which resulted in an increase in the EUA price with a high gradient. The flattening of the gradient and its renewed increase is detected likewise. Politically, these changes are aligned with an indicative vote by the EU parliament to align the EU 2030 emissions targets with the Paris Agreement (implying tighter emission targets and hence a tighter cap), and several reports that claimed in 2018 that EU carbon prices are set to double by 2021 (which they did) and could quadruple to EUR 55 per tonne by 2030 if policy actions of the European Union come in line with the Paris climate agreement. As political credibility had been re-established by the market stability reserve, EUA prices started to move upwards (see Figure 8.1 in Chapter 8, where we provide a detailed discussion on EUA prices). Various arguments support a further increase in the price of EUAs. Still, the perception of the market is that the EU will impose tighter control on emissions and push the cap upwards (see *Financial Times* (2021)). Several analysts expect the price to go up to about EUR 90, so speculative investment seems worthwhile.

[2]As change-point detection algorithm, we applied the pruned exact linear time (PELT) method (Killick *et al.*, 2012).

A standard correlation argument identifies EUAs as a diversification possibility. Obviously, EUA certificates are a natural hedge for portfolios with a heavy carbon footprint.

2.4 Carbon Credits

Carbon credits are generated from emission-reduction and emission-removal projects and are used to compensate for GHG emissions. To establish such markets, where (regulatory) allowances for emissions can be traded, this has been considered as an efficient tool to drive economy-wide decarbonisation by environmental economists for quite some time. So, within the Kyoto Protocol (Article 12), the clean development mechanism (CDM) was established. Companies from Annex 1 countries have the opportunity to compensate for emissions in their country of residence with regard to the emission policies in force there by establishing GHG emission mechanisms in developing countries predefined by the Kyoto Protocol. For every avoided tonne of CO_2e, a tradable certified emission reduction (CER) is issued. A CDM project must qualify through a registration and issuance process, which is lengthy and bureaucratic, before it is approved by the designated national authorities. For instance, it must satisfy a claim for additionality with respect to the amount of tonnes of emissions that have been avoided compared to the 'business-as-usual' scenario. In addition to the regulatory risk in the approval process, there is financial risk in terms of EUA price volatility, as the CERs are tradable with prices relating to the EUAs. Barrieu (2010) offers an explanation for the difference in CER and EUA prices. So, as the price for emission certificates within the EU ETS declined, the value of CERs fell and remained at a low level. CDM projects became very unattractive for companies and investors, and the market came to an almost standstill.

Parallel to these developments, voluntary frameworks, such as the Gold Standard (GS) or the Voluntary/Verified Carbon Standard (VCS) for carbon credits, have been created. A voluntary carbon credit is a certificate representing one metric ton of carbon dioxide equivalent that is either prevented from being emitted into the atmosphere (emission avoidance/reduction) or removed from the atmosphere as the result of a voluntary carbon-reduction project.

A voluntary carbon-reduction project needs to meet standards, such as GS and VCS for carbon credits to be issued. These different standards have different scopes of emission reduction, sometimes in combination with further social engagements as well as differing administrative requirements. Companies wishing to signal ecological and social responsibilities increasingly turned to the voluntary carbon market as the CDM imposed a heavy regulatory burden. As a consequence, the market had an early phase of activity with the Chicago Carbon Exchange (CCX) operating as the first centralised system from 2003 onwards. Also, the standards were consolidated and worked towards standardisation which decreased the frictions for users. However, this early phase came to an end when the financial crisis hit and the CCX, which was intermediated around 44% of voluntary traded CO_2e volume, shut down in 2010. Trading then took place over the counter (OTC), but due to falling prices (parallel to the certificate markets), the volume of transactions decreased steadily. It reached its low after the Paris Agreement became effective due to regulatory uncertainty. However, the Paris Agreement negotiations on a new international carbon market/mechanism are not finalised. In particular, the question whether carbon credits bought by private sector actors should be counted towards the post-2020 climate pledges of countries or only be incremental is unresolved.

In recent years, the market started to pick up again after several carbon-neutral initiatives were started. Carbon credits help in two ways to give credibility to carbon-neutral commitments. On the one hand, they can support projects which focus on emission avoidance and reduction, with investment into renewable energy, energy efficiency, and natural capital. On the other hand, their proceeds can finance projects for the removal of carbon dioxide from the atmosphere. So, they can generate negative emissions, which can compensate for residual emissions that will persist or even count against historical emissions. Figure 2.4 shows the development of the market in recent years.

With increasing commitments from countries and businesses to go carbon-neutral, a report led by Trove Research with UCL Geography predicts the market for carbon offsets could be worth up to USD 25 billion (GBP 18 billion) a year by 2030, compared with just USD 0.4 billion (GBP 300 million) today. Also, in February 2021, the Task Force on Scaling Voluntary Carbon Markets (TSVCM) (2021),

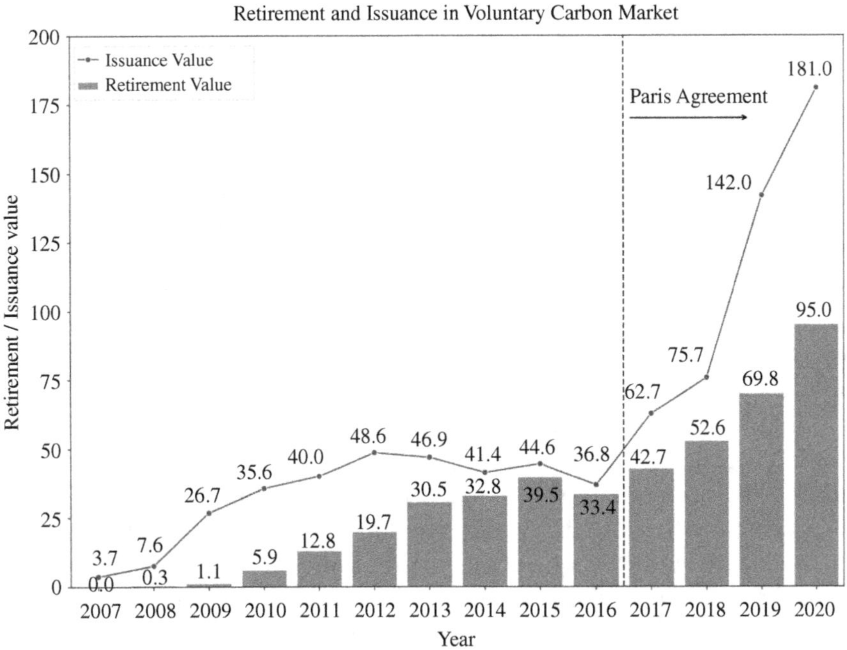

Fig. 2.4. Development of the carbon credit market.

backed by former Bank of England governor Mark Carney, published a report on what the new market might look like and estimated the market to be USD 50 to USD 100 billion per annum.

The carbon offsetting concept relies on the environmental integrity of the credits — specifically, the money paid for the offsets is used to reduce emissions or capture carbon dioxide from the atmosphere. Thus, the TSVCM has recommended setting core carbon principles — defining key criteria for a carbon credit — with an independent third party to check that the credits are consistent and of high quality. Older, low-quality credits should be moved out of the market, which will require a joint effort by registries, governments, and buyers. In view of recent developments in green bond markets (see Chapter 11), it may be buyers, pressured by public opinion, who will take a leading role here. The guidance could be issued by independent organisations advising buyers on the authenticity of the credits bought. Thus, classification (maybe in terms of a rating scheme) of high quality is needed (compared to the development of green bonds).

For a functioning market, price transparency, consistency, and clarity are the fundamental prerequisites. Thus, a credible global carbon market with a liquid, exchange-traded (spot and futures) contract at its core has to be established. That contract would also form the basis for an over-the-counter market that could reflect different types of carbon offsets. At present, with carbon credit pricing fluctuating significantly, there is a lack of transaction transparency, and project developers can sell directly to companies and individuals, or through brokers or exchanges. The TSVCM has emphasised the above requirements in its action plan.

Voluntary carbon offsets have been criticised by some environmental groups of greenwashing by companies that are not serious about cutting emissions and want to appear to be taking action. It is important to establish a link to absolute emission reduction, i.e., emissions as such. Analogous to green bonds, carbon credits can be linked to total emissions (given the data availability). However, some projects, such as investment in new technologies, do not have a direct impact.

So, greenwashing remains one of the biggest risks in forming a large, reputable market for carbon offset. In order to prevent companies from greenwashing, strong regulation, transparency, and link to carbon emissions are needed. Companies are expected to develop formal and concrete plans for reaching net-zero emissions that focus on reducing direct emissions and to use carbon offsets only as an additional tool for reaching the target. In some sectors, the transition to net-zero target is limited with the technology in use, and thus carbon offsets will play an important role during the transition. Sectors that will require great attention in the transition include the utilities and energy sector. Figure 2.5 shows a comparison of the median carbon intensity (defined as CO_2e divided by total revenues) of companies buying carbon credits and the ones who do not purchase classified as the utilities or energy sector. We can observe small differences in the actual carbon footprint of companies based on offsetting emissions and slightly higher carbon footprint for those companies that offset their emissions in comparison with those that do not. Thus, we can argue that at least for these two sectors, carbon credits are a means to additionally implement environment-friendly projects, which do

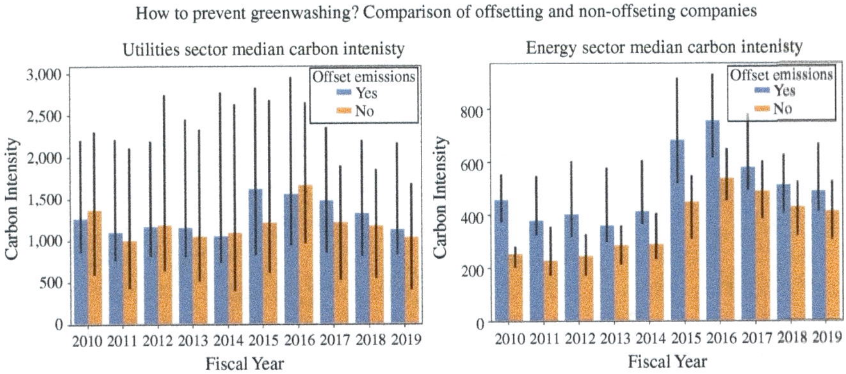

Fig. 2.5. Comparison of median carbon intensity of carbon offsetting and non-offsetting companies.

not necessarily have a direct impact on reducing carbon intensity (compared to green bonds).

Market participants and regulators are engaged in a discussion on appropriate market infrastructure that will enable scaling up carbon credit markets. Necessary infrastructure improvements include trade, post-trade, financing, and data verification and storage. Trade infrastructure is crucial and needs to be built to adhere to high cybersecurity standards and process a high volume of trading data. A study conducted by the World Bank's Carbon Markets and Innovation team and World Bank's Information Technology Services Technology and Innovation (ITSTI) lab (The World Bank, 2020) has shown that blockchain has the capabilities to simplify the data sharing and verification process due to the decentralised and immutable nature of the system. It has proven to be resilient against cyberattacks and to prevent manipulation of information. Proposed blockchain technology in the climate markets uses permissioned networks that reach consensus by agreement of the nodes rather than by mining (requires significant energy consumption) and allows flexible user roles and entitlements across different regulatory and organisational environments (see Chapter 7 for details).

In order to build competence in the carbon credit market, the action plan of the TSVCM emphasises the need for a reliable taxonomy, the establishment of core carbon reference contracts together with a trading infrastructure, and a consensus on the legitimacy of offsetting together with a market integrity assurance. We will return to this topic in Chapter 8, where we provide a detailed description of a possible market design.

Pricing and risk management of reference contracts can be provided via several avenues. Analogous to CER generated by the CDM, a link to an ETS and thus a price reference to the certificates traded can be established. Alternatively, a more fundamental approach (similar to the different variants of green bonds, see Chapter 11) can be established (which would honour the variability of the carbon credits) and thus a larger price band can be generated for variants of carbon credits. Providing classification and reliable price information remains a major issue to be resolved.

Chapter 3

Climate Risks

3.1 Carbon Risks

The transition to a low-carbon economy gives rise to a multitude of risks encountered by economies and firms in general, and banks and insurance companies in particular. The purpose of this chapter is to provide a classification of these risks and means of measuring them. We also discuss the class of carbon risks in the context of general sustainability.

Difficulties in capturing carbon risk for financial institutions arise from several sources. The decarbonisation pathway of the global economy is uncertain, and there are different choices at the national level in terms of levels of GHG emission constraints and technology options that will be incentivised. There exist no historical data for models available. Distributions of climate-related risks are skewed and have fat tails. Tipping points may alter the outcomes completely.

In addition, there is the shift in time horizon. Financial actors usually think in terms of one to three years, which is far shorter than the time for the materialisation of climate risks.

Climate-related risk refers to financial risk encountered by financial institutions due to their exposure to physical effects or adaptation measures to climate change.

We follow the, by now well-established, classification by Network for Greening the Financial System (2019) (see also Volz *et al.* (2020) for a detailed discussion on the transmission channels of climate risk in the international financial system).

A first high-level classification separates these risks into *physical* and *transition* risks. Physical climate risks refer to physical changes in climate, which lead to modifications of climate pattern, and frequency and severity of extreme weather events. These changes may alter the supply and demand pattern of many industries and lead to physical damages of assets, which may trigger adaptation costs and economic loss of value.

Transition risks emerge from the process of establishing a low-carbon economy, which will alter the financial viability of a part of the capital stock and business models. The associated financial risks and opportunities will change the performance of assets and portfolios. While such a transition is wanted, too rapid a transformation may have undesirable effects on financial stability and the broader economy. For instance, carbon-intensive sectors of the economy, such as utilities or heavy industries, may suffer from a transition that is too rapid.

As we pointed out in Chapter 1, many of these risks have already emerged and altered economic processes. However, the financial implications surface only slowly, but their magnitude is increasing.

Physical risks are driven by two major sources. News from extreme weather events, be it more violent storms, floodings, extreme heat or cold spells, arise with ever higher frequency. Locations hit by these extreme events may face relocation of businesses together with the corresponding workforce. Corporations, due to extra costs, and municipalities, due to reduced tax income, may see a decrease in their investment and debt repayment capacities. Thus, debt portfolios of banks and the liability side of balance sheets of non-insurers may see an increase of risk. In addition, asset managers and pension funds may have to restructure their portfolios.

The second driver of physical risk is the gradual shift in climate pattern. Rising sea levels or growing deserts may lead to migration of populations. These population shifts subsequently result in demand- and supply-side shocks.

Figure 3.1 displays an overview on the consequences of physical risks.

Transition risks are classified into three categories. First, we may see the introduction of strict climate-related mitigation policies, such as carbon taxes and emission trading schemes (see Chapter 2).

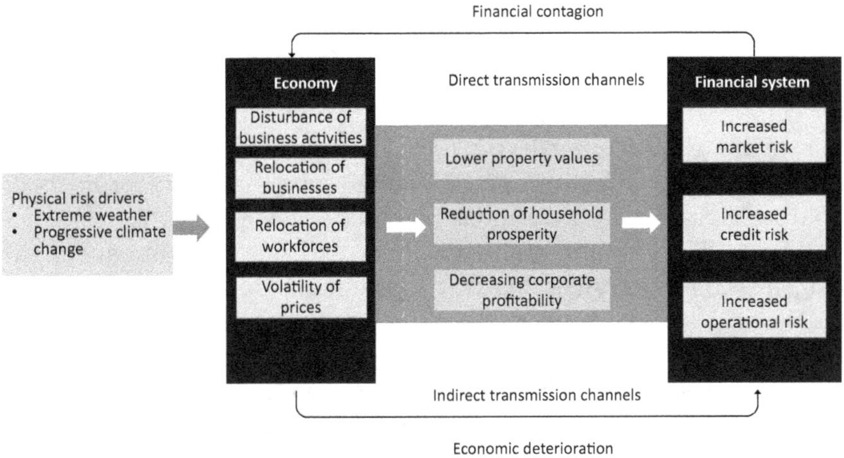

Fig. 3.1. Physical risks.

This could endanger business models and lead to a substantial reduction of the value of companies. For instance, the German utility sector has hugely suffered with the rise of renewable energy sources (and the simultaneous phase-out of nuclear power) during the last decade. Many of their power plants became stranded assets (see Section 3.4) as they went out of use and were no longer able to earn an economic return on past investment. The impact on investment funds can be likewise substantial. Overvaluation of companies (carbon bubble, see Section 3.4) can lead to a serious decline on investment return. We refer to Chapters 12 and 13 for details of the discussion. Ambitious restructuring programmes had to be put in place to revive the sector. A second source of transition risk arises from the technologies chosen. There is a risk to being in front of the curve as well as behind. A bet on a technology, which may not be advanced further, may result in huge sunk cost. Likewise, being too late may push businesses out of the market. Third, we already observe a shift in public sentiment towards a more climate-friendly behaviour. The younger generation not only demands policy changes within public movements, such as Fridays for Future, but also promotes already in their demand pattern, preferences, and expectations for a shift towards a low-carbon economy. In addition, increased litigation against companies involved in carbon-intensive sectors and production processes will result in financial costs and reputation risks. Companies even face legal risk for not sufficiently accounting for climate risk or not having disclosed relevant information concerning their carbon risks. This includes financial institutions, which will be under scrutiny concerning financing carbon-intensive projects or holding high-carbon investment portfolios.

Figure 3.2 describes transition risks and further summarises the transmission from transition risk to the financial system.

We will use the term *carbon risk* to denote the risks which are related to GHG emissions and affect corporates and financial institutions. These carbon risks are visible through various classical prudential risk types. Examples include the industrial carbon-related policy risk, which prices GHG emissions by an emission trading scheme or taxes (or both), and also carbon-related market constraints, which arise from changes in the demand and prices for energy linked to an energy transition. There is also the possibility of an increased uncertainty in market signals and increasing cost of raw materials. In addition, we have climate litigation risk from lawsuits that can create liabilities due to past emissions for targeted companies. Investment regulatory frameworks, which impose mechanisms that impact the cost and availability of capital and, in the

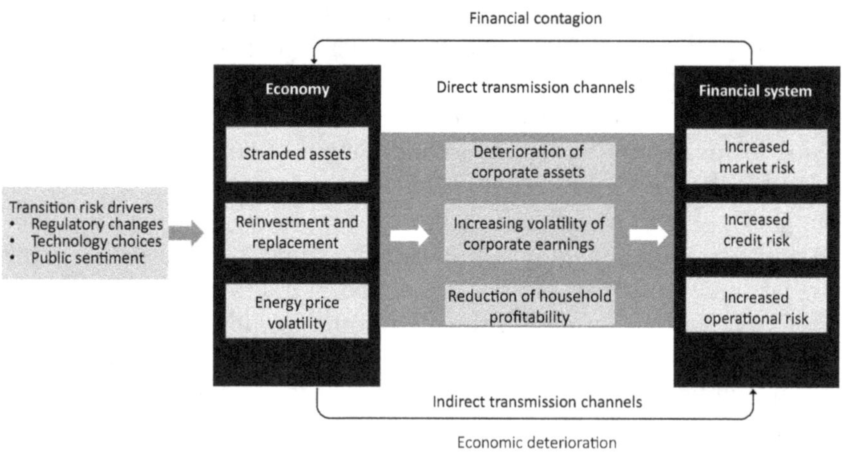

Fig. 3.2. Transition risks.

case of financial institutions, may translate into additional capital requirements. Moreover, stakeholders may voice their concern on stigmatised sectors and give negative feedback on investment strategies. Furthermore, fiduciary-duty-related litigation may arise from claims of negligence for institutional investors in the case of a rapid price assessment of companies affected by a carbon bubble. Summarising, carbon risk relates to regulation, litigation, competition, production, and reputation risks.

For our subsequent analysis, the main focus will be the effect of carbon risk on the standard prudential risks, in particular on market, credit, and operational risks. Let us start with the definitions according to the Basel Committee on banking supervision (see Hull (2018)).

Market risk can be defined as the risk of losses in on-and-off-balance sheet positions arising from adverse movements in market prices. From a regulatory perspective, market risk stems from all the positions included in banks' trading book as well as from commodity and foreign exchange risk positions in the whole balance sheet. Here, physical risks such as extreme weather events with destructions of infrastructure or transition risks, such as regulatory measures, could lead to a repricing of assets and debt, which will affect the value of the corresponding securities. So, carbon risk imposes a market risk and may require a carbon risk premium in prices. We discuss the possible existence of such a premium in asset and bond prices in Chapters 9–11.

Credit risk is most simply defined as the potential that a bank borrower or counterparty will fail to meet its obligations in accordance with agreed terms. Banks need to manage the credit risk inherent in the entire portfolio as well as the risk in individual credits or transactions. Clearly, physical and transition risks have an effect on individual credits and portfolios of credits. Extreme weather events may affect a whole region, while gradual climate change may lead to changes in demand and supply in certain regions and thus alter industrial sector structure, and finally, regulation may change the value of assets and make business models no longer maintainable. Again, credit risk may contain a part which is linked to carbon risk, and we will investigate this relation in Chapter 10.

Operational risk is the risk of loss resulting from inadequate or failed internal processes, personnel, and systems or from external events. There are seven categories (or types) of operational risk, namely internal fraud; external fraud; employment practices and workplace safety; clients, products and business practices; damage to physical assets; business disruption and system failures; execution, delivery, and process management. Clearly, carbon risk has an impact on operational risk in terms of physical and transition risks.

We will not specifically discuss the relation of carbon risk to liquidity and underwriting risk, but it is obvious that disruption by physical or transition risks will also impact these risk types.

A theoretical framework of the transition risk of the phase-out of carbon-intensive industries and the shift to low-carbon industries is given in Semieniuk *et al.* (2020). They also provide a discussion of the impacts on the financial system and the feedback from the financial system to the general economy.

3.2 Carbon Metrics

Total GHG emissions (or often CO_2e emissions) are apparently the simplest way to assess the exposure of a corporate to carbon risk. However, even to measure this quantity is a daunting task, as ideally the emissions of all activities of a corporate should be captured.

The current standard of measuring is specified by the Greenhouse Gas Protocol, which was jointly established by the World Resources Institute (WRI) and the World Business Council for Sustainable Development (WBCSD) — two non-government institutions seeking to promote environmental sustainability (see World Resources Institute (2016) for details (WRI and WBCSD, 2004)). The Greenhouse Gas Protocol divides emissions into three scopes, which — based on Bernoville (2020) — can be summarised as follows:

- Scope 1 emissions are direct emissions from resources either owned or controlled by a company. They can be further divided into the four categories of stationary combustion (e.g., fuels, heating sources), mobile combustion (vehicle fuel), fugitive emissions (GHG leakages, e.g., from refrigerators), and process emissions (released during industrial processes).
- Scope 2 emissions are indirect emissions resulting from the generation of energy purchased from a utility provider. They thus comprise GHG emissions released as a consequence of consuming purchased electricity, steam, heat, and cooling.

- Scope 3 emissions are all indirect emissions that are linked to the company's operations but not included under scope 1 or scope 2. These emissions occur as a consequence of company activities but are not directly owned or controlled by the company. An example of scope 3 emissions is the use of purchased goods or services.

Clearly, the question of a correct company-specific allocation arises immediately. Also, a normalisation of the GHG emissions is needed and can be done in several ways. Usually, the normalised quantity is referred to as carbon intensity (or footprint). The TCFD recommends to use the following:

$$\text{carbon intensity} = \frac{\text{tonnes of CO}_2\text{e}}{\text{revenue in millions of currency}}. \tag{3.1}$$

Normalisation will make it possible to draw comparisons between companies and is a proxy for a company's operating performance (the notion of efficiency). However, these figures become sensitive to the variability of denominators, which themselves have no link to climate issues and/or operational progress. So, if the data are available, we can opt for intensity levels with absolute physical indicators. However, to make sector-wide, business-wide, and intra-sector comparison possible, careful normalisation is needed.

Usually, the largest companies in the benchmark index are likely to be the companies with the highest GHG emission levels. Ignoring this circumstance will tend to be a bias against the largest companies. Normalisations adapted to each sector are preferable, for example, dividing CO_2 emissions by the following:

- tonnes of output in the oil and gas sector;
- revenue from transporting one tonne over a certain distance in the transport sector;
- total GWh electricity production in the electric utility sector;
- square footage of floor space in the housing sector;
- total sales in the retail sector.

There are different organisations, which provide carbon footprint measures, such as Trucost, South Pole Group, and MSCI ESG Research. GHG emission measures are divided into the three scopes, but as there is no systematic, standardised reporting of these emissions, different organisations may report different values for the same company.

The carbon footprint (intensity) faces several limitations. We will discuss data issues in Chapter 6. Besides that, the carbon footprint is backward-looking rather than forward-looking.[1] As we use historical data, we cannot immediately judge the dynamics of companies towards a low-carbon economy. We are not able to distinguish a dynamically moving company from a stagnant company using just a single number. Unlisted assets may not provide the relevant data to compute carbon intensity. There may be varying denominators being used for carbon intensity measurement, which makes it difficult to compare the numbers across companies. Also, there may be stranded assets which might not be in any production process in the future, as companies may change their business plans.

3.3 Sustainable Finance

In this section, we discuss the difference in environmental social governance (ESG) or sustainability risks and carbon risks. Carbon risks were subsumed under the 'E' dimension of ESG and have only recently won prominence on their own. Figure 3.3 shows that sustainability risks result from various sources and impact the corporate sector in several dimensions.

ESG risks can have a significant impact on products, service and production processes, costs, and demand. As a result, ESG factors have an impact on P&L, CF statement as well as balance sheet. ESG risks can lead to disruptions in value chains or the exclusion of suppliers (e.g., caused by violation of human rights).

As we already discussed for carbon risk, ESG risks have an influence on the existing risk types. Credit risk may arise from potentially higher probability of defaults as well as lower recovery rates. As ESG risks have a direct impact on profitability and the valuation of companies, market risk is affected. Also, financing non-sustainable sectors or fossil fuels can lead to reputation risk.

[1] Although some studies, e.g., Trinks *et al.* (2020), report a high persistence of carbon intensity.

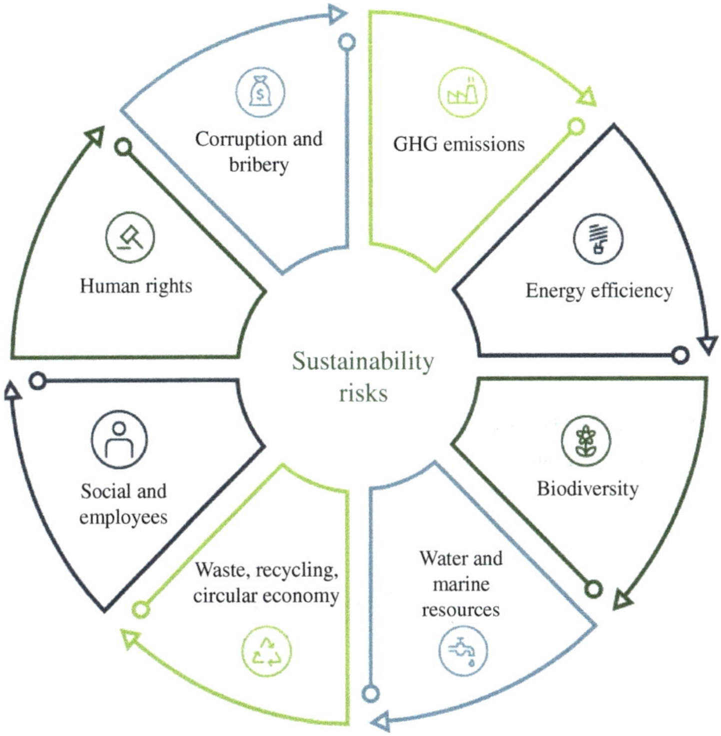

Fig. 3.3. Sustainability risks.

ESG risks have been addressed in the EU action plan on financing sustainable growth. The EU also established a classification scheme for sustainability activities. Figure 3.4 outlines the dimensions of this taxonomy. The action plan tries to create an instrument that supports investors, companies, issuers, and project promoters in the transition to a low-carbon, resilient, and resource-efficient economy. It provides the definition of performance thresholds (known as 'technical screening criteria') for economic activities that substantially contribute to at least one of the six environmental objectives and simultaneously do no significant harm to any of the other five, if relevant, and meet other minimum safeguards (such as OECD guidelines or UN guidelines). As such, it is a means to finance sustainable growth.

Another aim is to take sustainability into account in prudential regulation. This, of course, involves the European Central Bank (ECB) which released similar guidelines. The guidance describes ECB's

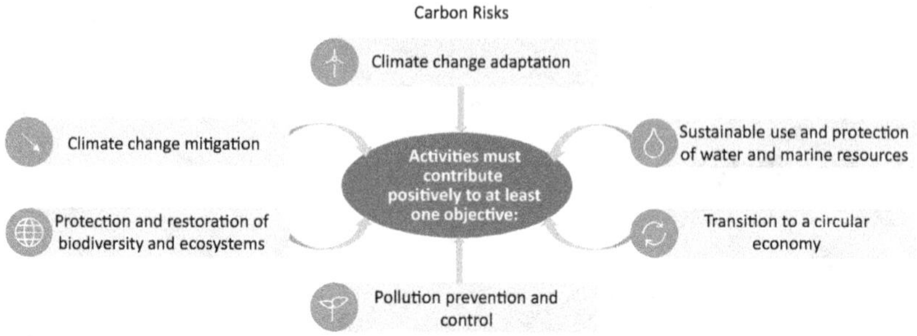

Fig. 3.4. EU taxonomy on sustainability.

supervisory understanding of how to deal with climate and environmental risks in relation to business model and strategy, governance and risk appetite, risk management, and disclosure (see also Chapter 12).

3.4 Stranded Assets and Carbon Bubble

Meinshausen *et al.* (2009) stated that if global average temperature was not to exceed 2°C above pre-industrial levels by 2050, strict limits on the total emissions would be required. They predicted that to meet the 2°C goal, less than one-half of the world's proven economically recoverable oil, gas, and coal reserves could be emitted during 2007–2050. Thus, much of the world's fossil fuel would be stranded and therefore potentially worthless under the climate change scenarios examined. This could trigger a sharp reduction in energy firms' valuations because their financial statement reserves make up a significant part of that value.

Subsequently, Carbon Tracker (2013, 2015) introduced the concept of a *carbon budget*, which links the rise in temperature to the amount of GHG emissions, as the amount of warming is linked to cumulative annual emissions. So, for rise in temperature deemed acceptable, there is a GHG emission budget, namely the carbon budget. The budget is linked to a specific temperature rise, covers a certain period of time and states a level of likelihood. Clearly, a higher budget reduces the likelihood of restricting warming to particular temperature (see Chapter 1). One can express the carbon budget in terms of years remaining at a given level of emissions to stay with a given probability below a specific temperature rise. For instance, based on the 2019 level of emissions

($43.1\,\text{Gt}\ CO_2$), 11.5 years remain for a 50% probability of a 1.5°C warming (Carbon Tracker).

To stay within a carbon budget, GHG emission have to be limited. As Meinshausen *et al.* (2009) point out, this leads to fossil fuel energy reserves and known resources which physically cannot be burned. This generates *unburnable carbon* as an overhang of available fossil fuels.

According to Spedding *et al.* (2013), the combination of reduced oil and gas prices (from lower demand) and unburnable fossil fuel reserves places at risk some 40–60% of the market capitalisation of the world's top 200 energy companies due to the short-term valuation models used. This could translate to a substantial wealth loss for these firms' shareholders, thereby bursting what some analysts and commentators have termed a *carbon bubble* from the mispricing of fossil fuel reserves. Thus, investors should divest from investments tied to unburnable carbon. As we will see in Chapter 13, there are various additional tools available to limit exposure to those assets. In contrast to financial markets, where bubbles arise from market sentiment or policy implications, the size of a potential carbon bubble depends on the specific temperature goal and the corresponding physical and transitory risks. A transition driven by technological developments, for instance, could cause a negative shock to electricity producers, while reducing production costs for some other sectors. Apart from the energy sector, broader economic changes related to energy use will also impact a range of other high-carbon and climate-related sectors, notably utilities, transport, and manufacturing sectors. Governments owning fossil fuel reserves would be faced with a fall in revenues, reducing the value of the sovereign bonds they have issued. Already, Meinshausen *et al.* (2009) pointed out that the need to leave a significant part of fossil reserves in the ground leads to impairment of assets. By now, assets that are not able to earn an economic return for the full timespan envisaged at time of investment, due to the transition to a low-carbon economy, are called *stranded assets*. The specific factor of an asset stranding can be physical, economic, or regulatory. German utilities exhibit several examples of stranded assets in their many modern coal and gas power plants, which were shut down due to financial and regulatory reasons.

As for the targets of the Paris Agreement, McGlade and Ekins (2015) report that more than 80% of global coal reserves, almost half of the gas reserves, and around one-third of global oil reserves cannot be burned in order to reach the 1.5°C target. Thus, industries with an exposure to fossil fuels would be severely impacted. Also, many currently productive industry sectors have to alter their production methods or business models.

The immediate reaction of stock markets to the first publications in 2009 was muted. Griffin *et al.* (2015) show that stock prices of the relevant companies declined by 1.5–2% over a three-day period around the publication of the nature. Further news over the years on energy firms facing stranded assets show an even smaller reaction. Maybe investors anticipate technology improvements, such as carbon capture and sequestration (CCS), or were sceptical of the willingness of governments to enforce rigid carbon standards.

3.5 Tail Risk

Based on the IPCC (2014) AR4 physical sciences report (Meinshausen *et al.*, 2009; Millner *et al.*, 2013), Figure 3.5 presents the estimated probability densities of climate sensitivity from 19 published climate studies. Climate sensitivity is measured as the equilibrium increase in global mean surface temperature associated with a doubling of GHG concentration. It features in many integrated assessment models as a summary statistic of the response of global mean temperature to increases in GHG concentrations. Although these estimated probability densities are based on different climate modelling approaches, they indicate that the global average temperature response is governed by a distribution with 'fat right tails'; thus, extreme increases are possible with a low probability.[2]

It is important to understand the effect of fat-tailed distributions. Of course, we can address an increase and variation in empirical observations of temperatures in terms of increasing the expectation and variance (maybe with a time-dependent component), but then we would model a temperature distribution with less colder and more hotter weather with some variations, but we would not have more record hot weather. To put it in different words, we would see the same type of patters only with higher mean temperatures and more variations around the centre of the distribution. The story is different in our current

[2]Millner *et al.* (2013) also point out that Figure 3.5 reveals ambiguity — a fact we will address in Chapter 4.

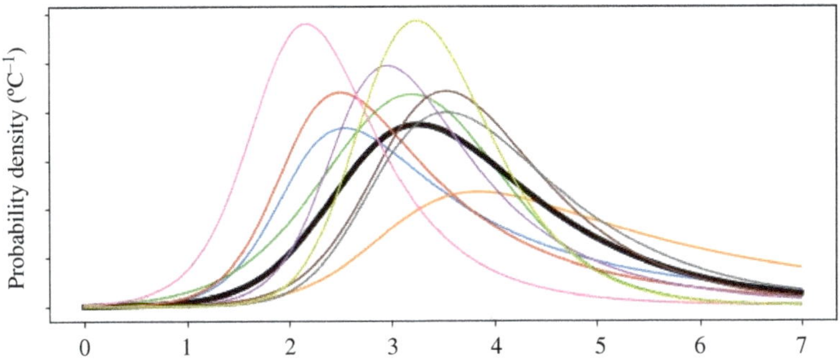

Fig. 3.5. Estimates from different forecasts.
Source: Meinshausen *et al.* (2009).

context — we see higher averages, more variability, and more frequent and higher extremes. Taking climate tipping points into account, the situation becomes even more complicated as we need to model events we have not seen on the basis of available data. Extreme-value theory is the mathematical approach that is developed precisely for estimation problems in such a context. For a detailed discussion, we refer the reader to Embrechts *et al.* (1997); see also Fasen *et al.* (2014) for the analysis of a temperature dataset.

Let us assume the random variable (process) T models global temperature above some pre-industrial (in a region and at a certain time) average, which is governed, in the light of the discussion by a (right-) heavy-tailed distribution. In climate modelling, the economic costs of climate change are expressed in terms of a damage function $d(.)$, with the global mean temperature T as argument (see Stern (2007a)). So,

$$d(T) = cT^{\beta}, \tag{3.2}$$

where c is a constant and β the damage-function exponent. For ease of interpretation, $\beta = 2$ was a frequent choice (as this implies linear marginal benefit function), but higher values are more realistic (see Stern (2007a) and Dietz (2011)). So, as the temperature distribution already has heavy tails, the distribution of climate damages will inherit this property.[3]

[3]As an illustrative example, take a Pareto distribution with density f_{α} and $0 < \alpha \leq 1$. Then, not even the expectation exists and the asymptotic of the

The next step of welfare analysis of climate change specifies a social welfare function, which features a weighted utility function of CRRA type. Take the following example:

$$u(c) = \begin{cases} \dfrac{c^{1-\gamma}}{1-\gamma} & \gamma \neq 1, \\ \log(c) & \gamma = 1, \end{cases} \tag{3.3}$$

where c is consumption per capita and γ is the elasticity of the marginal utility of consumption. In this specification, γ specifies the relative risk aversion and simultaneously aversion to inequality in consumption over regions and time. The economics of climate change suggest one to assume $\gamma > 1$, and thus, utility tends to minus infinity as consumption tends to zero, and marginal utility u' tends to infinity as consumption tends to zero.

From this, it follows that society's marginal willingness to avoid zero consumption is unbounded. So, if there is a future state in which the value of climate damage is at least as great as baseline consumption, society's marginal willingness to pay to avoid that is unbounded. As the damage distribution has heavy tails, such an outcome is very unlikely but possible! So, climate economic models need constraints to avoid damages higher than baseline consumption. Dietz (2011) discusses ways to address this problem in great detail, and we refer the reader to this enlightening piece of work.

Of course, the discussion in the previous paragraph is related to the 'dismal theorem' (see Weitzman (2009, 2011)). We now use a simple example from Weitzman (2014) to explain the dismal theorem and the importance of tail probabilities for the analysis of climate risks.

Let us use a two-period model with the times $t = 0, 1$. Normalise present consumption $c_0 = 1$, and take future consumption after climate change damages as random C_1. Welfare W is

$$U(C_1) = U(1) + \beta \mathbb{E} U(C_1),$$

with a utility function $U(.)$ and a discount rate β. Now, suppose that each unit of carbon abatement shifts future consumption upwards with

---

density is $f_\alpha(t) \sim \frac{1}{t^{\alpha+1}}$, $t \to \infty$. For the damage function, the tail asymptotic is $f_d(t) \sim \frac{1}{t^{\frac{\alpha}{\beta}+1}}$, $t \to \infty$, and as $\beta > 1$, this tail is even heavier than the tail of the temperature distribution.

a multiplicative factor $\theta > 0$. The social cost of carbon (SCC) is now (negative of) the quantity paid at $t = 0$ for abatement and still obtaining the same level of welfare as before. Now, assume that the damage distribution has a point mass probability p at a low consumption bound C_p. We just use this outcome (and ignore the contribution of the remaining probability $(1-p)$) to obtain a lower bound of the SCC:

$$\text{SCC} \approx \rho\theta p C_p^{1-\gamma}.$$

It is clear that with $\gamma > 1$, the quantity $C_p^{1-\gamma} \to \infty$ as $C_p \to 0$, so the convergence of SCC needs to be analysed. In order to display the asymptotic behaviour in terms of the thickness of the tail, we again follow Weitzman (2014) and change the variable. So, let $x = -\log C_p$, and call $p(x)$ the probability of x (which moves the 'low consumption' now in the right tail as we are used to with the damage function). So, in terms of x,

$$\text{SCC} \approx \rho\theta \left(p(x) \exp\{(\gamma - 1)x\}\right). \tag{3.4}$$

So, it is immediately clear that for a normal distribution like point mass $p(x) \sim \exp\{-x^2\}$, the SCC in (3.4) remains finite. In fact, the probability only needs to decline in x faster than exponential (thin tails) for SCC to have a finite limit. For a polynomial decline, as in the Pareto case, we have $x^{-\alpha}, \alpha > 0$, and so, the SCC in (3.4) will be unbounded. So, the SCC can be infinite even if the probability of zero consumption or infinite damage (a catastrophe) is zero as long as the probability of consumption per capita is dominated by the marginal utility. This is what Weitzman (2009) calls the 'dismal theorem.' He also listed various reasons why the 'dismal theorem' is an absurd result. However, as Weitzman (2014) puts it, 'the "dismal theorem" should serve as a warning flag that a credible economic analysis of climate change should seriously consider extreme tail values of damages and their probabilities.'

The work by Dietz (2011) contains a much more detailed analysis of low-probability high-impact events and finds significant tail effects under several plausible specifications. As the author does a simulation exercise, an asymptotic analysis is, of course, not possible, but additional assumptions, such as an upper bound on the damage function and a lower bound on consumption, are discussed and investigated. The importance of the right tail of climate sensitivities is also discussed in Quiggin (2017) as the central policy implications of the 'dismal theorem.'

Summarising, the presence of heavy-tailed distributions in physical climate science implies an increasing effect with additional emissions. As damage functions are convex, this translates to greater total and marginal damages associated with an additional degree of warming. From the concavity of the utility functions, an increase of the risk-adjusted present value of additional damage at the margin follows.

A possible way to circumvent the problems' fat-tailed distributions cause in climate change analysis is to set bounds on the variables and functions of interest, as Dietz (2011) does on consumption. Taking the effects of climate policy, in particular abatement policy, into account, Millner (2013) and Hwang *et al.* (2016) show that fat-tailed distributions imply more stringent abatement policies, but the social cost of carbon remains finite.

Chapter 4

Theory of Carbon Risk

4.1 What Should the Price for Carbon Be?

Figure 3.5 in Chapter 3 reflects not only the tail risk of highly relevant climate risk parameters (in this case, climate sensitivity, which plays an important role in integrated assessment models) but also a high degree of uncertainty. In the following section, we discuss how discrete models which try to specify optimal carbon policies and by implication carbon prices take this uncertainty into account.

So far, systematic modelling of the various levels of uncertainty has been largely lacking (see, for example, the classifications in the IPCC Report, IPCC (2007) and Kunreuther *et al.* (2014)). We describe the basic framework for optimal climate policies and discuss which role uncertainty modelling plays in this context.

4.1.1 *Utility Framework*

As today's climate policy decisions have long-term effects, the discounting of their far-reaching consequences is of particular importance. Stern (2007a) and Nordhaus (2007) (and others) describe the social discount factor as the most important decision variable in the context of climate policy proposals. Stern (2007b) uses a discount factor of 1.4% and receives a carbon price 10 times higher compared to that of Nordhaus (2008), who proposes a discount factor of 5.5%. The central question of intertemporal discounting refers to today's assessment of the benefits of different consumption and investment decisions at different points in time. In particular, a comparability of the utility values, which relate to different points in time, needs to be achieved. Today's investment in emission-reduction measures involves costs that reduce consumption and investment in other sectors of the economy, but not investing may result in rising climate damage leading to future costs. We will not discuss this issue in very much detail and only mention aspects in calculating the discount rate in passing. We refer to Gollier (2012), Stern (2010), and Tol (2019) for a much more in-depth discussion.

Let us now start to consider the utility-based modelling framework, in which we will increase the complexity from model to model. The starting point are models that take into account a realistic description of risk preferences, time preferences, and ambiguity aversion, and pursue an intertemporal utility maximisation of current and future generations.

We start with pure time preference. It is usually assumed that the decision maker prefers today's consumption to future consumption. The farther away the consumption lies in the future, the lower it is weighted. Pure, in this context, means that the preference is made independent of the risk assessment.

Then, there is the growth-related time preference. In general, a positive growth rate is assumed. This implies that more consumption will be available in the future than it is today. Consequently, future generations are richer, and today's consumption is preferred over future consumption.

The final ingredient is the uncertainty. Obviously, the question of how confident we are that the future consumption is really available to us must be taken into account. So, we need to put some probabilistic framework around the magnitude and availability of the future consumption. The probabilistic framework then is subject to various degrees of uncertainty, which range from a fixed probability measure, to various probability measures, and to no probability assessment possible at all. Let us use a two-period model with the time points $t = 1, 2$ for illustration. In each period, a consumption pair c_1, c_2 is available. Each possible consumption pair provides a benefit represented by an additive utility function $U(c_1, c_2)$. So, it is

$$U(c_1, c_2) = u(c_1) + e^{-\delta} u(c_2). \tag{4.1}$$

The growth rate of the economy can also be represented in this notation as $g = \log(c_2/c_1)$. If a constant relative risk aversion (CRRA) utility function with $u(c) = c^{1-\gamma}/(1-\gamma), \gamma > 0, \gamma \neq 1$ is assumed for the function $u(c)$, the discount factor is given by the Ramsey equation $r = \delta + g\gamma$. The Ramsey equation separates the discount factor r into two components. The first represents the pure time preference rate δ. The larger the δ chosen, the more important that today's consumption is compared to that later. As a result, the discount factor r also increases. A higher discount factor means that the current value of future cash flows is lower. The second component of the Ramsey equation is the product of the growth rate and the level of relative risk aversion. The larger the growth rate g, the more consumption will be available in the next period. At the same time, this means that there is little interest in giving up today's consumption in order to profit from it in the future, which is reflected in a higher discount factor.

The parameter γ plays a role both in specifying the discount factor and in specifying the relative risk aversion within the utility framework. The consequence is that only two variants for combinations of risk attitude and time preference can be specified. Either a low risk aversion together with a greater willingness to postpone today's consumption into the future (low γ) or a high risk aversion with a little willingness to forego consumption today (high γ) can be realised. Within the simple CRRA framework, it is not possible to combine low/high risk aversion with low/high willingness to postpone consumption. So, in the context of climate policy, a model based only on CRRA utility may not be flexible enough and a separation of risk and time preferences is desirable.

4.1.2 *Risk Aversion and Intertemporal Substitution*

Let us assume that future consumption is stochastic and described by a random variable C_2 defined on a specified probability space $(\Omega, \mathcal{F}, \mathbb{P})$ (see Appendix A). We now use a recursive framework to separate risk aversion and attitude towards intertemporal variation in consumption. Here, the idea is that some increasing and concave function f, the so-called aggregator, combines current consumption and some 'present value' of future consumption (see Munk (2013),

Section 5.7). Let us use the certainty equivalent $\mu(C_2)^1$ as this present value and an iso-elastic time aggregator function. Thus,

$$U_1 = \left(c_1^{1-\rho} + \beta \mathbb{E}[\mu(C_2)^{1-\rho}]\right)^{\frac{1}{1-\rho}}, \tag{4.2}$$

where $\beta \in (0,1)$ represents the pure time preference (with $\delta = \log((1-\beta)/\beta)$, in (4.1)), the parameter $1/\rho$ represents the elasticity of intertemporal substitution (EIS), and γ is the risk aversion parameter. So, risk aversion and time preferences are separated. Let us interpret this framework immediately in a carbon risk context using an example examined by Ha-Duong and Treich (2004). Divide the consumption variable into two parts: an exogenous value y_t and an endogenous control e_t, which represent the CO_2 emissions in period t. The initial inventory of pollutants in the atmosphere is m_0, and during the transition from one period to the next, a proportion q (with $0 < q < 1$) of the pollutants remains in the atmosphere. In addition, pollution increases due to emissions, so $m_t = qm_{t-1} + e_t$ for $t = 1, 2$. Consumption in period 1 and the associated emissions reduce consumption in period 2 due to climate damage by $D(X) = m_2(1 - X)$. So, climate damage is proportional to the pollution m_2 and represents the consequences of consumption and emissions. The random variable X describes the uncertainty in climate damage resulting from emissions. The consumption in the two periods is given as

$$c_1 = y_1 + e_1 = y_1 + m_1 - qm_0, \tag{4.3}$$

$$C_2 = y_2 + e_2 - D(X) = y_2 - qm_1 + Xm_2. \tag{4.4}$$

We now use the utility framework in (4.2) to optimise utility and to obtain optimal consumption levels and resource use. So, plugging in the explicit form of the certainty equivalent, the objective is

$$\max_{(m_1,m_2)} U_1 = \Big((y_1 + m_1 - qm_0)^{1-\rho} + \beta \mathbb{E}[(y_2 - qm_1 + Xm_2)^{1-\gamma}]^{\frac{1-\rho}{1-\gamma}}\Big)^{\frac{1}{1-\rho}}. \tag{4.5}$$

We can solve (4.5) in two steps. First, as all quantities are positive, it is enough to look at $\mathbb{E}\left[(y_2 - qm_1 + m_2)^{1-\gamma}\right]$, and the first-order

[1]The certainty equivalent $\mu(C)$ of a future consumption C is defined as $\mu(C) = \mathbb{E}(u(C))$ (see Munk (2013), Section 5.6).

condition is

$$\frac{\partial}{\partial m_2}\mathbb{E}\left[(y_2 - qm_1 + Xm_2)^{1-\gamma}\right]$$
$$= (1-\gamma)\mathbb{E}\left[X\left(1+\frac{m_2}{y_2 - qm_1}X\right)^{-\gamma}\right] = 0.$$

So, writing k for the solution of $\mathbb{E}\left[\tilde{x}\left(1+k\tilde{x}\right)^{-\gamma}\right] = 0$, we find

$$m_2^* = (y_2 - qm_1)k. \tag{4.6}$$

Define $\mu(\gamma) := \mathbb{E}\left[(1+k\tilde{x})^{1-\gamma}\right]^{\frac{1}{1-\gamma}}$; then, the certainty equivalent of future consumption is

$$\mu(C_2) = (y_2 - qm_1)\mu(\gamma). \tag{4.7}$$

Now, we plug the optimal m_2^* in (4.5) and solve for m_1. The first-order condition is

$$(y_1 + m_1 - qm_0)^{-\rho} - \beta[(y_2 - qm_1)\mu(\gamma)]^{-\rho}q\mu(\gamma) = 0,$$

which gives

$$m_1^* = \frac{qm_0 - y_1 + y_2\mu(\gamma)(\beta q\mu(\gamma))^{-\frac{1}{\rho}}}{1 + q\mu(\gamma)(\beta q\mu(\gamma))^{-\frac{1}{\rho}}}. \tag{4.8}$$

We can now compute the optimal consumption in period 1 as

$$c_1^*(\gamma,\rho) = \frac{\frac{y_2}{q} + y_1 - qm_0}{1 + \beta^{\frac{1}{\rho}}(\mu(\gamma)q)^{\frac{1}{\rho}-1}}. \tag{4.9}$$

The explicit form of the consumption in the first period allows one to analyse sensitivities easily. We notice directly that consumption is increasing in exogenous endowment y_1, y_2 and decreasing in the initial pollution level, the decay factor q, and the discount factor β (which corresponds to an increase in the discount rate r).

To analyse the solution with respect to the interplay of the risk aversion and time preference, we calculate the total derivative of c_1^*:

$$dc_1^* = \frac{\partial c_1^*}{\partial \rho}d\rho + \frac{\partial c_1^*}{\partial \gamma}d\gamma. \tag{4.10}$$

Thus, we can disentangle the effects of the risk aversion and intertemporal substitution. We calculate the partial derivatives to see that

$\frac{\partial c_1^*(\rho,\gamma)}{\partial \gamma} < 0$ if and only if $\rho > 1$. As $\rho > 1$ can generally be assumed, we find that risk aversion has a negative effect on the consumption of the first period. With rising risk aversion, i.e., a rising fear of future climate damage, consumption and associated emissions are reduced.

The intertemporal substitution effect works in the opposite direction, i.e., $\frac{\partial c_1^*(\rho,\gamma)}{\partial \rho} > 0$ if $\beta q \mu(\gamma) > 1$, which is the case if $\mu(C_2) > c_1^*$. An increasing substitution effect means that consumption is distributed as evenly as possible, and therefore, consumption from the richer future shifts to the present (as there is a positive growth rate).

Let us, in passing, consider uncertainty about the growth rate g. Assume g is modelled as a random variable: $g \sim \mathcal{N}(\mu_g, \sigma_g^2)$. Thus, the parameter μ_g can be interpreted as the expected growth rate. In the pure additive setting of (4.1), this implies $r = \delta + \gamma\mu_g - \gamma^2 \frac{\sigma_g^2}{2}$. We observe that uncertainty about the growth rate lowers the discount factor, which in this case, without explicit time preferences, increases the current value of future consumption. In the current setting (4.2), we find

$$r = \delta + \rho\mu_g - (\gamma - \rho + \rho\gamma)\frac{\sigma_g^2}{2}. \tag{4.11}$$

With the standard assumption that risk aversion is greater than the intertemporal risk aversion ($\gamma > \rho$), future consumption will be discounted at a lower rate. So, the benefits of future consumption are discounted to a lesser extent and given a higher weighting compared to current consumption. See also Gollier (2012) for a discussion, which includes the case of an uncertain volatility.

4.1.3 *Ambiguity and Uncertainty*

Let us now extend the approach in (4.2) to include uncertainty about the future probability distributions. Here, we follow the ideas of the 'Smooth Ambiguity Aversion' developed in Klibanoff *et al.* (2005). The probability distribution for future events is replaced by a probability distribution *over the possible probability distributions* for future events. For our framework, the recursive variant of Klibanoff *et al.* (2009) is relevant. We immediately consider the inclusion of ambiguity in our example. The uncertainty within the model depends on the random variable X. However, we are uncertain about its distribution (as we are about the precise form of the damage function, which could be treated in a model risk framework), and we will use a whole class of distributions, $\mathcal{D}$, to capture this. The recursive approach now requires one to average over this so-called second-order uncertainty distribution (see Klibanoff *et al.* (2009)). For this step, we assume that the class of distributions $\mathcal{D}$ can be parametrised by a parameter space Θ. Then, possible probability distributions are indexed by a parameter $\theta \in \Theta$, denoted by $\mathbb{P}(\theta)$, and we assume the existence of a probability distribution π on the space Θ that specifies the likelihood of events. In order to introduce ambiguity preferences, we use an increasing and concave function ϕ ($\phi' > 0, \phi'' < 0$). The extended utility function with ambiguity is now

$$U_1(\Theta, \pi) = \left[c_1^{1-\rho} + \beta\phi^{-1}\left\{\int_\Theta \phi\left[\mu(C_2, \theta)^{1-\rho}\right] d\pi(\theta)\right\}\right]^{\frac{1}{1-\rho}}, \quad (4.12)$$

where $\mu(C, \theta) = \mathbb{E}_{\mathbb{P}(\theta)}(u(C))$ is the certainty equivalent corresponding to the specific distribution labelled θ.

As closed-form solutions cannot be obtained in the general case, we report on a few results from a simulation exercise. For $\xi > \rho > 1$, we use

$$\phi(u) = \frac{-(-u)^{1+\xi}}{1+\xi}. \quad (4.13)$$

For parameter choice, we use typical values $\rho = 1.5$, $\gamma = 2$, and $\xi \in [5, 10]$ (see Millner *et al.* (2013)). Our simulations show that an increase in ξ, i.e., an increase in ambiguity aversion, leads to an increasing effort to avoid emissions. Thus, consumption in the first period is reduced. A similar effect can be observed in terms of the distribution π, which governs the probability of the damage distribution. In case the probability weight on distributions with higher expected damage and/or higher variability of damages is increased, consumption in the first period is likewise reduced. Generally, an increase in ambiguity aversion puts more weight on states with low expected utility and less weight on those with high expected utility. For the case $\gamma = \rho$, a multi-period discussion using a DICE model is done by Millner *et al.* (2013). Furthermore, Traeger (2014) offers a detailed discussion on the effects of ambiguity on the discount rate. His findings are in line with our results in that ambiguity aversion will decrease present consumption. See also Gollier (2012), Chapter 6, for a discussion on the effect of uncertain volatility.

4.2 Asset Pricing Approaches

We now embed the question of pricing carbon emissions in an asset pricing framework. In this context, GHGs in the atmosphere are considered as a negative payoff asset. We start with a multi-period discrete model, which operates in an Epstein–Zin recursive utility framework and complement this with various dynamic continuous-time models.

4.2.1 *Discrete-Time Models*

Here, we follow a representative agent model suggested by Daniel *et al.* (2016). There are periods $t \in \{0, 1, \ldots, T\}$ and in each period, the agent has a certain base amount of the consumption good c_t^b available. Now, the agent can mitigate in each period a fraction $0 \leq x_t \leq 1$ of emissions, which costs a fraction $\kappa_t(x_t)$ of his/her endowed consumption parts. Additionally, climate change damage reduces his/her consumption. The damage function is given as $D_t(\bar{x}_t, X_t)$ and depends on the cumulative GHG mitigation $\bar{x}_t$ and a random variable X_t which captures the uncertain effect of GHG concentration in the atmosphere and consumption damages.

Thus, the consumption stream for $t \in \{1, 2, \ldots, T\}$ is given by

$$
\begin{aligned}
c_0 &= c_0^b(1 - \kappa_0(x_0)), \\
c_t &= c_t^b(1 - D_t(\bar{x}_t, X_t) - \kappa_t(x_t)), \quad t \in \{1, 2, \ldots, T-1\}, \\
c_T &= c_T^b(1 - D_T(\bar{x}_T, X_T)). \qquad (4.14)
\end{aligned}
$$

The agent's optimisation problem determines the optimal mitigation strategy $x_t^*(X_t)$, $t \in \{0, 1, \ldots, T\}$ to maximise his/her utility.

As in our discussion in Section 4.1, and as also pointed out by Daniel *et al.* (2016), it is important to separate time and risk preferences. Thus, they use the Epstein–Zin (4.2) specification. Thus, utility is represented as

$$
U_t = \left(c_t^{1-\rho} + \beta \mathbb{E}_t[\mu(U_{t+1})^{1-\rho}]\right)^{\frac{1}{1-\rho}}, \quad t = 0, 1, \ldots, T-1, \qquad (4.15)
$$

with $\mu(U_{t+1})$ the certainty equivalent of future lifetime utility with coefficient of relative risk aversion γ. Utility at the final time point

T cumulates all future utility and is calculated as a perpetuity; see Daniel *et al.* (2016) for details.

In order to calibrate the model, estimates for marginal abatement costs over time and pricing emissions in terms of a tax rate are linked with consumption loss. As long as technology does not change the consumption loss function, κ is assumed to be time-invariant. Technology change is brought into the model by defining a multiplicative technology change cost factor. The damage function is specified in terms of temperature change $\Delta(T)$ until the final time point T. Temperature distributions at other time points are specified by the functional form

$$\Delta(t) = 2\Delta(T)(1 - e^{-\frac{t}{T}\log 2}),$$

which implies a decreasing magnitude of temperature increase over the years. Economic loss is then associated to temperature increase using a specification from Pindyck (2012) based on data from the fourth assessment report, IPCC (2007). In addition, probabilistic assumptions on tipping points causing extreme damage are included.

Daniel *et al.* (2016) calibrate the model for a five-period case starting in 2015, which is used for the starting values of emissions and consumption and proceed in 30-year interval steps. The results of their simulations show that carbon emissions should be priced higher early (well above USD 100 per tonne of CO_2e emission), which should then decline over time. They also demonstrate the importance of including tail risks, which increases the carbon price substantially with a stronger effect in case risk aversion and time preferences are separated. The decline of carbon prices reflects the degree by which uncertainty is resolved and also the potential for technological progress.

Of course, as in Section 4.1, uncertainty on future effects can also be reflected in using smooth ambiguity models. Again, with a prior π, which reflects the beliefs and/or information of the representative agent over the different possible distributions, recursive utility can be formulated as follows. In total, we get

$$U_t = \left(c_t^{1-\rho} + \beta\left(\int_\Theta \mathbb{E}_\theta[\mu(U_{t+1})]^{1-\xi} d\pi(\theta)\right)^{\frac{1-\rho}{1-\xi}}\right)^{\frac{1}{1-\rho}}. \qquad (4.16)$$

The parameter ξ now reflects ambiguity aversion, and increasing ξ will result in a higher level of carbon prices.

4.2.2 *Continuous-Time Models*

Continuous-time stochastic equilibrium models allow a mathematically elegant formulation of optimisation problems. Typically, a Hamilton–Jacobi–Bellman (HJB) equation can be stated, for which optimal strategies can be obtained as solutions of partial differential equations (see Appendix A for details). We present an application of this technique developed by Hambel *et al.* (2020).

In this setting, models for the carbon dioxide concentration in the atmosphere, the global average temperature, and the global gross domestic product (GDP) together with their interaction are provided. Let us outline the specifications in the following sections.

4.2.2.1 *Carbon Dioxide Model*

Anthropological and natural shocks increase, while natural sinks, such as oceans and forests, decrease the CO_2 concentration in the atmosphere. The models address both effects. Start with the total current CO_2 concentration in the atmosphere, which is specified as

$$Y_t^S = \tilde{Y}_0 + Y_t, \tag{4.17}$$

where $\tilde{Y}_0$ is some pre-industrial age starting concentration and Y_t is the anthropogenic amount of atmospheric CO_2. Its dynamics are given as

$$dY_t = Y_t[(\mu_y(t) - \alpha_t)dt + \sigma_y dW_t^y], \tag{4.18}$$

with W^y a standard Brownian motion. The process μ_y models the expected growth rate of atmospheric CO_2, i.e., the business-as-usual scenario. Additional abatement strategies are captured by the process α and change the overall growth rate. Technology restrictions are used to put an upper bound on the feasible abatement strategies. W^y models unexpected shocks with volatility σ_y. In addition, the process X, which measures the total quantity of atmospheric CO_2 that has already been absorbed by natural sinks, is included. X and Y are connected by a system of stochastic differential equations, for which we refer the reader to the original exposition.

4.2.2.2 *Climate Model*

The climate model employs the link of atmospheric CO_2 concentrations to global warming:

$$T_t = \eta_\tau \log\left(\frac{Y_t^S}{\tilde{Y}_0}\right).$$

The average global temperature dynamics are given by

$$dT_t = \frac{\eta_\tau Y_t}{Y_t^S}(\mu_y(t) - \alpha_t)dt + \frac{\sigma_\tau Y_t}{Y_t^S} dW_t^{y,\tau} + \Gamma_\tau(T_{t-})dN_t^\tau, \tag{4.19}$$

where $W_t^{y,\tau} = \rho_{y\tau} W_t^y + \sqrt{1-\rho_{y,\tau}} W_t^\tau$ with a Brownian motion W^τ independent of W^y and $\rho_{y,\tau}$ a correlation parameter. N^τ is a point process independent of the Brownian motions with intensity λ_τ and jump size distribution Γ_τ, both of which may depend on the temperature process T_t. Thus, the temperature process is a jump diffusion process[2] and as such has a right-skewed heavy-tailed distribution, which is in line with our discussion in Section 3.5.

4.2.2.3 *Economic Model*

Here, the dynamics of global GDP C is considered in a stylised production economy. Global warming has a negative effect on the drift of global GDP. The representative agent (society) can only indirectly influence this effect by choosing abatement strategies. As in Section 4.1.1, a factor K_t^α capturing abatement cost under abatement policy α and a damage factor D_t dependent on climate change are introduced. In the current context, real GDP C_t is the economic variable to be considered:

$$C_t = \bar{C}_t K_t^\alpha D_t, \tag{4.20}$$

with $\bar{C}_t$ the shadow GDP without climate change impact. Its dynamics are

$$d\bar{C}_t = \bar{C}_t(g(t)dt + \sigma_c dW^{y,\tau,c}), \tag{4.21}$$

where $W_t^{y,\tau,c} = \rho_{c,y} W_t^y + \rho_{c,\tau} W_t^\tau + \rho_c W^c$ is a further Brownian motion independent of the Brownian motions W^τ, W^y and the point process N^τ. $\rho_{c,y}, \rho_{c,\tau}$, and ρ_c are correlation parameters (which can be

[2]For general properties and variants of these processes, i.e., Lévy processes, see Bingham and Kiesel (2004).

explicitly computed). g is the growth rate which may depend on a consumption rate χ.

Hambel *et al.* (2020) consider two variants of the damage function. They use a level impact $D_t = D(T_t)$, where damage only depends on the current temperature. A more realistic model links damage to the whole path of temperature change $D_t = \exp\{-\zeta_d \int_0^t T_s ds\}$, with ζ_d a scaling parameter. Lasting damages, such as crossing tipping points, are possible within this variant. Defining the cost process $K_t^\alpha = \exp\{-\int_0^t \kappa(s, Y_s, \alpha_s)ds\}$ with κ the instantaneous growth effect, they arrive at real GDP dynamics:

$$dC_t = C_t((g(t,\chi) - \zeta_d T_t)dt + \sigma_c dW^{y,\tau,c} - \kappa(t, Y_t, \alpha_t)). \quad (4.22)$$

Now, all is in place to formulate the representative agent's time t utility $J_t^{\alpha,\chi}$, with Epstein–Zin type preferences:

$$J_t^{\alpha,\chi} = \mathbb{E}_t\left[\int_t^\infty f(C_s^{\alpha,\chi}, J_s^{\alpha,\chi})ds\right], \quad (4.23)$$

with the aggregator function depending on the same parameters and same interpretation as usual, namely the relative risk aversion γ, the elasticity of intertemporal substitution ρ, and a pure rate of time preferences δ.

The representative agent has a set $\mathcal{A}$ of admissible abatement–consumption strategies α, χ to maximise time t utility at every time point t. The optimisation is done depending on the current value of the variables C, X, Y, and T:

$$J(t, c, x, y, \tau) = \sup_{(\alpha,\chi)\in\mathcal{A}} \{J_t^{\alpha,\chi} | C_t = c, X_t = x, Y_t = y, T_t = \tau\}. \quad (4.24)$$

So, the Hamilton–Jacobi–Bellman (HJB) equation is[3]

$$0 = \sup_{\alpha,\chi}\Bigg\{ J_t + c(g - \zeta_d\tau - \kappa)J_c + \frac{1}{2}c^2\sigma_c^2 J_{cc} + y(\mu_y - \alpha)J_y$$
$$+ \frac{1}{2}y^2\sigma_y^2 J_{yy} - \delta_y(x)yJ_x + \frac{y\eta_\tau}{y + \tilde{Y}_0}(\mu_y - \alpha)J_\tau + \frac{1}{2}\left(\frac{\sigma_\tau y}{y+\tilde{Y}_0}\right)^2 J_{\tau\tau}$$

[3]Subscripts of J denote partial derivatives.

$$+ \frac{y^2}{y+\tilde{Y}_0}\rho_{y,\mathcal{T}}\sigma_y\sigma_{\mathcal{T}}J_{y\mathcal{T}} + cy\rho_{c,y}\sigma_y\sigma_c J_{cy} + c\sigma_c\rho_{c,\mathcal{T}}\frac{\sigma_{\mathcal{T}}y}{y+\tilde{Y}_0}J_{c\mathcal{T}}$$

$$+\lambda_{\mathcal{T}}\left[J(t,c,y,\mathcal{T}+\Gamma_{\mathcal{T}})-J\right]+f(\chi c,J)\Big\}. \tag{4.25}$$

The HJB (4.25) can be solved by numerical methods, e.g., using finite differences. We will also not present the calibration procedure but state the main results directly.

Importantly, the analysis sheds light on the difference of modelling the impact of climate change on output in terms of level vs. growth. In case the impact is on the level of output, the optimal abatement policy, and thus the social cost of carbon (i.e., the price of carbon), varies highly with temperature. In this setting, risk aversion and the elasticity of intertemporal substitution have a significant effect on the choice of policy. In the case of a growth impact, the importance of risk aversion diminishes. In contrast to the results in Section 4.1, the price of carbon is increasing during the whole time period under consideration (which ends in 2200).

Barnett *et al.* (2019) also rely on a similar continuous-time model and recursive utilities and focus on the modelling of uncertainty and its impact on policy decisions explicitly. For that, they include ambiguity and aspects of model robustness (uncertainty about models) in their investigation. To address ambiguity, they use the smooth ambiguity setting (see Klibanoff *et al.* (2005) and Section 4.1). Their results reveal a substantial impact of uncertainty on the SCC, which account for roughly half its value. Again, the SCC increases over the period under consideration (the next 100 years). A very detailed analysis on how uncertainty affects the SCC is the focus of Lemoine (2020). Precautionary saving, the scaling of damages with consumption, and the covariance between future consumption and the impact of present emission reductions on future consumption growth are identified as the major channels through which the SCC is affected. Through numerical simulations, it is shown that uncertainty substantially increases the SCC and the uncertainty about the effects of climate change on consumption is especially important.

Cai and Lontzek (2019) study a stochastic generalisation referred to as the DSICE model. They emphasise the importance of climate tipping points as thresholds to an irreversible transition to a different climate process. Their approach is based on high-dimensional Markov chains and requires substantial computational resources. They also find that uncertainty substantially affects the SCC. In particular, the inclusion of tipping points substantially increases (more than triples) the SCC.

The results we presented show, very convincingly, the power in mathematical models to analyse the impact of climate change on society. They also emphasise the importance of using such models carefully in terms of interpretation and robustness of results. However, properly handled, they provide insight on possible risk-management measures — in this context, abatement strategies — to alter the risks arising from climate change.

4.3 What Do the Markets Think?

4.3.1 *Green Impact Investing*

Here, we discuss the question whether corporate GHG emissions (or intensity) may be driven by the pressure applied by green investors, i.e., by green (impact) investment. Obtaining insights into the mechanism that influences corporate abatement and mitigation decisions is also of importance for the discussion of the role of large portfolio investors (and even for central banks). Green investors screen companies and exclude (by divestment) or underweight carbon-intensive (measured by some form of carbon intensity) companies. Thus, they internalise the expected financial impact of future environmental externalities of companies in which they invest. These externalities can be positive or negative depending on the transition, physical, or litigation risk a company is exposed to.

To discuss green investing, we follow a simplified version of a dynamic continuous-time framework provided by De Angelis *et al.* (2020). The securities market model uses an n-dimensional Brownian motion as the source of randomness. There are n risky stocks, numbered $i \in \{1, \dots, n\}$ and trading is possible at $t \in [0, T]$, i.e., until a terminal date T. Thus, the market model is free of arbitrage and complete (see Appendix A for definitions). Each stock is a claim on a single liquidating dividend D_T^i at T, so $p_T^i = D_T^i$ with p_t^i the equilibrium price processes. The n-dimensional vector of terminal dividends is given as

$$D_T = D_0 + \int_0^T \sigma_t dB_t, \tag{4.26}$$

with σ_t a deterministic volatility (n, n)-matrix and B_t a standard n-dimensional Brownian motion[4] defined on a filtered probability space $(\Omega, \mathcal{F}, \mathbb{F}, \mathbb{P})$. The underlying interpretation is that the terminal dividend is driven by a sequence of cash flow events given by $\sigma_t^i dW_t^i$ for each stock i. The dividend forecasts are given by the conditional expectations $D_t = \mathbb{E}(D_T|\mathcal{F}_t)$.

Two types of investors act in the market with different expectations regarding the cash flow news. These are regular investors, whose information is given by the framework of the previous paragraph, and green investors, who internalise the financial impact of the expected environmental externalities of the companies they invest in, which results in an additional drift term in equation (4.26). In particular, the drift term is given by a decreasing function $\theta_i(\psi_t^i)$, where ψ_t^i are the emissions (or a related quantity) of firm i at time t. In vector notation, the process D_t has a deterministic drift $\int_0^t \theta(\psi_s)ds$, the terminal dividend for green investors is

$$D_T = D_0 + \int_0^T \theta(\psi_t)dt + \int_0^T \sigma_t dW_t \tag{4.27}$$

and its conditional expectations $\mathbb{E}(D_T|\mathcal{F}_t) = D_t + \int_t^T \theta(\psi_s)ds$.

Regular (r) and green (g) investors trade in the available assets with (n-dimensional) trading strategies $\varphi_t^{r,g}$, which specify the quantities of asset i held at time t. So, they have wealth processes[5]

$$W_t^x = w + \int_0^T (\varphi_s^x)' dp_s, \quad x \in \{r, g\}, \tag{4.28}$$

[4]We will typically use W for Brownian motions; however, as a wealth process is needed in this section, we change the notation. Both types are used in the literature.

[5]For vectors x, y, x' denotes the transposed vector and $x'y$ the usual vector multiplication.

with w the (equal) initial wealth of investors. Now, investors maximise the expected utility of terminal wealth W_T:

$$\mathbb{E}\left(1 - \exp\{-\gamma W_T^x\}\right) \quad x \in \{r, g\}, \tag{4.29}$$

γ specifies the absolute risk aversion of the investors and is assumed to be equal across the investors.

This allows one to obtain the asset prices in equilibrium:

$$\begin{aligned} p_t = D_t - \int_t^T \mu_s ds \quad \text{with } \mu_t = \gamma_t \Sigma_t \mathbf{1} - \frac{1}{2}\theta(\psi_t) \\ \text{and } \Sigma_t = \sigma_t' \sigma_t. \end{aligned} \tag{4.30}$$

Here, $-\frac{1}{2}\theta(\psi_t)$ is the externality premium and links the asset price to emission schedules. The optimal trading strategies for regular and green investors can now be obtained as

$$\varphi_t^r = \frac{1}{2}\left(\mathbf{1} - \frac{1}{\gamma}\Sigma_t^{-1}\theta(\psi_t)\right) \tag{4.31}$$

and

$$\varphi_t^r = \frac{1}{2}\left(\mathbf{1} + \frac{1}{\gamma}\Sigma_t^{-1}\theta(\psi_t)\right). \tag{4.32}$$

Let us outline the steps to prove the above results before we discuss the interpretation. Details of the proofs (in a richer model) can be found in De Angelis *et al.* (2020). Now, as the market is complete and free of arbitrage, there exists a unique equivalent market measure, which we call the risk-neutral measure. Investors, regular and green, solve their optimisation problems assuming their respective asset price dynamics induced by the different news processes. To find the optimal terminal wealth, a standard Lagrange multiplier argument can be used (optimised subject to a budget constraint). Observe that this optimisation problem searches for a random variable in a set of admissible random variables. The next step uses the market clearing condition, the sum of the terminal wealth of the investors must be the dividend payments at T, to identify the risk-neutral measure. From the martingale condition, the asset price dynamics can be computed. To find the optimal trading strategies, the completeness of the market is used. Indeed, the optimal terminal wealth of the (regular and green) investors is a contingent claim and can be replicated by trading the assets. The trading strategies for replicating the optimal terminal wealth of the regular and green investors are the optimal strategies.

Equation 4.26 shows how asset prices react to the adjustment by the externality premium. Prices increase with the financial impact of future environmental externalities via the internalisation by green investors driven by the function θ. De Angelis *et al.* (2020) provide a richer model which also allows for different initial wealth of green and regular investors. They show that prices also increase with the proportion of green investors' wealth relative to total wealth. In summary, asset prices for brown companies will be lower than those of green companies (and conversely equilibrium returns higher).

In a further extension, De Angelis *et al.* (2020) include uncertainty about environmental externalities in their analysis. As climate risks are characterised by fat tails and tipping points (see Section 3.5), point processes should be used to model this additional uncertainty. Thus, a time-inhomogeneous Poisson process N with (n-dimensional) intensity (Λ_t) and independent jump sizes $(Y_k)_{k\geq 1}$ are used to express the vector of terminal dividends as

$$D_T = D_0 + \int_0^T \sigma_t dB_t + \sum_{k+1}^{N_T} Y_k. \tag{4.33}$$

So, in the time interval $[0, T]$, a random number of shocks N^i with jump sizes Y_k^i occur. When uncertainty about the realisation of future environmental externalities is internalised in this way, green investors reduce the share of investing in green companies, and expected returns for brown companies decrease and increase for green companies. This highlights again the need for transparency and accuracy of GHG emission data for companies (an issue discussed in Chapter 6).

De Angelis *et al.* (2020) also include the optimisation of companies on their emission schedule in their framework. The optimal schedule balances the cost saving of not putting abatement measures in place and the negative effect of the environmental externalities. They show that emissions decrease as the function of the proportion of assets managed by the green investors and their environmental stringency and increase with the cost of reducing environmental externalities. Thus, it is important to give companies access to low-cost technology solutions to reduce emissions, which justifies the support to greener technology development.

In Chapter 13, we discuss the empirical evidence for these effects.

4.3.2 *Green vs. Brown Stocks*

For our discussion, we use a simplified version of a model introduced in Pastor *et al.* (2020). Consider a single-period model, $t \in \{0, 1\}$, with n firms, a continuum for investor u time points. The (excess)[6] return vector is

$$R = \mu + \epsilon, \tag{4.34}$$

with μ the equilibrium (excess) returns and $\epsilon \sim \mathcal{N}(0, \Sigma)$. Firms have a carbon-characteristic $g = (g_i)$, which is positive in case they generate positive externalities or negative in case the externalities are negative. We call the first type of firms *green*; the second type is labelled *brown*. Investors care about this and have a carbon sensitivity $d_u \geq 0$ (increasing d_u means a higher importance). The initial, time $t = 0$, wealth of investors is w, and their wealth at time $t = 1$ is $W_u = w_u(1 + x_u' R)$, with x_u the vector whose ith elements specify the fraction of wealth of investor u invested in asset i.

The utility of investor u is

$$U(W_u, x_u) = -\exp\{-\gamma_u W_u - x_u' b_u\}, \tag{4.35}$$

with $b_u = d_u g$.

Let us assume that investors have identical relative risk aversion $\rho = \gamma_u w_u$. To obtain the optimal portfolio weights, we use the normality assumption (in particular, we use the formula for the moment-generating function of a normally distributed random variable) and evaluate the first-order conditions:

$$\begin{aligned}
\mathbb{E}[U(W_u, x_u)] &= \mathbb{E}\left[-\exp\left\{-\rho(1 + x_u' R) - x_u' b_u\right\}\right] \\
&= -e^{-\rho}\mathbb{E}\left[\exp\left\{-\rho x_u'\left(R + \frac{b_u}{\rho}\right)\right\}\right] \\
&= -e^{-\rho}\exp\left\{-\rho x_u'\left(\mu + \frac{b_u}{\rho}\right) + \frac{\rho^2}{2} x_u' \Sigma x_u\right\}.
\end{aligned}$$

[6]We assume that the risk-free rate is zero.

Differentiating with respect to x_u, we obtain the first-order condition

$$-\rho\left(\mu + \frac{b_u}{\rho}\right) + \frac{\rho^2}{2}\Sigma x_u = 0,$$

and so,

$$x_u = \frac{1}{\rho}\Sigma^{-1}\left(\mu + \frac{b_u}{\rho}\right). \tag{4.36}$$

Let $\omega = \int w_u du$ be the total initial wealth and $\omega_u = w_u/\omega$ the investor u's relative share of total wealth. Then, define $\bar{d} = \int \omega_u d_u du \geq 0$ the wealth-weighted mean of carbon sensitivity across investors. Now, using the market-clearing condition, we find for the weights x_M of the market portfolio

$$\begin{aligned} x_M &= \int \omega_u x_u du = \frac{1}{\rho}\Sigma^{-1}\int \omega_u\left(\mu + \frac{b_u}{\rho}\right)du \\ &= \frac{1}{\rho}\Sigma^{-1}\mu + \frac{\bar{d}}{\rho^2}\Sigma^{-1}g. \end{aligned}$$

From this, we obtain the market equity premium

$$\mu_M = x'_M\mu = \rho\sigma_M^2 - \frac{\bar{d}}{\rho}x'_M g, \tag{4.37}$$

with σ_M^2 the variance of the market return. With the natural assumption that the market is carbon-neutral, i.e., $x'_M g = 0$, we find (this is proposition 1 in Pastor *et al.* (2020))

$$\mu = \mu_m\beta - \frac{\bar{d}}{\rho}g. \tag{4.38}$$

Here, $\beta = \frac{1}{\sigma_M^2}\Sigma x_M$ are the market betas. So, for $\bar{d} > 0$, the expected return of stock i is decreasing in g_i, i.e., expected returns are decreasing in the stocks carbon characteristics. Equation (4.38) also implies that the alpha of stock i is

$$\alpha_i = -\frac{\bar{d}}{\rho}g_i, \tag{4.39}$$

and thus, green stocks (recall $g_i > 0$ for these stocks) have a negative α, and brown stocks have a positive α.

The framework also allows one to obtain insights into betas of green and brown stocks in case there are random shocks due to environmental concerns. We only give a brief outline and refer the reader to the detailed analysis in Pastor *et al.* (2020). To include environmental shocks, assume that there are macroshocks Z_h and consumers' demand shifts due to environmental matters. In addition to the exposure to environmental consumer risk, stocks are also affected by investor concerns, so that stocks are exposed to a carbon risk factor Z_g. Let h and g be the sensitives of firms regarding these shocks. Returns are given by $R = Z_h h + Z_g g + \epsilon$. After calculating the market portfolio weights x_M, the market return is $R_M = (x'_M h)Z_h + (x'_M g)Z_g + x'_M \epsilon$. Now, $x'_M g = 0$, and so, it turns out that the beta regarding the green factor is positive as long as $\mathbb{C}\text{ov} Z_h, Z_g > 0$. This implies that the market beta of a green firm increases with a carbon factor and that of a brown firm decreases. So, green firms perform better than brown firms when markets move up and vice versa during market downward movements.

Part II
Carbon Finance — Data

Part II is devoted to applicable statistical techniques, the analysis of data requirements, and the implementation of 'Big Data' solutions. Any attempt to make sense of high-dimensional data requires the formulation and calibration of mathematical models that seek to capture causal relationships prevailing in and between nature, economy, and society. Past experience suggests that in many cases, linear and additive models, in which a dependent variable is modelled as a weighted sum of various inputs plus a random error, are not flexible enough to perform this task in a reliable manner. The great challenge that results from this finding is the need to develop and implement types of models that are flexible enough to accommodate the complexity of the dependence relationships under investigation, while at the same time being sufficiently transparent to perform a number of basic plausibility checks and to enable a causal analysis of deviations between actual and expected model outputs should the need arise. Under the umbrella term 'Big Data Analytics,' a variety of tools and algorithms have been developed, through which these challenges can be addressed. Examples include non-relational databases for the efficient storage of large quantities of raw data, artificial neural networks or regularisation techniques for solving complex classification or regression problems with large numbers of inputs, and various visualisation tools that facilitate the graphical representation of high-dimensional datasets. Their competent application in the intersection of climate science, macroeconomics, and finance thus promises significant contributions to the development of applicable solutions in these fields.

Chapter 5

Carbon Finance and Artificial Intelligence

Artificial intelligence (AI) or machine learning (ML) techniques have recently gained attention in asset pricing, hedging, and generally, the valuation of financial assets. ML is a collective term for processes that apply computer algorithms which improve themselves automatically through experience and by the use of data. It is commonly regarded as a part of AI, which is a summary term for all applications in which machines perform human-like intelligent acts, such as learning, assessment, or problem solving. The use of these techniques often creates the opportunity of performing timely, system-spanning evaluations of large and complex data structures, which lead to the identification of previously unknown interrelations. Often, such activities require the extraction of rather elementary pieces of information from high-dimensional and complex data. The process of transforming data from a high-dimensional space into a low-dimensional space, so that the low-dimensional representation retains some meaningful properties of the original data, is referred to as dimensionality reduction.

Exemplary application of related techniques in a business context involves the calibration of bond spreads by using a combination of market data and meta-information. This includes (among others) the bond's currency, the timing, nature and magnitude of its coupon payments, its seniority and collateral as well as the credit rating, the country of residence, and the sector affiliation of the issuer. The linkage of carbon-related data with market data for the analysis of the impact of carbon risks to credit spreads, stock price performance, and volatility is another typical application. We will see that identifying and measuring the linkage between carbon risk and cost of equity/debt, traditional risk factors (industry, country, etc.), and the interrelation between carbon risk exposure and financials are potential outcomes of the application of such techniques. A completely different but popular example is text mining, i.e., the algorithm-based process of transforming large amounts of text into quantitative information. Applications in the context of carbon risk include the construction of climate news indices or simply the extraction of carbon risk-related information from company reports. Dixon *et al.* (2020) report many more applications in finance.

5.1 A Brief Introduction to Machine Learning

Let us start with the basic statistical techniques, which form the point of departure for the more advanced and data-intensive ML methods.

5.1.1 *Linear and Generalised Linear Models*

We assume an underlying probability space and variables X and Y defined on that space. In the simplest case, we assume we have two sets of observations $x = (x_1, \ldots, x_n)$ (generated from X) and $y = (y_1, \ldots, y_n)$ (generated from Y). Our aim is to understand the relationship between X and Y. Thus, we consider the pairs (y_i, x_i). We call the y_i dependent variables (or response) and the x_i independent (explanatory) variables. The underlying assumption is that there exists a functional relationship

$$Y_i = \varphi(X_i) + \epsilon_i, \quad i = 1, \ldots, n,$$

where $\varphi : \mathbb{R} \to \mathbb{R}$ is called the regression function and $\epsilon_i : \Omega \to \mathbb{R}$ is an error term. In the simplest case, this relationship is linear. Then the regression function is given by

$$\varphi(x) = \alpha + \beta_1 x.$$

We want to estimate the vector $\beta = (\alpha, \beta_1)$ of regression coefficients and obtain confidence intervals for its components. We also want to test whether the components have a 'significant' influence on the output.

Typically, estimation is done by minimising the mean squared error

$$\varepsilon(\alpha, \beta) = \frac{1}{n} \sum_{i=1}^{n} (y_i - (\alpha + \beta x_i))^2. \tag{5.1}$$

We obtain

$$\alpha = \bar{y}_n - \beta \bar{x}_n \quad \text{and} \quad \beta = \frac{s_{xy}^2}{s_{xx}^2},$$

with $s_{yy} = \frac{1}{n-1} \sum_{i=1}^{n} (y_i - \bar{y}_n)^2$, $s_{xx} = \frac{1}{n-1} \sum_{i=1}^{n} (x_i - \bar{x}_n)^2$, and $s_{xy} = \frac{1}{n-1} \sum_{i=1}^{n} (x_i - \bar{x}_n)(y_i - \bar{y}_n)$. Under the standard assumption of independent identically distributed error terms, these are also the maximum likelihood estimators and thus standard properties (e.g., unbiasedness, asymptotic normality) are obtained.

We can generalise the simple linear regression above so that the response variables $Y_i, i = 1, \ldots, n$ can depend on vector-valued explanatory variables $(X_{11}, \ldots, X_{1m}), \ldots, (X_{n1}, \ldots, X_{nm})$, i.e.,

$$Y_i = \varphi(X_{i1}, \ldots, X_{im}) + \varepsilon_i.$$

The regression function φ is given by

$$\varphi(x_1, \ldots, x_n) = \beta_0 + \beta_1 x_1 + \cdots + \beta_m x_m.$$

Again, we want to estimate the coefficients β_j. We assume deterministic explanatory variables and define the following matrices:

$$Y = \begin{pmatrix} Y_1 \\ \vdots \\ Y_n \end{pmatrix}, \quad X = \begin{pmatrix} X_{11} & \ldots & X_{1m} \\ \vdots & & \vdots \\ X_{n1} & \ldots & X_{nm} \end{pmatrix}, \quad \beta = \begin{pmatrix} \beta_1 \\ \vdots \\ \beta_n \end{pmatrix}.$$

X is called the design matrix. We try to find a vector $\hat{\beta}$ such that the mean squared error

$$\epsilon(\beta) = \frac{1}{n} \sum_{i=1}^{n} (Y_i - X_i \beta)^2$$

is minimised (where X_i denotes the ith row of the design matrix). We obtain[1]

$$\hat{\beta} = (X'X)^{-1}X'Y.$$

Under the assumption that the error terms ε_i have zero mean, variance $\sigma^2 > 0$, and are uncorrelated, an F-test for lack of fit and a t-test can be derived for the significance of single components. In addition, confidence intervals can be estimated for each element β_i of β, and joint confidence bands can be obtained for β.

Generalised linear models link a discrete response to explanatory factors. In the binary case, we have responses $Y \in \{0, 1\}$, explanatory variables X, and we are interested in the conditional probabilities

$$\mathbb{P}(Y = 1|X) = 1 - \mathbb{P}(Y = 0|X). \tag{5.2}$$

We assume a functional form

$$\mathbb{P}(Y = 1|X) = F(X, \beta) \quad \text{and} \quad \mathbb{P}(Y = 1|X) = 1 - F(X, \beta). \tag{5.3}$$

Again, β is a d-dimensional parameter vector that shows the impact of the components of X on the conditional probability. In many cases, the normal distribution Φ has been used, which leads to the so-called probit model:

$$\mathbb{P}(Y = 1|X) = \int_{-\infty}^{X'\beta} \phi(t)dt = \Phi(X'\beta). \tag{5.4}$$

A frequently used alternative is the logit model:

$$\mathbb{P}(Y = 1|X) = \frac{\exp(X'\beta)}{1 + \exp(X'\beta)} = \Gamma(X'\beta). \tag{5.5}$$

The logistic distribution has a shape similar to the normal, only the tails are considerably heavier. For both approaches, the parameter estimates can be obtained by maximum likelihood.

With increasing model complexity, the variability of predictions can also increase. Furthermore, with too many parameters, the model can overfit the data, modelling noise rather than the underlying trend and leading to poor generalisation to unseen data. For a deeper discussion of these issues, applications, and ways to handle model complexity, we refer the reader to Greene (2018) and James *et al.* (2017).

---

[1]We denote by X' the transposed vector (matrix) of a vector (matrix) X.

5.1.2 *A Classification of ML Methods*

5.1.2.1 *Supervised Learning*

In supervised learning, we are given labelled data, i.e., pairs $(x_1, y_1), \ldots, (x_n, y_n)$, where x_i are generated from a random variable X and y_i from a random variable Y, and the goal is to understand the relationship between X and Y. Each x_i is referred to as a feature vector, and y_i is the response. This approach is important for the analysis of risk premia on financial markets (see Chapters 9 and 10).

Supervised learning methods have in common the requirement of a large system of linear equations to be solved. Popular examples are the kernel estimation (local smoothing) and (locally) weighted linear combinations. Advantages of such types of methods are well-known theoretical properties and the fact that the impact of individual components can be retraced rather easily. The drawback is the limited capability to deal with nonlinear relationships of unknown form. Artificial neural networks (ANNs) are also a prominent class of methods. They are a natural extension of the linear models as now a nonlinear map $\phi(X)$ over a high-dimensional input space is estimated using hierarchical layers of abstraction. An ANN is a set of interconnected model neurons or units organised in input layers, hidden layers, and output layers. The input of a unit is the superposition of a weighted sum of states of units in the previous layer with a rather simple nonlinear function, e.g., standard logistic function or maximum of argument and zero. The back-propagation algorithm is used to effectively train a neural network and is obtained by using the classical Newton method and derivations via chain rule. ANNs are highly flexible and can be parallelised very well. Deep learning refers to the fact that a higher number of layers improves performance. In addition to the structural components, the number of hidden layers and neurons per layer, the so-called hyper-parameters, are needed to fine-tune the forecasting performance. These are algorithms to optimally train the network, the structure of the training set, the number of training repetitions, and several more. One of the drawbacks is that the choice of network architecture is often more an art than a science. Multi-layered (deep) networks can become arbitrarily complex; therefore, establishing a causal relation between inputs and results is often barely possible. Regression trees are useful for incorporating multi-way predictor interactions. The idea is to spatially split a dataset into increasingly small subsets typically based on a single-feature value. Besides classification, decision trees can also be used for piecewise linear regression. A random forest is an ensemble of classification and regression methods that consists of many decision trees. The predictions of the decision trees are combined to the random forest's predictions by an averaging procedure. Underlying is the idea that the combination of many slightly different decision trees make better predictions than any of them alone. A key advantage of decision trees compared to NNs is that the rules they use to classify data are human readable, and thus, the reasons that lead to a particular classification can be easily traced.

5.1.2.2 *Unsupervised Learning*

In unsupervised learning, we are given unlabelled data $x_1, \ldots, x_n$, and the goal is to derive exploratory information about the data, most often some sort of grouping or hidden structure. Typical forms of unsupervised learning include clustering, i.e., the formation of groups of entities, either based on mutual proximity/similarity or on the proximity to a common central point. Moreover, they contain anomaly detection, i.e., the identification of entities that appear so distant even from their closest peers that they give rise to the suspicion that a data recording/processing error has occurred or that the underlying real-world phenomenon constitutes an exception from commonly known empirical regularities. Classical mathematical procedures for category formation (clustering) include centroid-based (e.g., K-means) clustering, where clusters are represented by a central vector and the objects are attributed to the nearest cluster centre. Moreover, there is connectivity-based (e.g., k-nearest-neighbour) clustering, which is based on the idea of objects being more related to nearby objects than to objects farther away. A further method is density-based clustering (e.g., DBSCAN), in which case clusters are defined as areas of higher density than the remainder of the dataset. These procedures have been studied and tried out extensively, but limitations still exist. For example, small differences or variations in location of data points may cause an object to be rigidly assigned to one or another cluster. We will encounter these techniques when trying to group firms, e.g., according to their disclosure of climate-related data.

A selection of methods and terms used in ML can be found in Table 5.1.

5.1.3 *ML-Based Estimation of Carbon Intensities*

We conclude this section with an example of an ML application to a key question of carbon finance, namely the estimation of carbon intensities. We will use random forest regression for this task as it enables us to integrate a broad set of environmental, fundamental, and company-specific variables to our model setup. The output can be calculated with competing model specifications, estimation procedures, and assumptions on functional forms of the regression. The target of the model is to condense a multidimensional set of variables into one single value. This will allow us to identify companies that perform generally better or worse compared to their close peers with respect to their carbon intensity. As we will see, carbon intensities are needed to study the carbon risk of financial assets (see Chapters 8–11). As model setup, we use a regression of the form

$$Y = f(X, Z, W) + \epsilon. \tag{5.6}$$

The dependent variable Y describes the carbon intensity, here calculated as CO_2e emissions/revenues. For CO_2e emissions, we used the sum of scope 1 and 2 emissions. X collects the fundamental variables, e.g., total assets/total revenues and number of employees/total revenue, operating profit margin (higher profitability might indicate more investments in clean energy and less exposure to carbon risk), and the capital intensity (companies that invest more are in better position to decarbonise their portfolios). Z collects sectorial and geographical decomposition, e.g., the sectorial revenue decomposition (NAICS mapping) in percent of the total revenue for the company each year, the region of company headquarters, and the country income level measured by GDP PPP per capita. Finally, W contains environmental indicators, for example, Boolean variables such as the clean technology (does the company develop clean technology, say wind, solar, hydro, geo-thermal or biomass power?),

Table 5.1. ML terms.

Acronym	Long form	Domain	What it does
CNN	Convolutional neural network	Images	Filters adjacent subsections of an image in a predefined manner, e.g., along vertical lines
	Deep fakes	Images, text	Deceptively realistic replicas, mostly of (animate) pictures; often produced by GANs (see the following)
DNN	Deep learning neural network	All	Artificial neural network in which several layers are superposed
GAN	Generative adversarial network	Images, text	A model employed to distinguish between originals from counterfeits; can be used to automatically generate deceptively similar imitations
LSTM	Long short-term memory	Texts	Comparable to RNN (see the following), but partially extending over short distances and partially over long distances between words
NSL	Neural structured learning	All	Enhancement of learning procedures for neural networks, achieved by using structured signals in addition to feature inputs
PCA	Principal component analysis	Linear methods	Ordering of eigenvectors according to the size of the eigenvalues; rejection of the least relevant ones
	Random forest	All	Applicable if there is a very large variety of candidate inputs; consists of averaging the results obtained with several rivalling combinations of explanatory variables

Table 5.1. (*Continued*)

Acronym	Long form	Domain	What it does
RL	Reinforcement learning	All	Trial and error with feedback, e.g., indicator for winning, drawing, or losing a game of chess; may also be applied to itself in order to learn
RNN	Recurrent neural network	Text	Application of a given filter across the time axis; very similar, in purely mathematical terms, to CNN
SVM	Support vector machine	Linear methods	A method for describing a learner with a rather small number of parameters (L1-penalty, ...)
TL	Transfer learning	All	An attempt to apply a model that was trained on A to B with little effort

awareness of climate change risks/opportunities, emission-reduction objectives/target emission reductions (has the company set any targets or objectives to be achieved with respect to an emissions reduction?), and emission trading (does the company participate in any emission trading initiative?).

In the heatmap (Figure 5.1), average results have been plotted in the form of residuals for each sector–region combination. High values, which are marked in red, indicate that the actual emissions are higher than the average expectation, while low values, marked in green, indicate the opposite.

The methodology is an important input for several additional applications, such as the building of company clusters based on relative emission exposures or for an estimation of carbon risk beta, based on statistical models. Possible models to be applied contain, for example, the portfolio model, the cost of equity model, or the credit spread model. Moreover, the methodology can be used for risk reporting at the corporate, regional, and sector levels.

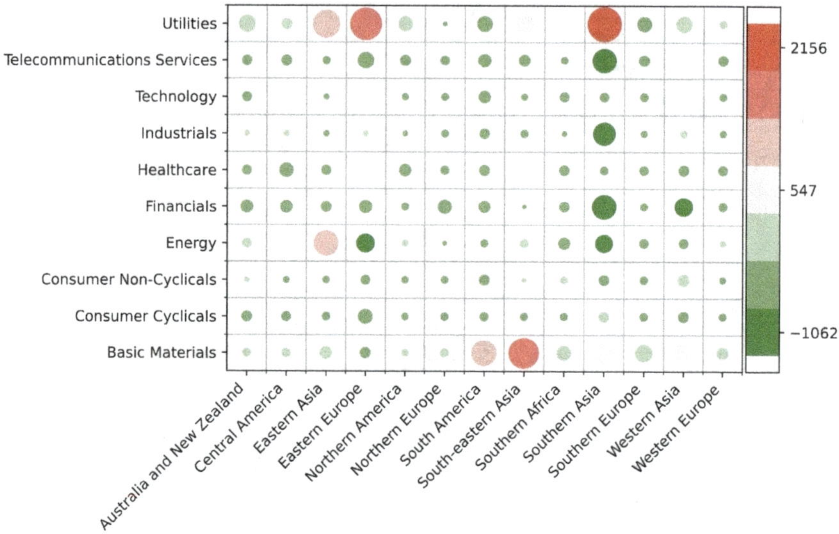

Fig. 5.1. Heatmap.

5.2 Applying AI to Carbon Risk

5.2.1 *Motivation*

In the following, we describe the most important challenges when applying AI techniques to relevant use cases in carbon finance. This (depiction) includes the quality and amount of available data, selection of the adequate techniques and models, interpretation of results, data sharing as well as data privacy and security, and moreover, the availability of enough powerful hardware and capable software.

However, the application of artificial intelligence and machine learning is far from being a cure for many cases of use in carbon finance. There are numerous risks and uncertainties regarding the question of how the transition to a low-carbon world can be achieved. Various measures at the European and global levels are under consideration, such as emission trading, taxation, subsidies, and promotion of technologies. Financial market participants tend to think in time frames of one to three years. Relevant historical data are often not available, which is why results from different models need to be aggregated. There is a high degree of uncertainty due to the fact that estimated statistical distributions of relevant quantities (e.g., the change in temperature in response to a doubling of the CO_2 concentration) often have fat tails. Given these obstacles, traditional approaches from mathematical finance and risk management alone will often not be sufficient to build an effective and systematic approach for identifying, measuring, and managing carbon risks. However, the biggest challenge is the complexity of the problem itself, as economic and financial carbon risks are derived from the complex response of the climate system on GHG emissions and implied physical and political risks. The assessment of the extent to which a company is exposed to climate risks and the effectiveness with which it manages these risks shows itself to be challenging. For example, information must be extracted as inhomogeneous data from the different data sources in aggregated and analysed forms. Equally problematic are companies which do not report such information at all or only do so in a fragmentary manner. However, it is essential that these companies are assigned to clusters of comparable firms.

Another challenge that comes up in the process is, for instance, the automated formation of carbon clusters, in a way that the within-cluster variation of feature values relating to carbon intensity is low, while the differences between clusters are large and statistically significant. Striking a balance between these poles is a typical task for machine learning or artificial intelligence.

Moreover, the successful implementation of an automated mapping of investees and issuers in an investment portfolio to a unique carbon intensity cluster also enables an automated generation of reports on the carbon intensity of the portfolio as a whole. A professional consideration of carbon risks in the practice of portfolio management requires the integration of the relevant risk factors in the valuation and risk models in use. A data-centred strategy creates the opportunity of automatically evaluating carbon-relevant data for large investment portfolios in a timely and comprehensive manner. It enables the assignment of single issuers to carbon clusters under due consideration of a variety of factors as well as the identification of relevant linkages between groups. We will see that a combination of modern techniques described in Figure 5.2 will support us in tackling important challenges, starting with the management of carbon-related risks and ending by using distributed ledger techniques to build an adequate infrastructure for carbon credit trading.

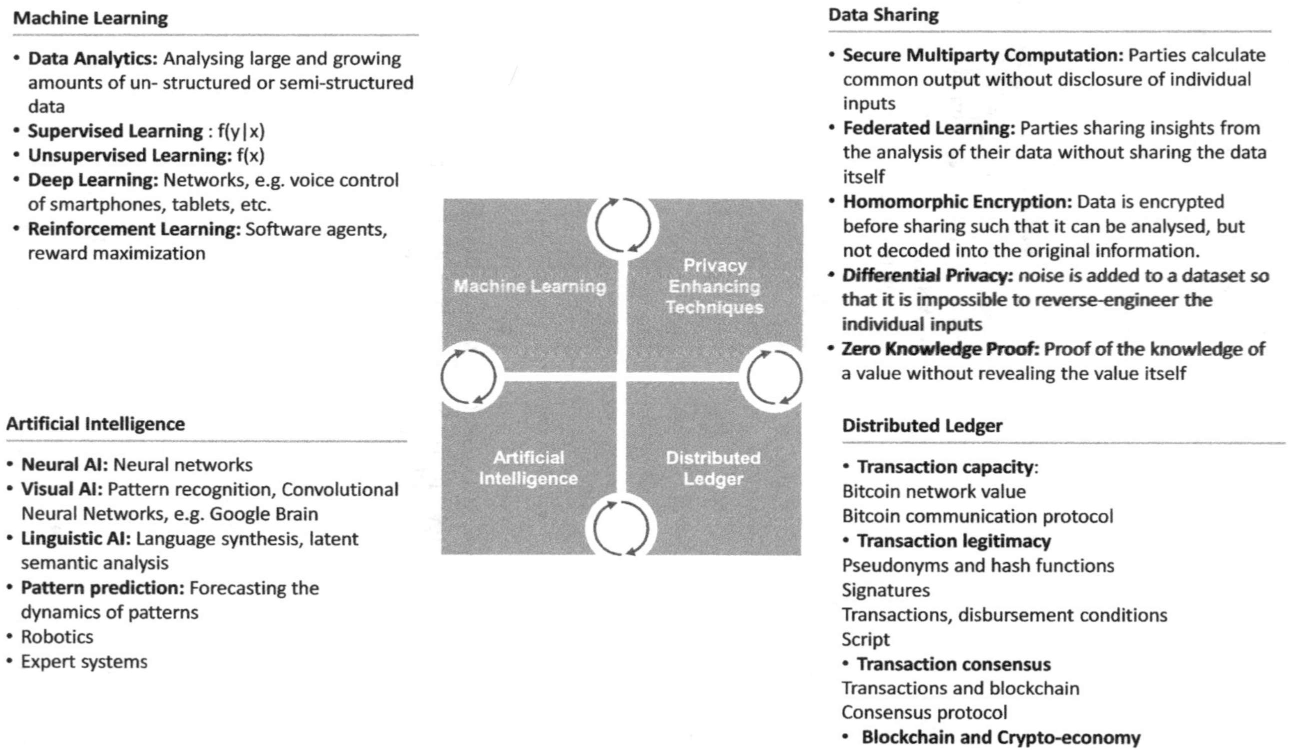

Fig. 5.2. Dimensions of applying AI.

As relevant data often comes from distributed sources subject to different legal and regulatory restrictions, the necessity to share data is not without risks. However, an emerging set of technologies called 'privacy-enhancing techniques' has the potential to reduce or even mitigate these restrictions.

An important example of a privacy-enhancing technique is federated learning. This type of machine learning is based on the iterative aggregation of local and global models. Once a party has trained a model on a local dataset, it transmits the trained local model parameters to a third party, which aggregates local models into a global model. We will see that a successful implementation of such distributed or decentralised techniques can be helpful to close today's existing data gaps.

5.2.2 *Building an AI model*

5.2.2.1 *Data Handling*

At the onset, the relevant information in the data is expressed in terms of vectors of real-valued numbers. This is achieved by a number of nonlinear and, in most cases, irreversible transformations. Often, this step is the most time-consuming stage of the entire process. It involves different steps, for example, data cleansing, which deals with the fact that there are errors in virtually all large datasets. Whenever these errors impede the fulfilment of the task to be performed, these errors either have to be corrected or the related datasets must be identified and excluded. This is a major obstacle in the practice of distributed computing or federated learning. The next step can be referred to as the removal of information items/features considered irrelevant. An example in this case would be text mining applications, in which font information is irrelevant.

Then, there is tokenisation, i.e., the assignment of integer numbers to different categories. This is akin to numbering the words in a dictionary and subsequently referring to the number of a word as the word itself.

The next step deals with the encoding of letters or categories by creating binary indicators. These indicators either take a value of 0 or 1, depending on whether a certain condition has been met or not. An example in this context would be an additive colour model, in which a distinction has to be made between red, blue, and green light. These three categories can be encoded as red = (1, 0, 0), blue = $(0, 1, 0)$, and green = (0, 0, 1).

Then, there are word embeddings, i.e., representations of words for text analysis, typically in the form of real-valued vectors. Each of them encodes the meaning of the word in such a way that the words that are closer in the vector space are taken to be similar in meaning. Since the process of doing so involves a mathematical embedding from a space with many dimensions per word to a continuous vector space with a much lower dimension, this can also be treated as a machine learning task of its own. An example application in this case is natural language processing (NLP), as exemplified by Google's bidirectional encoder representations from transformer (BERT).

5.2.2.2 *Selection Strategy for ML Methods*

When dealing with text or images, ANNs will often be the preferred choice because the inevitable nonlinearities in the underlying, complex relationship make it impossible to find a reasonable linear solution. For some of these applications, excellent pre-trained networks with practice-proven geometries exist. The use of such network geometries as a starting point can significantly lower the effort and the required development time.

For other cases, it is preferable to first examine the results attained by classical linear methods and only switch to more complex, nonlinear models if the first results obtained are not satisfactory. It can even be useful to apply partially linear model specifications, in which the results obtained with a linear submodel can be nested.

Clustering techniques are, generally speaking, only suitable if applied in the context of unsupervised learning or anomaly detection. In most of the other cases, the fact that these techniques are intrinsically discontinuous will turn out to be mathematically detrimental.

The more flexible the model, and the less complex and extensive the informational content of the underlying dataset is, the greater the risk of overfitting or fitting the noise becomes, i.e., the higher is the likelihood of mistaking purely random variations in the data for indications of systematic relationships. Applying such an overfitted model to data from outside the original sample very likely results in a poor predictive quality.

5.2.2.3 *Model Size and Complexity*

With respect to the size and complexity of models, with respect to the related hardware requirements, clear distinctions need to be made between different classes of models.

The results of centroid-based clustering methods are usually least demanding because in this case, only the coordinates of the cluster centres need to be stored in order to enable the assignment of data points to cluster. Procedures based on systems of linear equations are not too demanding either because in these cases, we typically have a massive over-determinacy of the systems of equations employed, which by implication, leads to relatively small model sizes.

The opposite is true for artificial neural networks, where the size and complexity of the models in use can be extreme. Take, for example, on-screen keyboards for which a standard application pre-installed in customary mobile phones requires around 37 MB of storage. A high-performance solution, such as Google's Gboard, however, comes with a storage requirement of 183 MB. This suggests that around 150 MB are needed for the underlying AI model employed for the prediction of the following word. Even if only half of this amount were required to store training weights, the size of the model would nevertheless amount to the equivalent of 10 volumes of the *Encyclopaedia Britannica.*

Such dimensions render the underlying models intrinsically unstable in the training process and imply that great efforts must be incurred in order to train them and stabilise the results obtained.

5.2.2.4 *Dependence on Training Data*

Only if the training data fed into a model is of high quality (which means that it captures the relevant aspects of reality in the way we want), the outcome of the calibration procedure will have a chance of being reliable. Prominent examples of model failures are environment recognition for autonomous driving, classification of possible employees, and medical image processing.

The AI models currently in use require substantial amounts of high-quality input data to perform trivial tasks. Consequently, the computational costs associated with their applications can be enormous. The main reason for this is that AI algorithms fail to distinguish between details a human observer would consider essential on the one hand and those a human observer would consider irrelevant on the other hand. Current AI models tend to focus on the microstructure of the input data rather than on what humans would call the big picture. Moreover, as long as the structure of a text fed into a text-processing algorithm conforms to commonly used standards, AI systems are often unable to tell what most humans would likely consider complete nonsense from meaningful texts. Besides, unlike AI algorithms, humans often only need one image of an object to recognise it, which indicates that humans tend to make more efficient use of the information provided than the present-day AI algorithms.

Training data always constitute a selective and hence biased excerpt of reality. It follows that the magnitude of the likely predictive errors derived from training data will always tend to be smaller than the actual errors resulting from an application of the model to real-world data.

5.2.2.5 *Generalisation vs. Overfitting*

The term *overfitting* applies to a situation where a model reproduces the relevant informational content of a training dataset very well but fails to produce results that are generalisable for data outside the training dataset. The dilemma is that generalisable solutions tend to produce far worse results than overfitted models if applied to the training dataset only. However, by evaluating the results obtained for a training dataset in isolation, it is rarely, if ever, possible to decide whether a reliable solution has been obtained or whether there is an overfitting problem.

A possible strategy which takes these observations into account, for example, would be the addition of meta-information (regularisation), such as the inclusion of a penalty function that discourages oversized parameter values, the normalisation of the sum of certain weighting factors to unity, or the imposition of an upper limit on the predicted probabilities of certain outcomes.

Often, the use of certain empirical regularities of human perception mechanisms as a guide for model specification also proves valuable. The fact that the human brain has a tendency to supplement missing or imprecise inputs with expectations, mostly without us recognising it, can be, for instance, interpreted as a biological equivalent of a regularisation procedure.

Finally, a proven strategy consists in the termination of iterative search procedures (or training cycles of neural networks) after passing a certain amount of computing time, regardless of whether further improvements appear likely or not. A key requirement is the availability of independent test datasets that are used only once. The best practice would probably be to separate them completely from the remaining data and to keep them under external control, so that the only context in which they are actually used is the final review of the proposed solution. To this, the following rule of thumb applies: First, if the application of a model to a test dataset not used for training leads to errors that resemble those obtained with the training dataset(s) in terms of nature, structure, and magnitude, a high degree of generalisability has (probably) been obtained. Second, among several solutions that share the above property, it is advisable to choose the one with the smallest overall error. If a solution looks too good to be true, it probably is.

5.2.2.6 *Explainable Machine Learning (XAI)*

Many models are akin to a black box — it is not possible to obtain a comprehensive understanding of how, and why, certain results are generated. Image recognition is a case in point with the well-known example of separating dogs from wolves. Photographs of wolves can be more easily obtained in the wild and on snow. In contrast, dogs mostly live in towns or villages. Photographs which were easier to obtain were more frequent in the relevant sample. So, the ML procedure when given the task of separating wolves from dogs ended up separating human settlements from (winter) landscapes.

By now, depending on the specific method(s) in use, there are techniques available by which the transparency of such processes can be enhanced. Examples for these techniques that are applicable to neural networks are, on the one hand, a layer-wise relevance propagation (LRP), which comprises a set of analytical instruments. These instruments enable the identification of those input data items that have the highest impact on the results obtained. It is, however, closely coupled with the specific network geometry in use.

On the other hand, the counterfactual approach aims at identifying those specific changes in individual input data items to which the network reacts most strongly (or most weakly). Due to the fact that this approach is based on numerical derivatives, it can be implemented without any knowledge of the network geometry.

5.2.2.7 *Societal Implications*

ML algorithms reproduce (in a condensed and transformed manner) the information that has been fed into them. Among these pieces of information, they tend to place greatest emphasis on easily recognisable signals. Prejudices, racist, and sexist attitudes prevailing in society may therefore inadvertently enter mathematical models in spite of the obvious neutrality of the latter. A wrongly calibrated model, or a model fed with inadequate input data, can cause significant reputational damage. In contrast to inadequate outcomes obtained from the application of classical statistical methods, such damages cannot be reversed by a mere bug fix. In most cases, the consequence would be the abandonment of the model as a whole. The perception that the model was just fine but it was just the input data that were the bad does not offer any comfort. In the practice of ML, the input data cannot be separated effectively from the model, and users of these technologies bear the responsibility for the outcomes. Perhaps the most obvious piece of evidence supporting this statement is the fact that Google and Facebook generously share their algorithms but meticulously protect the input data they use.

Humans tend to treat results from ML as the truth rather than just as one more source of information. Take, for example, credit scores: No matter how the actual situation of a client is, vendors tend to rely on the scoring outcome to a very large extent. This behaviour is understandable because someone whose decision differs from the recommendation issued by the machine is unlikely to gain any significant advantage if they are right but will have to fear undesirable consequences if the outcome of their decision is negative. Thus, these results from ML are expressions of opinion from a machine, and not a divine truth, which must be clearly communicated. At the very least, the error margin of a model's predictions needs to be communicated.

5.2.3 *Data Protection/Differential Privacy*

Most database queries can lead to the disclosure of potentially sensitive information. This is highly relevant for ML because the related algorithms very often require several database queries. The theoretical target of differential privacy is giving an individual approximately the same privacy that would result from having their data removed from the database. A pure anonymisation of information does not lead to a sufficiently high degree of protection. Even what remains after anonymisation can be as unique as a fingerprint.

Examples for this are media consumption behaviour in which all user IDs and all movie identifiers in a database were replaced by randomly chosen values; still, a substantial number of both users and movies could be reidentified by adding information from an outside source (e.g., IMDb). In the case of a medical research study based on completely anonymised data, 40% of all participants could be identified indubitably on the grounds of other publicly available data coming from sources, such as address databases.

Disclosure should only be an option for absolute necessary information. Desirable is a method for sharing information about a dataset without disclosing information about individuals in the dataset. An example can be found at airports, where the use of a sniffer dog is privacy-preserving (because the dog can only tell explosives from harmless substances), but X-raying of luggage is not privacy-preserving.

The underlying idea of differential privacy is that the impact of an arbitrary substitution of a single record from the database is not sufficient to infer much about any individual. Expressed differently, the removal of a single record from the database should not impact the end result, and the learning methodology applied to the database should not depend significantly on the data of any one individual. As this is one important quality criteria for machine learning, this means that differential privacy does not conflict with the objective of successful learning. Rather, it is the desired result.

Possible actions to achieve differential privacy consists in adding noise to the input data. The advantage of this method is that it is very safe and simple; its drawback, however, consists in the fact that the amount of data required to attain reliable results increases significantly. Alternatively, noise could be added to the results. With this approach, the same level of privacy as above can be obtained with significantly smaller errors compared to the alternative of adding noise to the inputs.

Still, a significant drawback is that the choice of the random number to be added needs to conform to certain criteria that are specific to the content of the query, and the underlying distribution must exhibit heavy tails. A number of helpful results from theory are available if one uses the Laplace distribution ($\sim e^{-|x|}$); however, even then, details of the specification and implementation are rather complicated.

5.3 Federated Learning

Often, we encounter a situation where the relevant data are not concentrated in a single database but are widely distributed instead. In each of the individual databases in use, there are not enough relevant signals to make a reasonable statement. Federated learning is a machine learning technique that trains an algorithm across multiple distributed data samples without exchanging them. Federated machine learning is often based on the iterative aggregation of the so-called local and global models.

5.3.1 *Horizontal Federated Learning*

Federated Learning can be applied to scenarios in which datasets share the same feature space but are different in sample. This can be referred to as horizontal federated learning. For example, the persons responsible in the individual hospitals know the answers to the following yes-or-no-type questions: (i) Should an individual patient be provided with artificial respiration because of COVID-19? (ii) Did an individual patient take Aspirin? In order to assess whether Aspirin affects the probability of survival positively, negatively, or not at all, information from a large number of individuals must be combined, but information on individual cases from a single hospital alone is not sufficient for this purpose.

Often, it is not possible to merge the information from the individual case into a common database because this would violate the principles of data protection/differential privacy. The duty to maintain the principle of differential privacy remains with the providers of the individual databases. Applying the principle of distributed learning does not relieve them of this duty.

A combination of federated learning methods with techniques from secure multi-party computations is often necessary in order to aggregate locally updated model parameters to a global model by a central instance. The latter is often realised by methods belonging to the field of secure multi-party computation or federated computing. The goal of secure multi-party computation for parties is to jointly compute a function over their inputs, while keeping these inputs private. An example can be found in secure multi-party computation: Let us assume that Alice, Bob, and Charly want to determine their average wage $a + b + c$ without revealing what they earn on an individual basis. At the start, Alice determines a random number z, adds her wage a, and tells Bob $z + a$. He tells Charly $z + a + b$, and Charly tells Alice $z + a + b + c$. She subtracts her private random number, divides by three, and tells everybody $(a + b + c)/3$. Under the condition that none of them collaborates, nobody could ever determine the other ones' wages.

Obviously, the method presented in the example is very error-prone and open to fraud; however, there are well-founded mathematical alternatives.

Multi-party computation, in principle, enables one to attain a fully encrypted model, in which only the owner of the model knows the weights on which it is based. A further goal consists in obtaining fully encrypted input data, which implies that only the owner of the respective data knows their plain content. A result is calculated together as if neither the model nor the data had been encrypted.

Take, for example, a company that has developed an extremely precise diagnostic system for diseases, which must not fall into the hands of competitors. However, there is a patient who is unwilling to send his or her sensitive, health-related information to this company. Nonetheless, both agents can jointly determine the diagnosis, and only this piece of information becomes known to both. Even the latter can be circumvented by engaging a neutral third party, who is bound to secrecy.

Currently, this is mainly interesting from a theoretical viewpoint rather than from the perspective of the practitioner because depending on the nature of the model in use, a significant amount of computing time is required. Mathematical operations such as adding and subtracting can be performed fast, multiplication and comparisons at a reasonable speed, but division is not productively doable at the current state of techniques.

So, an optimal application, as of today, is the calculation of sums or arithmetic means across distributed databases.

Federated Learning often has a design of exchanging parameters from distributed or local models instead of exchanging raw data. There are several implementation strategies available.

Distributed models may link directly into a central model. Here, the central instance specifies a model design; each participating party trains its own model and reports it to the central instance, and the weights are aggregated to form a central model. Many of the classical models that can be traced back to systems of linear equations can be calibrated in this way. This allows for multi-party computation to fulfil the purpose of increasing security. When applied to other types of models, it cannot be taken for granted that a meaningful result is obtained.

Alternatively, distributed models train a central model. Now, each participating party trains its own model. The central instance queries every single model in order to find how the result obtained for certain datasets looks and takes the resulting outcomes as a training dataset. Then, the central instance uses these artificial data for its own training process. This sequence of steps is particularly suitable in cases where the local models are not at all identical. It does not allow for multi-party computation, but it is rather secure nevertheless.

Finally, a central model with local updates specifies a model first. Afterwards, one after the other, the optimal model updates are calculated locally; these are then immediately entered into the model. Although this is easy to program, it is questionable with regard to speed and precision. Therefore, convergence cannot be taken for granted. In a variant, the local updates are aggregated. At the beginning, the central instance specifies a model. Then, the optimal model updates are computed locally. Since these are derivatives, they can be added! In the following process, the central instance integrates the average of the local model updates and calculates a new model.

This procedure is applied in the case of the smart keyboard (Google, Apple) on a cell phone. It implies that hardly any local private data leave your own cell phone, and nevertheless, all users train the model. This approach can also be applied to classical numerical methods. It allows multi-party computation with the goal of increasing security.

5.3.2 *Vertical Federated Learning*

In some scenarios, the relevant databases contain completely different data for a given individual. Vertical federated learning is applicable to cases in which two datasets share the same sample space, but differ in feature space.

For instance, the credit score is in the ownership of a national credit monitoring agency, information on the shopping behaviour for everyday purchases is on Payback, information on media consumption is on Netflix, and health data is with the health insurance company.

In such cases, the standard techniques start with the central instance specifying one model per participant. Then, using multi-party computation, the individual models are aggregated to form a joint result. This only involves rather simple operations. Afterwards, the gradients for the optimisation procedure are calculated and assigned to the individual participants. At the end, the participants modify their local models accordingly.

Also, in this case, the participants are responsible for protecting the data. This procedure will only work if the information on the existence of a dataset as such is not a secret worth protecting! There are methods to slightly improve this, but perfect privacy cannot be obtained.

5.3.3 *Rationale for the Use of Federated Learning*

Distributed learning may be expensive for the participants. The costs involve data collection and maintenance, provision of the data with an individualised interface, audits relating to data protection law, hardware for distributed computing, and moreover support, communication, and electricity.

Concepts exist to distribute the revenues fairly and thus to make participation palatable for the participants of the distributed learning processes. However, these concepts are apparently still in their infancy, since the relevant contribution of each individual is very difficult to quantify in a visible and traceable manner. Against this background, only two scenarios currently remain realistic: Either the calibrated model gives each of the participants a greater advantage than the alternative of calibrating the model on one's own or one participates in a cooperative effort in which the benefits, as a whole, exceed the costs/drawbacks.

5.3.3.1 *Attack Scenarios*

Dealing with tasks in a distributed manner requires significant communication between the participants. In this case, the problem of a possible attack on this communication is typically under control.

We have to assume that an attacker from outside can send any number of queries to the model. This implies that such an attacker can perform a targeted search for parts of the input data that can be reconstructed from the model. This can be prevented by ensuring that the model is well generalised and that the input data into the model has already been secured by differential privacy. From this, it follows that the possibility of attacks from outside constitutes a technical issue but is not a problem in principle.

When dealing with a malicious participant, there are hardly any useful technical countermeasures that can be used in practice. In such a situation, possible attacks include, *inter alia*, artificial generation or the deliberate omission of data, communication of incorrect results, sabotaging of jointly performed calculations, and performance of model poisoning attacks, which consist of modifying the overall result of a machine learning model by feeding it with data specifically generated to pursue selfish purposes.

If carried out skilfully, many of these attacks can be designed in a way that the remaining participants have no chance of detecting them. It follows that if there are reasons to believe that individual participants are malicious, we should not even initiate any joint calculations nor alternatively resort to methods which withstand even a small number of malicious participants.

The standard case treated in the literature is the one of an honest but curious participant. Such a participant always answers honestly; yet, this does not necessarily mean that the answers given are exact. Still, for example, the answer, 'The result is $X + Y$, and Y is a random variable with a distribution Z' would be considered honest in this sense. The fact that the participant under consideration is described as 'curious' means that he has the right to analyse all information others make available to him in any way he wants and to draw conclusions about the original data of other participants if necessary. It is the responsibility of the remaining participants to adequately protect their own data. The positive side effect of this is that a significant part of the attacks from outside is fended off *en passant* if even an insider cannot reconstruct any data.

Chapter 6

Disclosure and Data Requirement

6.1 Disclosure

6.1.1 *The Need for Disclosure Standards*

Climate-related financial disclosure currently occupies a central stage in the academic, regulatory, and public discussion (see *The Economist* (2021a) and *Financial Times* (2021)). In a recent speech, Governor Lael Brainard (Brainard, 2021) points out the importance of data quality, disclosures, and modelling techniques for reducing the uncertainty around the potential magnitude of carbon risks.

It is obvious that a proper risk management of carbon risk relies on the accessibility and quality of relevant data. The Task Force on Climate-related Financial Disclosures (TCFD) already published in 2017 (with an update in TCFD (2020a)) recommendations and guidelines for asset managers and asset owners for the disclosure of climate-related risks and opportunities. In addition, they suggested several metrics for quantification. As we have seen, climate-related transition and physical risks come in different facets for different sectors, industries, regions, and organisations. However, climate-related opportunities, generated by adaptation and mitigation (such as new energy sources, development of new products and services, or the access to new markets), can positively affect the firm value.

Climate-related financial disclosure is also included in the International Accounting Standards Board (IASB) conceptual framework for financial reporting (CDP, CDSB, GRI, and SASB, 2020), where the consistency of financial accounting standards and sustainability-related financial disclosure standards is emphasised. Clearly, a common climate-related financial disclosure standard would be beneficial as sustainability and climate risk matters influence enterprise value and generate feedback effects.

In a recent consultation document, the TCFD (2020c) points out the importance of forward-looking metrics. Examples of this type of metric include the implied temperature rise and the climate value at risk.

The implied temperature rise (ITR) is a numeric degree rating, which links current GHG emissions and assumptions on expected future emissions associated to a projected increase in global average temperature that would occur if all companies in corresponding sectors had the same carbon intensity as the selected asset(s). With a climate VaR, loss attributable to climate-related financial risks can be quantified with the standard VaR methodology. To calculate it, the value of assets in a world on a particular transition path are compared to their value in a world without climate change. Dietz *et al.* (2016) provide an early example by utilising an integrated assessment model to specify transition scenarios.

Also, the use of forward-looking metrics is an important aspect to establish credibility of commitments of countries and firms, which flag net-zero promises. So far, many ratings tend to focus on firm policy and disclosure levels, which may merely reflect symbolic activities rather than actual impacts and associated risks. An aim lays out, by means of a forward-looking metric which can be measured in a transparent way, a strategy for the future and is more valuable than a report on missed opportunities of the past.

6.1.2 *Current State of Disclosure*

For its most recent report, the Task Force on Climate-related Financial Disclosure (TCFD, 2020b) reviewed financial filings, annual reports, integrated reports, and sustainability reports of 1701 large companies from 69 countries in eight industries covering the period 2017–2019. An AI algorithm based on statistical language models was employed for this data-intensive task. The findings reveal the following:

- nearly 60% of the world's largest companies support and/or report in line with the TCFD recommendations;
- disclosure of TCFD-aligned information increased on average by six percentage points between 2017 and 2019;
- the leading sectors on reporting were energy companies (40% reporting), and materials and building (30% reporting);
- only one in 15 companies provided information on the resilience of its strategy to cope with carbon risk.

Overall, the level of disclosure remains unsatisfactory, and it comes as no surprise that the poor reporting has intensified the pressure on companies of big asset managers, such as BlackRock and Aviva Investors to disclose their climate risks (see *Financial Times* (2021)).

A similar investigation was done for Germany, Austria, and Switzerland by the consultancy PwC (Behncke *et al.*, 2020). Using a similar AI technology, they find that more than 90% of DAX30, MDAX, ATX20, and SMI 20 report on climate-related topics. Emission data (scopes 1 and 2) are revealed by about 80%, but a risk assessment is only done by 68%. When it comes to setting carbon risks in relation to standard financial figures, only 30% of these companies provide information.

The market interest in carbon risk disclosure is further highlighted by the wide range of investor-backed initiatives fostering corporate disclosure and reduction of carbon emissions, including the Carbon Disclosure Project (CDP),[1] the United Nations Principles for Responsible Investment (UN PRI),[2] the United Nations Environment Programme Finance Initiative (UNEP FI),[3] and Climate Action 100,[4] which aim to pressure the world's largest carbon emitters to decarbonise their activities.

The extent to which data on carbon emissions is available differs strongly among geographical regions and economic sectors. Table 6.1 from Bajic *et al.* (2021) summarises the availability of yearly greenhouse data by region of company incorporation. The number

[1] https://www.cdp.net/en/info/about-us/what-wedo.

[2] https://www.unpri.org/pri.

[3] https://www.unepfi.org/about/.

[4] http://www.climateaction100.org/.

Table 6.1. Company disclosure by region of incorporation.

Fiscal year	East Asia and Pacific	Europe and C. Asia	L. America and Caribbean	M. East and N. Africa	North America	South Asia	Sub-Sah. Africa
2002	14	89	0	0	37	0	0
2003	16	110	1	0	53	0	0
2004	90	175	1	0	77	0	0
2005	153	292	2	0	151	0	0
2006	187	363	2	0	199	0	0
2007	267	463	7	0	246	3	1
2008	320	493	20	2	302	6	10
2009	391	613	31	4	445	13	16
2010	528	663	67	11	499	25	40
2011	551	701	74	13	538	28	56
2012	602	725	78	15	547	29	92
2013	641	766	78	15	499	38	91
2014	671	812	87	15	495	40	92
2015	746	881	99	22	563	42	91
2016	812	915	127	22	612	49	88
2017	974	984	145	24	655	48	93
2018	1036	1222	143	28	669	53	92
2019	871	1024	67	14	390	54	84
2020	20	54	0	1	13	10	7

of disclosing companies is the largest in Europe and Central Asia followed by East Asia, and Pacific and North America. More than 90% of all emission disclosures come from these regions.

6.1.3 *Data Provider*

Carbon Tracker is an independent financial think tank that carries out in-depth analysis on the impact of the energy transition on capital markets and the potential investment in high-cost, carbon-intensive fossil fuels (from their webpage). Carbon Disclosure Project (CDP) is a not-for-profit charity that runs the global disclosure system for investors, companies, cities, states, and regions to manage their environmental impacts (from their webpage).

To help regulators and investors to identify and assess the risks and opportunities created by the new carbon-constraining policies, Carbon Market Data offers the EU ETS company database.

Firm-level carbon emissions data are assembled by the following seven main providers: CDP, Trucost, MSCI, Sustainalytics, Refinitiv,

Bloomberg, and ISS. All these providers follow the Greenhouse Gas Protocol[5] that sets the standards for measuring corporate emissions.

A comparison of main providers by Busch and Pioch (2018) has shown that there is very little variation in the reported scope 1 and 2 emission data across the data providers.

According to Bajic *et al.* (2021), basic materials, energy, and utilities are the most greenhouse-gas-intensive sectors when measured in total emissions as well as in carbon intensity. This is confirmed by several previous studies. In *et al.* (2019) use Trucost firm-level GHG emissions data from 2005 until 2015 to rank utility, materials, energy, and industrials as the most carbon-intensive ones, while financials and telecommunications have the lowest intensity. This is confirmed by a study from Trinks *et al.* (2020) using Trucost data covering the period 2008–2016.

6.2 Data Quality

This section reports on the results from Bajic *et al.* (2021), to which we refer for further details. They used a sample consisting of 29851 company years made available from a major data provider covering the period 2002–2020. As discussed in the previous section, many companies report their GHG emissions according to the standards set by the Greenhouse Gas Protocol. However, there is some variation in the reports of the different types: scope 1 (direct emissions), scope 2 (indirect emissions), and scope 3 (additional emissions in the process of operations).

Typically, major data providers collect GHG emission data and further ESG-related data from publicly available documents of companies. These include corporate social responsibility reports, company websites, and annual or 10-K reports. Questions regarding contradictory or inconsistent data are resolved by directly contacting the investor relations team of a company. In addition, based on the information collected, scores on various emission-related categories

[5]When companies do not disclose emission data based on Greenhouse Gas Protocol, data providers publish emission values related to methodology company uses for the calculation.

are given. These include emission-reduction policy and whether there is a strategy to implement it.

In the next step, total GHG emissions are calculated based on direct and indirect (scopes 1 and 2) emissions from the company. In addition, scope 1, scope 2, and in some cases scope 3 emissions are reported separately. The gap between companies that report aggregate GHG emission data and those that disclose all three scopes is still of the order of 50%. With more companies reporting, the size of this gap increased in absolute terms, but it decreased in relative terms. Due to the complexity of measuring and consolidating, reporting scope 3 is still a substantial problem for many companies.

Several problems with the reliability of GHG data arise concerning the aspects of time consistency. Often, GHG data are only published with a lag of 6–18 months. In addition, they are often updated in later reports.

A basic statistical analysis of the carbon intensity on a year-by-year basis shows the mean well right of the median, indicating the presence of extreme values in the right tail of the distribution. This indicates significant outliers in the dataset, which are most likely generated by data faults. Indeed, Bajic *et al.* (2021) highlight several examples where outliers can be traced back due to unreasonably small numbers in the denominator used to calculate carbon intensity. They show that it is not enough to treat the data using some standard approach, such as winsorizing, to remove outliers. Rather, even after winsorizing, the structure of the data remains the same, and suspicious data values remain.

On the level of company reporting, inconsistencies mainly arise from the company's disclosure of only scope 1 or scope 2 emissions. As total emissions are defined as the sum of scope 1 and 2 emissions, this causes a downward bias in emissions. Hence, separate scope 1 and scope 2 reporting is preferred. In cases where both are reported, there is a substantial number of cases where total emissions do not equal to the sum of scopes 1 and 2. Also, the presence of ties between companies and/or conglomerates sometimes results in double-counting of the published emission values. The most common cases are subsidiaries and dual-listing companies. Finally, companies may change the structure of their reports which leads to inconsistencies with previous reports. All in all, the handling of scope 1–3 data and their interactions (they are summed to a total, substituted for other, as in the case of scopes 1 and 2) is one of the main sources of error. This type of error can only be identified by a careful analysis on a year-by-year basis.

A review on the main sources of climate data together with a critical discussion of data quality is also given by Tantet and Tankov (2019). We will discuss the effect of disclosure on key financial indicators in Chapters 9 and 10.

6.3 Federated Disclosure and Sustainability Ratings

6.3.1 *Methodology of Ratings*

To measure the sustainability of corporate activities, a variety of criteria and a range of weighting and aggregation schemes to aggregate these measurements into summary sustainability ratings have been proposed. Such ratings enable lenders or investors to make different companies comparable with respect to the intensity and the success of their efforts to render production of goods and services carbon-friendly and sustainable. Due to the multitude of possible measurement criteria and aggregation schemes, substantial uncertainty prevails as to how a well-founded and reliable rating approach might look.

Thus, an economic dilemma arises: On the one hand, a consensually developed, comprehensive, and reliable rating methodology would be a valuable collective good for all market participants because it pools and balances the different pieces of expert knowledge from several players. On the other hand, the supply of such a good would require every player in the market to disclose details of his or her own rating methodology, and since reliable and comprehensive rating systems are a key to competitive advantage, competing institutions are unlikely to engage in such behaviour.

We will now use the federated learning techniques outlined in Section 5.3 to generate a common assessment of these individual rating outcomes without the necessity of inducing the participants to revealing their own respective criteria, methodologies, and assessments.

In order to ease the exposition later, we collected some definitions and explanatory notes in Table 6.2. Passages printed in *italics* indicate terms defined in the other sections of the table.

Table 6.2. Federated rating terms and definitions.

Term	Definition
Company	The entity to which a *rating* relates.
Institution	An entity that evaluates and assigns *rating* grades to *companies.*
Server	A trusted, non-affiliated entity which orchestrates the whole operation.
Rating (grade)	A key for a summary assessment result that describes an *institution's* opinion on a *company.* Typical ratings/rating grades are often coded as sequences of characters (e.g., AAA, AA, A, BBB, ...) or as integer numbers lying inside a predefined range.
Ranking	A relationship between a set of items such that, for any two items, the first is either 'ranked higher than,' 'ranked lower than,' or 'ranked equal to' the second. Rankings reduce detailed measures to a sequence of ordinal numbers and thus facilitate the summary evaluation of the outcomes of a complex assessment procedure.
Rank	A number assigned to a *company* as the result of a *ranking.* If company A is 'better' than company B, then the rank of A is higher than that of B (cf. Appendix B.1.2).
Global rank	The best estimate for a *rank* of the *companies* that can be obtained by combining all relevant pieces of information from all participating *institutions.*
Local rank	An *institution*'s best possible estimate of the *global rank* of a *company* it rated (cf. Appendix B.1.5).
Mapping	A function which translates a *rating* to a *local rank* (cf. Appendix B.1.5).
Federated counting	A procedure akin to a ballot, as a result of which a free and secret 'yes-or-no'-type answer on a predefined question is obtained from each of the *institutions.*
Robust federated aggregation	A procedure at the start of which each *institution* has a certain (secret!) number, and the participants engage in a joint effort to aggregate these individual numbers without any participant revealing its secret to the others. In this context, the word 'robust' means that the form of aggregation is not affected by a small number of incorrect values (cf. Appendix B.1.1).
Differential privacy	A system for publicly sharing information about a dataset by describing the patterns of groups of items within the dataset while withholding or obscuring information about individual items. By applying this method, participants in a federated learning process can further ensure the confidentiality of their secrets, i.e., of those pieces of information they intend to withhold from others. The result of its application will be that even if one participant is questioned several times, none of the other players will be capable of determining the secret content.

Initially, to start the process, the participating *institutions* anonymously determine a set of potentially interesting *companies*. For each of the participating institutions, a company it is interested in is not necessarily the one for which it holds information itself. This leads to a mild form of *differential privacy*. Through *federated counting*, the *institutions* determine, separately for every potentially interesting *company*, the number of institutions that possess enough information to issue a *rating*. All companies for which this number does not exceed a predefined threshold are discarded. Then *institutions* initialise an individual local *mapping*.

Then, the following steps are repeated until a predefined criterion (see (Termination) in the final step) has been achieved:

(1) For each company separately, the *institutions* employ the *mapping* to derive the *local rank* from the respective *company*'s rating. This is performed in a *differentially private* manner.
(2) Using *robust federated aggregation*, the *local ranks* are combined to an estimate of *the global rank*.
(3) From this estimate, the *server* derives a *global rank*. The following inequality holds: If the estimate obtained for company A is smaller than the one relating to company B, then the rank of A is also smaller than the one of B.
(4) The *server* broadcasts the *company ranks* to all *institutions*.
(5) Regarding their own *rating* methodology, the *institutions* improve their *mapping* in order to match the *global rank* more closely.
(6) Depending on the step size of the update it needed to perform, each *institution* decides whether it considers the stability of the *global rank* to have been attained. The outcomes of the decisions reached by the individual institutions are then aggregated via *federated counting*.
(7) (Termination) If either a predetermined maximum number of iterations has been reached or a vast majority of *institutions* considers the result sufficient, the loop is terminated.

We will now consider several key aspects of the strategy. A precise algorithm is provided in Appendix B.

6.3.2 *Risks*

As mentioned in the introduction, financial institutions face a dilemma: On the one hand, their rating methodologies and the outcomes of their application reflect, at least in part, proprietary knowledge of markets, clients, success factors, and methods, which are sources of competitive advantage. As a result, institutions will have a strong and legitimate interest in protecting this information from unauthorised access by outsiders. On the other hand, this very aspiration for secrecy prevents institutions from comparing their own methodology and results with standard benchmarks or industry best practices and thus from recognising and realising potentials for improvements.

Issuing a specific opinion about a client in public can have severe consequences for the institution; cf. e.g., Deutsche Bank vs. Leo Kirch, 2002 (Atkins, 2014). Therefore, providing an unrestricted secrecy guarantee is of the highest importance. Individual contributions of the institutions may under no circumstances, neither by accident nor on purpose, be revealed.

It should also be noted that the joint computation of a financially relevant parameter has significant potential for fraud. Perhaps the most obvious evidence for this potential is the LIBOR scandal of 2012 (New York Times, 2012). The LIBOR rates were computed from the joint contributions of 17 heavily regulated major international banks. It was found that individual institutes had collaborated to manipulate these rates in a way that favoured their own market position. It follows from the above that whenever participants in a joint calculation process can achieve financial gains by feeding biased inputs into the calculation procedure, it cannot be taken for granted that the reported quantities are trustworthy. This applies in particular if the institutions can expect an unrestricted secrecy of their contributions, so that the probability of any fraudulent activity being discovered is rather low.

In cases where the free use of a benchmark generated through joint calculations is conditional on the active participation in the calculation, this generates additional potential for fraud. In such cases, there is an incentive to maintain one's own research efforts at a low level and misuse the high level of privacy protection to cover up the submission of biased or low-quality information, with a view to receiving aggregate information of high level from the other participants in exchange.

In our description of the proposed procedure, we will show that these issues can be either solved or at least mitigated by applying mathematical methods. For ease of exposition, we assume that only two ways exist in which malevolent agents may sabotage the calculation process: (1) by the deliberate submission of wrong statements by one participant (or a minority of participants); (2) by free-riding, i.e., the use of data that are publicly available or have been poached from other providers in order to generate seemingly independent contributions that could then be fed into the calculation procedure with a view to obtaining additional valuable information from it.

In cases where the set of participating institutes is not stable over time, the first source of spurious signals is practically impossible to protect against. Moreover, allowing for the random entry of institutions into the group of participants will change the composition of this group, allow inferences on the new participant and thus not be compatible with the principle of privacy. Thus, we assume for now that we have a stable group of participants.

Possibly the biggest challenge is that some malevolent institutions collaborate covertly in order to pursue a common objective (e.g., distorting the rating grade distribution of a certain subgroup of companies to make it appear considerably better or worse than it would be perceived in an undistorted rating process). If such a group of conspirators succeed in 'infiltrating' the rating process and remain undetected by the honest participants, the latter have no chance of either detecting or counteracting the placement of such fraudulent inputs. However, the very nature of this problem indicates that it cannot be fully resolved by technical means because even requiring all participating institutions to submit each of their ratings openly to a central server will not be an effective remedy if the conspirators limit their activities to a small subset of companies.

The only alternative action which could mitigate this problem to some extent would be to supplement the overall result by adding information on the number of individual assessments on which the overall assessment is based. As the aggregation procedure and the iterative solution process are based on rank statistics, disseminating this information will enable each institution to individually decide which outcomes to trust and which ones to discard as unreliable.

What has to be kept in mind is that merely searching the outer ends of the observed rating grade distribution for suspicious-looking concentrations of data points is not sufficient because agents engaging in fraudulent activities may also seek to distort calculation results by conspiring to place grouplets of companies with unfavourable characteristics near the median of the overall distribution. Hence, the pragmatic, approximate solution we are advocating here is to exclude companies from the calculation procedure where the number of assessments falls short of a predefined threshold from the sample.

Defending against participants who enter the calculation process with the intention of exchanging low-quality inputs of their own for valuable information provided by the community is virtually impossible from a merely technical point of view too. However, by disconnecting the right to access the joint computation results from the willingness or unwillingness to make own contributions, most of the economic incentive to participate with inputs of low quality can be removed.

To conclude, we emphasise that joint computations can only work as desired if the majority of participants behave honestly when submitting its contributions.

6.3.3 *Security Techniques*

We distinguish two different layers of data security. In the case of *moderate security*, we consider the security provided by joint computation as sufficient. Pieces of information that can be gathered on this include whether an institution assigned a rating to a company and whether an institution is content with the recent level of approximation.

These measures, regarding the methodology employed, can be attacked either by the server or by other participants, in case enough of them collaborate. Such a collaboration can actually happen involuntarily; it just takes one new participant to enter and compare before and after.

For more sensitive data, we add a second layer of security, namely federated computing on differentially private data *complete security*. This approach is applied especially to company-specific ratings. The level of necessary modifications is dependent on the unknown number of questions, the unknown distribution of the ratings, the distribution of the rating categories, etc.

Therefore, we act pragmatically. We will add as much noise to the data while copying the data to the server, such that one gets a satisfactory overall result.

We use the interpretation of differential privacy from Dwork and Roth (2014): A query is differentially private if and only if the query is designed in way that one cannot infer any substantial information regarding singular data points, even if one has access to auxiliary outer information (see, for example, Section 5.3). This is achieved by modifying a real-valued number by a random number for which both Laplace or Gaussian distributed random variables are often used. We use the latter in the subsequent discussion.

An important notion regarding multi-party computation is the concept of additive homomorphisms. When we have an encryption $< \emptyset >$, this means

$$< \emptyset > (\mathrm{a}+\mathrm{b}) = < \emptyset > (\mathrm{a}) + < \emptyset > (\mathrm{b}),$$

i.e., the relation between encrypted elements stays the same despite the encryption. As the data keep their underlying structure, identical mathematical operations yield identical outcomes whether they were performed on the original or encrypted data.

In the following, the only federated algorithm we need will be federated counting. All others will be derived from this one. We deliberately did not make the federated counting differentially private. This step, if necessary, needs to be performed by the module, which delivers a number to the counting, i.e., is performed indirectly. We assume that the result of the counting is correct in all cases. Now, we present different possibilities to implement federated counting and their evaluation with respect to data security.

Federated counting and secret voting are virtually identical problems, i.e., every algorithm which allows secret and secure voting over insecure connections is capable of fulfilling our needs. We collect the properties in Table 6.3.

For homomorphic multi-party computation with zero-knowledge proofs, we choose any homomorphic encryption method with the following properties:

(1) zero-knowledge proof if number is either 0 or 1, i.e., one can prove to any other party that one has encrypted a 0 or a 1 without revealing what value it actually is;
(2) multi-party addition, i.e., one can jointly add up numbers without revealing which number one actually contributed;
(3) decryption of small numbers by trial and error;
(4) additive homomorphism.

Again, we summarise the properties in Table 6.4.

To implement secret sharing, we use an additive method which has 0 and 1 available and is an additive homomorphism. The first point could be solved by a signed and secured communication module, which just accepts input 0 or 1 and signals any manipulation. Table 6.5 lists the properties.

Finally, let us look at the signal to server security. Individual numbers are sent to the server via a secure line. The server performs the computation on plain data. Table 6.6 reports the security properties.

6.3.4 *Application and Outlook*

In Appendix B, we provide a detailed description of an algorithm and test it in a simulation study. The conclusions of this study on a use case situation are summarised in the following.

Table 6.3. Secret voting.

No fraud possibility by institution	Yes
No fraud possibility by server	Yes
Data stay a secret for the other institutions	Yes
Data stay a secret for the server	Yes
Computational/implementation efforts	High

Table 6.4. Homomorphic encryption.

No fraud possibility by institution	Yes
No fraud possibility by server	Yes
Data stay a secret for the other institutions	Yes
Data stay a secret for the server	Yes
Computational/implementation efforts	High

Table 6.5. Secret sharing.

No fraud possibility by institution	No (Number could not be 0 or 1)
No fraud possibility by server	No
Data stay a secret for the other institutions	Yes
Data stay a secret for the server	Yes
Computational/implementation efforts	Mediocre

Table 6.6. Server security.

No fraud possibility by institution	Yes
No fraud possibility by server	No
Data stay a secret for the other institutions	Yes
Data stay a secret for the server	No
Computational/implementation efforts	Low

A real-life implementation needs to run on a truly distributed basis. This means the different institutions need to run on physically different servers. If these are in one location we need additionally artificially introduced lags on the communication and potential connection failures. Furthermore, the complete dropout of one institution due to connectivity or other issues must not impact the overall process to a large extent. If secret sharing is the implemented federated protocol, then we need three additional servers on which this task could be performed. Potentially, the clients will also require an independent security audit of both implementation and algorithm. As each client can individually augment their answers by differential privacy, this does not need to be decided centrally.

Additionally, it is important to note that the infrastructure provided is also open to any other rating methodology. The only necessity is the institution with this new methodology providing a map between their rating and the global rank and an updating procedure. This would conveniently operate with derivatives (i.e., Jacobians) as well, but this is not strictly necessary and could be decided locally. However, it would be favourable if the update speed locally is not slower than that of the other participating institutions. However, depending on the federation algorithm, it might be necessary to use a signed and precompiled communication platform.

Chapter 7

Markets for Trading Carbon Risk

In this chapter, we discuss the design and functioning of a market for trading carbon emission certificates. We will use the carbon credit market as our prime example as this market has rapidly gained importance recently (see Section 2.4). This market is also of particular interest as the rules on projects generating offsets are still diffuse and need to be tightened in the near future.

7.1 Carbon Rights and Offsets

7.1.1 *Definitions*

The term *carbon rights* refers to the entitlement to emit or substitute GHGs in a wide field of units, certificates, quotas, and allowances. Often, it is used in the context of two contrary, yet mutually interlinked, notions. On the one hand, such rights may give its holder the permission to emit a certain quantity of GHGs, thus seeking to establish and enforce a cap on the amounts emitted; on the other hand, such rights may entitle their holders to benefit from measured GHG emission reductions. In the first case, carbon units are issued to regulated entities as part of a cap-and-trade scheme such as the EU ETS (see Section 2.3, then often called allowances). In the second case, they are issued under a baseline-and-credit scheme, where polluters that cut their emissions by more than they otherwise would have had to are granted credits, which they can then sell to others who need them in order to comply with the regulations applicable to them.

Hence, carbon allowances represent a required permit to release a certain quantity of GHGs into the atmosphere, while carbon credits are often used for reducing and offsetting emissions.

In principle, both types of units mentioned above are mere accounting units that are tracked and recorded in specialised GHG registries. However, as of now, they are also tradable instruments that can be transferred among entities. Sections 2.3 and 2.4 provide an overview and brief descriptions of those types of tradable carbon rights under various legal frameworks.

In a cap-and-trade system (such as the EU ETS), a regulated entity is obliged to release a number of units (allowances or certificates) previously allocated to it whenever it has caused the emission of an equivalent amount of GHGs. Each unit of allowances is assigned a unique identifier and allocated to its initial holder, and the related information is recorded in a specialised register. Interested parties can then open an account in an associated registry and start buying and selling allowances on the basis of private law contracts.

Carbon credits can also be generated by an activity that reduces emissions or sequesters GHGs. Unlike emission allowances, carbon credits do not *per se* constitute a right to emit a defined quantity of GHG. Rather, they are used as rewards for reducing emissions. However, under jurisdictions where carbon credits are recognised under a regulated emission trading system (e.g., the Kyoto Protocol under international law or the EU ETS under EU law), they can offset GHG emissions and thus work like *de facto* entitlements. The incentives set by the carbon credit function derive from baseline-and-credit systems. Under such a system, reductions (or removals) of emissions are certified as the difference between the actually measured emission amount and what would have emitted in a business-as-usual scenario. Carbon credits can either be issued under public or private standards. Credits issued under private standards are typically based on measurement rules such as the Verified Carbon Standard, the Gold Standard, or the American Carbon Registry (among others) administered by an adequately qualified expert organisation, who also recognise and certify actual emission reductions achieved.

Although GHG emission decrease is a primary benefit of the voluntary carbon markets, there are also other important benefits to consider. The first one is financing a project that would otherwise have no chance of being started. Furthermore, projects are often launched in developing countries where financing projects have a much wider benefit for both emission removal and the entire community. Besides biodiversity protection and pollution prevention, those benefits include improvement in public health and job creation. Carbon credits also finance types of projects that are more oriented towards technology improvements. This can be, for example, projects that undertake a challenge of CO_2e removal and storage from the atmosphere.

7.1.2 *Current Status of the Voluntary Carbon Market*

The voluntary carbon market has grown substantially in recent years both from the supply and demand for carbon credits (see Section 2.4). On the supply side, there has been a rapid increase in the available credits, with total new issuances in 2020 amounting to 181 Mt CO_2e, an increase of almost five times compared to that in 2016. Supply has consistently been above demand, and it is unlikely that there will be shortages in the following three to five years. The consistent issue on the supply side is the quality of credits that are issued. It is extremely important to have well-defined criteria to award the project with carbon credits and verify it under one of the major standards (see Section 2.4).

On the supply side, major issues to be addressed are as follows:

- **Additionality:** Does the project yield emission reduction that otherwise would not happen?
- **Leakage:** Does the project result in increased emissions elsewhere, outside the project scope?
- **Permanence:** Does the project achieve permanent GHG reductions over several decades?

In this context, large-scale renewable energy projects, forestry, and land-use projects raise the most concerns.

On the demand side, there has also been a rapid increase in carbon credit retirements. From 2016, carbon retirements grew by almost three times and amounted to 95 Mt CO_2e in 2020. Fitch (2020) emphasises that with the expansion of climate policy to industrial companies, where adaptation costs are much larger than for utility companies, the increase of global demand will be substantial.

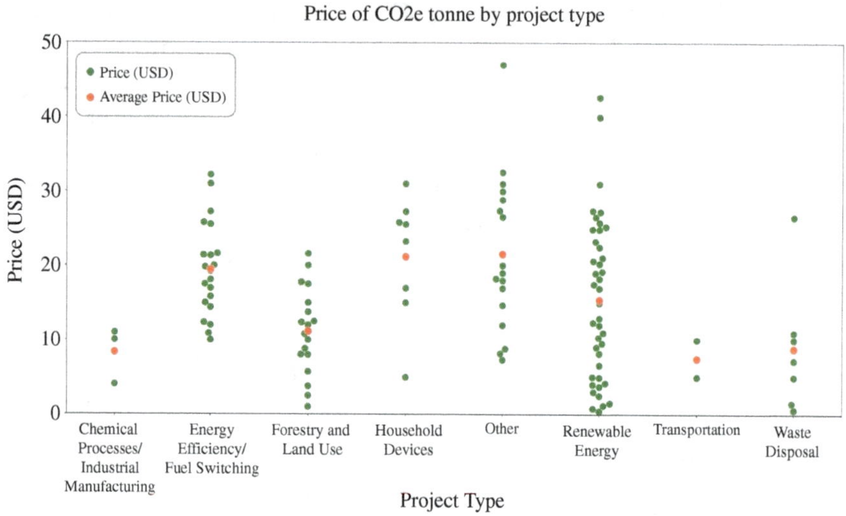

Fig. 7.1. Price of CO_2e tonne by project type.
Source: Allied Offsets, Deloitte Climate Finance Research.

In Figure 7.1, prices for various project types are presented. Data are obtained from carbon credit resellers that purchase carbon credits from project developers and sell them at the retail price. The price varies from USD 0.5/t CO_2e to more than USD 50/t CO_2e. Voluntary carbon markets (in contrast to compliance markets) function more like real-estate markets, where the location and type of the project play an important role for the buyer. Prices vary greatly across different geographical regions, project types, project maturities, and even project certification standard.

7.1.3 *Risks Associated with Tradable Carbon Rights*

Endogenous vs. exogenous risks: Within the totality of financial risks associated with carbon credit trading, a broad distinction can be made between endogenous risks, i.e., risks that arise from normal market transactions and the behaviour and organisations involved in them, and exogenous risks, i.e., risks resulting from external events on the one hand and changes in the legal and regulatory framework on the other.

Policy risk: Policy risk is the possibility of unexpected losses due to shifts in the political and regulatory environment in which carbon credit trading takes place. It is systemic in nature because such changes affect all market participants operating in areas where the relevant regulations or policy measures become effective.

The market for carbon allowances is more directly and profoundly impacted by policy changes because it is entirely policy-based and thus highly dependent on legal and institutional measures. This is largely due to the fact that the relative scarcity of the underlying assets (i.e., emission allowances) is determined by political and legal norms and decisions, so that the degree of continuity (or discontinuity) of environmental policy has a decisive impact on market conditions. Examples of regulatory and policy-related factors that affect supply and demand conditions on the CO_2 allowances are changes in the following:

- the allocation scheme (free distribution, fixed price sale, or auctioning) for newly issued certificates and in the rule set in which the number of newly issued allowances is being determined;
- the set of activities that are legally recognised as being climate-friendly and thus allows emitters of GHGs to dispose of certificates they would otherwise have had to hold;
- the extent to which governments support activities directed at reducing the carbon footprint of current economic activities (e.g., reforestation, carbon capture and sequestration, restoration of wetlands) or furthering a substitution of climate-damaging products and processes (e.g., renewable energy, eco-friendly cement alternatives).

Projects directed at reducing emissions often require large initial investments and have a protracted payoff period. A high degree of planning security is hence essential if profit-oriented market participants are to be incentivised to undertake such projects. Therefore, when seeking to identify policy risks, the timeliness, consistency, and long-term target orientation of public policy should be focused on.

Credit risk: Credit risk generally refers to the possibility of unexpected losses resulting from a failure by a borrower or a counterparty to meet its payment obligations. Often, information asymmetries prevailing between the parties in a contract are among the main factors to which the occurrence of such risks is to be attributed. In the field of carbon-related financial transactions, information asymmetry is exacerbated by the fact that disclosure requirements relating to the climate risk profiles of companies are by far not as comprehensive and ubiquitous as in the case of purely financial information. This may create an 'adverse selection' problem in the sense that the coverage and reliability of climate-related disclosures might be highest among firms with favourable climate risk profiles (at least compared to the peer group average), whereas those with rather unfavourable characteristics may have a tendency to remain, at least partially, in hiding.

Credit risks specific to carbon-related transactions also include the risk that holders of emission rights fall short of their emission-reduction obligations. This clearly indicates that financial and ecological risk factors are closely intertwined in this context.

Market risk: Market risk is the risk of unexpected losses due to adverse moves in the market prices of assets (or in the risk factors underlying them). Given the multitude of ecological, sociopolitical, technological, and economic factors that jointly impact the magnitude of future GHG emission reductions necessary, and the cost at which they can be achieved, it should be obvious that quantifying the market risks associated with holding or trading related emission rights or certificates is a formidable task, particularly because the datasets from which estimates of the ranges of variation for the associated prices can be inferred are so far limited, and the statistical processes generating these data probably change over time.

Operational risk: In line with the definition by the European Solvency II Directive for insurers, operational risk can be defined as 'the risk of a change in value caused by the fact that actual losses, incurred for inadequate or failed internal processes, people and systems, or from external events (including legal risk), differ from the expected losses.'

In carbon financial transactions, one of the examples of significant operational risks involves the losses that may arise from irregular market manipulations during which some participants (e.g., providers of brokerage services, trading platforms, or personnel) misuse their information advantages they have to engage in actions that distort prices, spread misleading information, and/or induce investors to make decisions that end up putting them at a disadvantage. Under many jurisdictions, such actions constitute breaches of the law and expose the perpetrators to the risk of penalties and reputational losses; but even if this is not the case, the resulting loss of confidence in the fairness of market processes can produce very negative side effects for the market as a whole.

Another example of operational risks relates to technology and human errors. Carbon certificates essentially are intangible virtual e-vouchers and exist only in the relevant registry system. System vulnerabilities in combination with negligent or malicious actions by a human can cause allowance theft and reuse. Since the triggering events of such developments often only take little time and the resulting losses tend to spread quickly, such processes can prompt chain reactions that lead to subsequent credit and market events that eventually result in massive losses.

Here is an example of carbon credit theft in the EU ETS, as quoted from Ying *et al.* (2018):

'Before the inception of the Union registry, the registry systems of some EU member states were attacked or hacked due to Internet technology security loopholes, which hindered the normal transactions of the carbon market. In 2010, Romanian registry accounts were stolen and 1.6 million tons of EU allowances (EUA) were lost. On January 28 the same year, the German registry was invaded by a Trojan virus and forced to close until February 4, when finally the account names and passwords of all users were reset. In this event, criminals obtained the account names and passwords of seven equipment operators by acting as the registry authority to send phishing emails to the users, and used their accounts in other registration systems to illegally transfer allowances the next day after invasion. In 2011, the registry hacking in some EU countries led to theft of three million tons EUA and economic losses of 50 million euros. Allowance theft incidents seriously impeded not only stable registry operation, but also market supply and demand balance, and dampened the confidence of market participants.'

Liquidity risk: Liquidity risk is the possibility of unexpected losses due to an organisation's inability to fulfil its payment obligations on time without having to incur significant additional costs. It may arise either from the unexpected loss of reliable and affordable funding sources (funding liquidity risk) or from the unexpected cessation of reliable and inexpensive opportunities to obtain cash or cash equivalents by selling assets in the market (market liquidity risk).

Financial institutions typically seek to quantify funding liquidity risk by classifying different funding sources according to their perceived stability and to model the risk of their discontinuation with the help of the so-called 'run-off' factors. Market liquidity risks are typically measured by studying bid–offer spreads, trading volumes and transaction frequencies of the instruments under consideration.

Both of these aspects of liquidity will also have to be studied when examining the liquidity risk impact of trading in carbon financial instruments.

7.1.4 *Role of the Trading Infrastructure*

For the carbon credit market, we are in the realm of OTC trades because they are extremely hard to standardise. This makes them vulnerable to any kind of wrongful double use, as demonstrated in the following.

A typical example of implicitly wrongful double use is the case of the operator of a hydropower station who sells its output to users in its own country and is assigned a certain number of carbon credits due to the sustainable manner in which its output was produced. It then proceeds by selling the associated certificates to some buyer abroad, who produces power from coal and buys the certificates in order to improve its climate footprint. As long as the contract between the operator of the hydropower station and the foreign coal power station operator is not disclosed, the customers of the water power provider will continue to think that they bought 'clean' energy, while actually, there is no longer any justification for this belief because their supplier absorbed part of the negative footprint of its foreign counterpart by selling the certificates.

An example of explicitly wrongful double use would be a company that reforests an area, receives a certain amount of carbon credits in return, and sells this given amount several times to a multitude of counterparties while leaving the transaction undisclosed.

An example of controversies that could arise from the lack of transparency that is the root cause of these problems is a recent dispute on the reforestation project 'Plant for the Planet': In the German newspaper *DIE ZEIT*, Knuth and Fischer (2020) published an expose of the alleged fraud committed by the organisation. Their article alleges that over the course of five years, the organisation claims to have planted trees in the Yucatan region of Mexico, where the existing forest was not threatened in the first place. However, extensive independent research conducted by Alt (2021) reached the conclusion that the allegations of Knuth and Fischer did not have a valid empirical basis.

This difficulty cannot be circumvented by classical means. Apparently, the only effective countermeasure is to ensure transparency of (at least) the most important parts of the contracts (e.g., the plot of land or the hydropower plant to which the contract is referring).

Generally speaking, trading in instruments of the types discussed here can take (at least) the following three forms:

- peer-to-peer trading (which is often only feasible for very big players for whom the cost of gathering and processing information is negligible compared to the volumes traded);
- trading via a trusted intermediary, e.g., a brokerage firm that acts as a seller to buyers and as a buyer to sellers (which often puts the intermediary into a powerful position and causes a significant share of the profit to be captured by the intermediary);
- auctioning at a trusted intermediary (which is often time-consuming and may, if performed online, give the auctioneer a comprehensive insight into the trading strategies and needs of its individual clients which could be monetised to their disadvantage).

In principle, auctions constitute a very efficient price discovery process; however, it follows from the last-mentioned point that only in combination with a technical and institutional setting that manages to reconcile the needs for confidentiality and freedom from manipulation the attainment of this advantage can actually be taken for granted. This is, at least in part, what motivates our solution approach: We seek to set up an alternative setting for such an auction that does not require an 'all-knowing' intermediary but rather employs cryptographic techniques to perform the role of the controlling instance.

7.1.5 *Market Integrity, Transparency, and Fairness*

One of the key functions of financial markets is to provide economic agents with reliable signals on what might be a consensus view of the intrinsic value and the risk content of the financial instruments that are being traded. This goal can only be attained if market participants have confidence in the fairness and equity of the conditions under which price formation processes take place.

One of the demands that can be immediately derived from this stipulation is that information asymmetries between different (groups of) participants should be kept to a minimum, which in turn calls for mandatory disclosure of material non-public information and simultaneous dissemination of such information to the public.

Against this background, it is vital that laws prohibiting the purchase and sale of financial instruments while being in possession of material non-public information as well as the leaking of such information also need to be observed when trading instruments relating to carbon rights.

Moreover, the objective of unbiased market processes implies the need to prohibit transactions that deceive fellow market participants, e.g., through the deliberate dissemination of false or misleading information or by engaging in activities that distort price and trading volume information. What deserves particular attention in this context is the possibility that two or more influential manipulators could collude to jointly secure a controlling position in an asset to manipulate its price or the price of a related derivative and extract injurious prices from any other players who need access to that asset. Manipulation examples include (but are not limited to) the following:

- 'pump and dump,' i.e., the act of driving the price of an asset upward by spreading exaggerated positive information;
- 'short and distort,' i.e., the act of spreading unverified negative news about an asset in order to profit from a related short sale;

- fictitious trades intended to give the impression that there is much independent trading activity going in the market, while in fact little or no such activities actually take place;
- front running, i.e., the prohibited practice of entering into a trade in order to capitalise on advance, non-public knowledge of a large ('block') pending transaction that will influence the price of the related security.

In general, transactions on over-the-counter markets are more vulnerable to such market abuses than trading activities on organised public exchanges. Moreover, unregulated or thinly regulated trading platforms, including 'dark pools,' may render the detection and prosecution of actions that undermine the trust in the fairness markets more difficult.

In carbon-financial transactions, market manipulation can frequently also mean that based on their own funds and information advantages, some brokerage service providers, trading platforms, and other market participants induce investors to make investment decisions without understanding the real situation of specific carbon-financial products or emission-reduction projects.

7.1.6 *Challenges in the Carbon Market*

Greenwashing: Voluntary carbon offsets have been criticised by some environmental groups of 'greenwashing' by companies that are not serious about cutting emissions and want to appear to be taking action. It is important to establish a link to absolute emission reduction, i.e., emissions as such. As with green bonds, carbon credits can be linked to total emissions (given the data availability). However, some projects — investments in new technologies — do not have a direct impact.

Greenwashing remains one of the biggest risks in forming a large, reputable market for carbon offset. In order to prevent companies from greenwashing, strong regulation, transparency, and link to carbon emissions are needed. Companies are expected to develop formal and concrete plans for reaching net-zero emissions that focus on reducing direct emissions and to use carbon offsets only as an additional tool for reaching the target. In some sectors, the transition to net-zero target is limited by the technology in use, and thus, carbon offsets will play an important role during the transition.

Liquidity: Voluntary carbon market is characterised by low liquidity, low risk-management service, scarce financing, and limited data availability. These elements and challenges need to be assessed one by one for the market to have a smooth and uninterrupted connection between suppliers and buyers.

7.2 Development of Carbon Credit Markets

An increasing number of companies are deciding to participate in the worldwide goal of meeting the Paris Agreement's objectives by offsetting their CO_2e emissions and reaching the 1.5°C target by 2030 and net-zero by 2050. Ideally, GHG emission reduction can be done through a direct decrease of GHG emissions by the company. For example, newly advanced, less-polluting technologies can be employed. When the company decides not to use any alternative technology (for example, due to a high price) or if there is no further possibility for GHG emission reduction within the currently available technology, companies turn towards voluntary carbon markets. The voluntary carbon markets allow businesses to purchase carbon offsets by directly financing different projects, which either avoid GHG production or decrease GHG emissions and in that way produce carbon credits traded in the voluntary market. This kind of carbon offsetting has been recognised as a company tool for GHG reduction, which has resulted in an increasing number of companies participating in the market.

Mark Carney, the co-founder of Taskforce on Scaling Voluntary Carbon Markets, expects the market to grow to USD 50–100 billion per annum as a result of the transition to a net-zero economy. Scenario analysis of supply and demand for carbon credits as well as expectations of the future price, conducted by McKinsey & Company, indicate the market size of USD 5 billion to over USD 50 billion in 2030. These estimates are backed by emission reductions required to achieve Paris Agreement goals, which require an increase in the carbon market size by at least 15 times by 2030, while an increase of up to 100 times is expected by 2050. These figures are backed by the increasing number of companies offsetting their excess emissions with currently more than 1000 companies with a net-zero goal in comparison to only 500 one year earlier.

A carbon credit, once issued, represents one tonne of CO_2e that will be offset once the carbon credit is retired. An increasing number of offset credits is an indicator of increasing demand or, in other words, more market participants have decreased their GHG emissions by buying carbon credits. When comparing the number of retired credits with FY 2017, in the last year, an increase in the retirement surged by more than twice, worth 95 million tonnes of CO_2e. Looking at the future trends, expectations made for FY 2030 indicate a future demand for carbon credits to reach 1.5–2.0 Gt CO_2e, while by the end of 2050, expectations are high as 7–13 Gt CO_2e.

According to expectations, the supply of carbon credits will come from the following four main categories: nature-based sequestration (e.g., deforestation), avoided natural loss (deforestation), GHG emission reduction or GHG emission avoidance, and technology-based removals of GHG emissions from the atmosphere. Overall supply by 2030 is expected to be worth 8–12 Gt CO_2e per year. The supply of carbon credits is very sensitive and has a high risk of decreasing due to external factors. These include high concentration of projects that avoid nature loss and nature-based sequestrations in a small number of countries. A further risk is a significant time lag between initial investment and the sale of credits. These risks alone lower expected carbon credit supply from 8–12 Gt CO_2e to 1–5 Gt CO_2e per year by 2030.

Future action fields — Carbon credit principles: Scaling up the voluntary carbon market according to TSVCM will have to assess key areas for future success. The first is creating common carbon credit features. This would be the main characteristic of credit quality, enabling faster matching between supplier and end buyer. Currently, carbon credits are heterogeneous, each having its features, and those inconsistencies and individual characteristics create friction that slows down the entire carbon credit purchase process.

The second key area for the improvement of the voluntary carbon market is to develop standardised contracts. As more credits would become uniform, the creation of 'reference contracts' would create liquidity and create a possibility for the purchase of a large number of contracts. 'Reference contracts' would allow the creation of a clear daily market price. Furthermore, as OTC trades will continue to happen, reference contracts could be a starting point for the negotiation.

The creation of consensus about the proper use of carbon credits is another area to be established. This includes core principles that would help ensure that companies are not taking an easy road. The goal of the carbon market is to reduce the maximum amount of GHG emissions as far as possible and use credits when there is no other possible way for the business to offset emissions any further.

Additional improvement to the voluntary market could come by establishing trading and post-trade infrastructure. Trading infrastructure would bring structured finance products for project developers to process a large volume of listings and reference contrast trades and their additional attributes. Other post-trade infrastructure would need clearing houses and meta-registries for future market development and counterparty default protection. From meta-registries, buyers and suppliers would get standardised issuance numbers for individual projects.

The voluntary carbon market, at the moment, lacks a mechanism for safeguard. This includes a mechanism that would prevent potential money laundering through an increase in market transparency. Digitalisation is another point that would bring about shortened payment terms, lower issuance costs, tracing of credits, improvement in corporate claims credibility, and acceleration of the issuance of credits and cash flow.

A final key area that would make carbon market trades more smooth is the clear demand signal. When suppliers know that there are buyers for their carbon credits, supply will be driven up. The ways to promote demand signal are to promote industry-wide collaboration where different industries can set a shared goal in emission reduction, improve standards and infrastructure for the developers, impose widely accepted guidelines for carbon offsetting by companies, and sell attractive carbon credits for the consumers.

7.3 Blockchains — A Short Introduction

7.3.1 *General Principles*

Blockchains were invented by David Chaum in 1982. The first widely usable implementation (Bitcoin) was provided by 'Satoshi Nakamoto' in 2008 (the identity of the author(s) is still unknown). Now, we will describe the building blocks of this technology. Due to its complexity, we refrain from describing the actual implementation and restrict ourselves purely to the properties.

The transactions on the blockchain are always traceable — a blockchain does not forget anything. Therefore, if more anonymity is required, a central, trustworthy agent which could provide this extra bit of privacy is needed.

It is important to keep in mind that a blockchain itself never confirms the validity information but only that the information was in a valid format, so correctness is only assured within its own ecosystem. The same is true for a wrong understanding of smart contracts. The smart contract is just a set of rules to compute a result based on data in the blockchain, e.g., as a result the ownership of an NFT pointing some real estate could change the owner. However, both the ultimate validity of the claim and the ownership of the property itself can only be enforced in real life.

Blockchains get huge and the valid stored information is a tiny part. All the rest is kept to make it tamper-proof. As there exists no 'delete,' it is impossible to consolidate the blockchain by removing obsolete records, and as they are stored on many devices, this problem multiplies. The only possibility is declaring a blockchain as obsolete as a whole. Therefore, it might be advisable to partition a bigger problem into smaller ones with separate chains.

Blockchain/cryptography	Real-world analogy
Hash	Seal
Merkle tree	A larger document sealed (German: Mit Schnur und Siegel)
Digital signature	Signature + Signature register
Database	Library with register

Distributed ledger	Cadastral register
Blockchain	Eternal library with register, where no document could ever be removed
Consensus mechanism	Expert opinion, if a document is forged or not
Proof of work	The one who contributed most decides
Proof of authority	The owner decides
Blockchain (colloq.)	Eternal library with register, every document is checked by an expert and can never be removed. There is a possibility to access every document from the internet
Cryptocurrency/fungible	Swiss bank with many numbered accounts
Wallet	Numbered bank account
Mixer	Shady money exchange on the street
NFT (non-fungible token)	Deed of ownership
Smart contract	Notary with a pre-described task
Cryptographic auction	Sealed auction with notary
Bulletin board	Bill-board with signatures for every message
Key chain	Authority granted from a superior to its subsidiaries (German: Teil-Prokura)

Hash: A hash is a possibility to sign any piece of digital information with a tamper-proof seal. Any change in the underlying information will change the hash value completely. For the hash functions in use, there is currently no feasible method known to generate a hash collision, i.e., a second piece of information which is different from the first and has the same hash value. There are strong indications that quantum computers will not jeopardise this security as long as the hash keeps a certain minimum size.

Merkle tree: If one wants to seal more than one piece of digital information, one can efficiently do that by a so-called Merkle tree. Hereby, one can bind together many information with one hash. In layman's terms: Generate the hash of every single document, write all hashes into a new document, and then generate the hash of the final document.

Digital signature: A digital signature is a possibility to sign any piece of digital information with a personal signature. The signature is split into two parts: a private one, which is necessary to sign digital information, and a public one, which gives just enough information to control a signed message but not enough to forge a signature.

There are strong indications that quantum computers will jeopardise the security of at least some algorithms for digital signatures.

Database: A database is a collection of documents with a central register to find the documents. A database allows the operations 'add' and 'delete.' The 'alter' operation can be realised by 'delete' and 'add' operations.

Distributed ledger: A database which has multiple copies such that every owner of the copy could later on control that no tampering of the original database has been performed.

Blockchain: A blockchain is a collection of 'add' operations for a database. For each of the add operations, one needs to prove that it is performed on the 'correct' database by providing the hash of the previous database. As the validity of the database up till now was already shown in the last block, referring to this one instead of the whole database is sufficient and does not compromise security. The ordering is typically performed by timestamps, i.e., each block contains the following:

- Information
- Timestamp
- Hash of previous block
- Block validity information.

If at any point the real hash of the last block and the newly computed hash of the last block do not coincide, the block and all subsequent ones are invalid.

Notably, one cannot remove any block from the blockchain, i.e., there exists no analogue to a delete operation. Instead, a flag 'deleted' is added explicitly or implicitly. Therefore, it is strongly advisable to keep the information stored within the blockchain to a bare minimum in order to prevent poisoning of the blockchain with illegal content which would render the whole chain illegal.

Consensus mechanism: It is impossible to alter any inner part of a blockchain. The only possibility is to give an alternative end of a blockchain. Therefore, in order to verify that one has the full correct blockchain, one requires a consensus algorithm, i.e., all (important) players need to agree that the current database is the correct one and not the other one with an alternative ending. The possible protocols are manifold; for our purpose, we want to single out the following ones: proof of work and proof of authority.

Proof of work: In a non-permissioned, i.e., public, blockchain, there is initially no way to say whose new block is the valid one. Therefore, one requires additionally that every contributor performs a piece of work (which is normally very energy-intensive!). This piece of work is stored in the block validity information, i.e., one puts some friction on the blockchain and generation of new blocks is hard. Now, the valid blockchain is the one with correct hashes and correct proofs of work and is accepted by the majority of the participants as the longest blockchain. Depending on the protocol, this requires either a simple majority or a qualified majority of honest participants.

Proof of authority: The proof of authority (PoA) is a consensus method in which a small and designated number of blockchain actors are given the power to validate transactions or interactions with the network and to update its registry. It works as follows: According to the chosen scheme, one or more validating machines are responsible for generating each new block of transactions that will be included in the blockchain. Depending on the configuration chosen, a new block can be accepted by a unanimous vote of the block generators or by a simple or qualified majority. The energy consumption of such a consensus method is considerably lower than in the case of a proof of work.

In the simplest form of a PoA, there is just one contributor who is able to sign that a new block is valid. He does so, for example, by adding his own signature to the block validity information.

Common use of the term 'Blockchain': In many related publications, the term 'blockchain' is used in a wider sense, denoting a combination of (a) a distributed ledger, (b) a blockchain operating on this distributed ledger, and (c) a related consensus mechanism. Only if a combination of these three elements is in place, the outcome is an open, tamper-proof, eternal database which could be used for proofs of ownership like a cryptocurrency or any other piece of digital information.

Cryptocurrencies — Ensuring fungibility: In its simplest form, a blockchain is just a database that contains two possible types of entries:

- signature 'Alice' owns initially x coins (normally as a result of mining);
- signature 'Alice' transfers y coins to signature 'Bob.' The order is signed by 'Alice.' Bob just needs to provide its public signature.

By doing that, we can always keep track of how many coins each signature possesses. The above set of possible entries ensures that coins are fungible as they are not unique and just a number in the database.

Wallet: In its simplest form, a wallet is nothing but a signature. In order to spend some money, one needs to know the private part of the digital signature in order to sign the transfer of money.

Mixer: Obviously, any transaction in a system of the type described above is pseudonymous in the sense that any party in a transaction only gets to know the account number of its respective counterpart but completely transparent in the sense that each party knows, or can get to know, which account transferred what amount to whom. If this degree of transparency is not wanted, a (bitcoin) 'mixer' could be integrated into the system. A mixer is a service that acts as an intermediary, i.e., collects many payments to a collection of own accounts and then passes on the amounts to be transferred to the receivers from different accounts. Obviously, an unlawful application of this kind of technique would be to apply it for the purpose of laundering money originating from criminal activities.

Non-fungible token: A token is an object that represents the rights to perform a predefined operation. A non-fungible token (NFT) is a unit of data stored on a blockchain, which certifies a given digital file to be unique. An NFT function is like a cryptographic token; yet, unlike cryptocurrencies, NFTs are not fungible. NFTs are created when blockchains string records of cryptographic hash onto previous records, thereby creating a chain of identifiable data blocks. This cryptographic transaction process ensures the authentication of each digital file by providing a digital signature that is used to track NFT ownership ((Boscovic, 2021)). However, ownership of an NFT does not inherently grant copyright to the digital asset the token represents.

Technically speaking, rather than capturing the number of coins in possession, an NFT stores the hash value of a piece of digital information in the personal wallet of the owner. In its simplest form, the related blockchain only contains just two possible types of entries:

- signature 'Alice' owns some unknown document D with hash value x;
- signature 'Alice' transfers ownership of hash value x to signature 'Bob.' Bob just needs to provide its public signature.

Additionally, there exists outside the blockchain a public or private database with document D. This document has the hash value x. It is of utmost importance that D stays completely unchanged because otherwise it is only possible to prove the ownership of something, but the actual object owned will remain unknown forever because no proof can be established that the outcome D' of an alteration of D (which has a completely different hash) has the same relevant content as D. Moreover, any usage of the hash value that does not constitute a legitimate transfer of ownership needs to be denied by the authorities.

Smart contract: A smart contract is a computer program or a transaction protocol which is intended to automatically execute, control, or document legally relevant events and actions according to the terms of a contract or an agreement. The objectives of smart contracts are the reduction of need in trusted intermediators, arbitrations and enforcement costs, fraud losses as well as the reduction of malicious and accidental exceptions.

If used in conjunction with a blockchain, the piece of information stored in the chain is a small list of commands to be performed at a certain time. When the time has come, a block with the result of this list of commands is entered into the validity information segment of a block. For this block to be accepted as valid, either the ultimate authority (in a permitted blockchain) or the majority of nodes (in a non-permissioned blockchain) need to verify that the result was correctly computed.

Cryptographic auction: There are many applications of cryptographic techniques aimed at securing the fairness of auctions and the unbiasedness of their implied price discovery process. For the purpose of this document, we focus on an application with the following properties:

- When bidding, the bidder does not know the number of bidders.
- All bids with the exception of the winning bid remain secret.
- Bids cannot be altered.
- The identity of the individual bidders remains secret in the sense that it is only identifiable for a single, trusted third party.
- The validity of the auction and the winning bid can be controlled by everyone.
- There is no need for an intermediary.

So, we have complete secrecy regarding the content but complete transparency regarding the process and the result.

Bulletin board: A bulletin board is a public storage of information where anybody could post a signed message. This is needed as the intermediate step for many other processes. If, for example, someone wants to perform a transaction on a blockchain, this party could announce this intention on a bulletin board and, in doing so, arrange for the authorities in the blockchain to include this transaction in the next block of the blockchain.

Key chain: Keys for a signature can be issued in such a way that the signature itself is verified by another signature. This is the standard procedure for all secure internet connections. There is one root certificate issued by a big trustworthy institution. This, in turn, issues certificates to smaller ones, which may or may not grant the right granted to sign more certificates itself. As a consequence, all signatures can be ultimately relayed to the original issuing body.

7.3.2 *Blockchains as Trading Infrastructure*

When it comes to trading financial instruments, the term 'trading infrastructure' is commonly used as a collective term for all institutional and technical arrangements that allow the placement, matching, execution, clearing, and settlement of orders as well as the safeguarding of assets. Traditionally, this set of activities have been performed, in a collaborative manner, by brokerage institutions, exchanges, broker/dealer networks, and trading platform operators as well as clearing houses and custodians.

A blockchain is a continuously expandable list of data records ('blocks') that are strung together using cryptographic processes. Each block typically contains a cryptographically secure string ('hash') generated from the previous block, a timestamp, and transaction data. Blockchains can be used whenever several participants are involved in the processes of maintaining and updating data in line with binding, predefined rules and the need arises to guarantee the correctness of the data in a way that is comprehensible and transparent for all parties involved. This is achieved by securing that any subsequent transactions build on previous ones and confirm them as correct by proving knowledge of the previous transactions. As a consequence, it is (virtually) impossible to manipulate or erase earlier transactions without at the same time destroying all the following transactions as well.

It is obvious from the above that whenever the security of data from unauthorised access, manipulation, or destruction is an imperative need, blockchain technology can be considered a means to these ends. There is little doubt that this condition is met when it comes to the trading and safeguarding of financial assets and related contracts: Blockchain technology can be used as an efficient means for keeping records on property rights (e.g., emission allowances and/or carbon credits granted for climate-friendly technologies or business practices) and the transfer of such rights between participating agents. This is due to the fact that its application enables the various entitlements of individual participants to be represented by tokens, i.e., software objects that enable the secure storage of the underlying information and facilitate its protection against unauthorised access, counterfeiting, or theft. The automated nature in which the assignment of new rights and the transfer of existing rights once initiated by the trading parties involved are performed and recorded helps keep transaction costs low and opens up opportunities for harmonising contract structures originating from different legislations.

Moreover, the decentralised manner in which the relevant data is held provides all interested parties with access to the system the opportunity to validate the informational content of the database and thus helps in strengthening the trust of the stakeholders in the congruence of proclaimed actions and achievements on the one hand and actual results on the other. This point is of particular importance because past experience has pointed out that markets for carbon emission allowances and credits are particularly vulnerable to improper trading practices that dilute the aspired ecological benefit of their introduction, which include the double counting of emission savings achieved as well as the practice of 'greenwashing,' i.e., the deliberate dissemination of distorted information on an organisation's ecological footprint.

The standardised, rule-based storage of information on the rights and obligations of market participants in specialised computer programs or protocols, referred to as smart contracts, also allows for a reconciliation of two legitimate yet seemingly conflicting objectives when it comes to the compensated transfer of property rights: (1) the need for an efficient, tamper-proof, and hence highly transparent price formation process; (2) the legitimate right of market participants to protect their valuable proprietary information on trading and risk-management strategies, resource requirements, and endowments against unauthorised access. The solution approach envisaged to resolve this apparent trade-off consists of the application of an auctioning procedure in which individual bidders are allowed to conceal their identity using a one-time pseudonym, while at the same time, the application of cryptographic techniques controls the conformity of individual actions with the applicable rules.

In order to achieve climate change objectives and reach the sustainability development goals (SDGs), OECD (2017) study shows an annual investment of USD 6.9 trillion is required until the year 2030. A huge amount of investments raises the question of financial infrastructure and the opportunities it can offer. Setting up a global trading platform that ensures clear and efficient processes, data transparency, and integrity of all participating parties is a prerequisite for investors to gain trust and engage in the market. Additionally, a combination of various data sources like satellite imaging or digital sensors, application of artificial intelligence to improve accuracy and speed, while utilising blockchain technology to ensure integrity, enables the development of a digital project cycle.

The carbon market is characterised by fragmented verification standards that result in numerous remote entities having access to valuable data for decision-making on infrastructure investments, financial forecasting, mitigation and adaptive actions. Since the current data governance is isolated and disintegrated, the integrity of data is not possible to comprehensively assure. Additionally, cross-border transactions face difficulties in realisation due to the huge amount of manual interactions and non-transparent data trails. Blockchain provides a method to maintain, monitor, and analyse data based on a single book of accounts and without compromising data privacy and sovereignty. Reliable and timely analytics services based on trusted and obtainable data trails enable close interaction of decision-making and investment flows.

7.4 A Blockchain-Based Trading Infrastructure for Carbon Credits

The solution we propose has the following attributes, which we consider desirable:

- The minimal feasible solution can be implemented on a supranational level and is open to new participating countries. Technically, it can be set up and run without requiring a political decision by any government, but the quality of results obtained will, of course, greatly improve the more national governments 'dock' with the framework.
- The proposed system is operational in a heterogeneous environment in the sense that it is compatible with different country-specific blockchains.
- It is tamper-proof due to the usage of blockchains.
- Another advantage of the use of blockchains is the system's transparency and the fact that it is 'democratic' in the sense that everyone can access the platform and thus contribute to the detection of fraudulent actions.
- If possible and desired, the actual identity of the trading partners involved can be kept secret.
- Governments of all participating countries are given every opportunity to assert compliance with the relevant laws of their countries for those companies operating under these laws without requiring outside information.
- Regulations can be set, and supervisory oversight can be performed at the national level.
- Carbon credits become easily tradable.
- Trading is open to any system.
- A secure trading facility with price transparency is provided due to the use of multi-party computation.

An immediate implementation of the entire framework in every relevant country is not practical because a gradual introduction of the system, starting from a small subset of countries, provides its makers with better opportunities to fine-tune the proposed solution in line with demands that may be voiced only during the implementation process. Hence, we proceed by always presenting the initial and final states of this process. We will use proof of authority (rather than proof of work) as a consensus algorithm for all our blockchains. This has two reasons: First, it seems inconsequential to first set up a framework intended to protect the planet by reducing CO_2 emissions and then to let this framework itself consume the vast amounts of energy that are, under present-day conditions, usually consumed when running proof of work consensus algorithms. Second, should either a legal dispute or a case of suspected fraud arise, the individual countries and their judicial and law enforcement authorities are required to step in anyway. Therefore, a proposed solution that could, on the one hand, be interpreted as a declaration of mistrust in the state authorities (by not involving them in the consensus-building process), while on the other hand relying on their power when it comes to settling legal disputes or prosecuting punishable offences seems inconsistent and may easily turn out to be politically not viable. If carbon credits or unused emission allowances are traded, they indicate the absence of something (i.e., greenhouse gases) rather than the existence of an asset. Hence, the potential for fraud is probably much higher in this case than in situations where tangible evidence for the outcome of some productive activity is easier to produce (see Haya and Orenstein, 2008). This applies even more against the background that the ostentatious purchase of such certificates is often used in the context of advertising campaigns directed at providing incorrect or biased information on the environmental soundness of a company's products and processes. If prospective sellers of carbon credits are mainly commercially motivated, they will seek to 'produce' negative CO_2 emissions, and to package them into carbon credits, at minimal cost and (possibly) with the lowest regulatory oversight. On the other hand, a prospective buyer who intends to purchase carbon credits to neutralise an otherwise too high emission amount will usually want to do so at the lowest possible price. The general public usually lacks the data and information-processing capabilities necessary to exert effective control. It thus seems obvious that the responsibility for control should be conferred to independent, adequately specialised verification agents who benefit from, and hence have the greatest interest in, an effective and unbiased oversight. Hence, our approach stipulates the introduction of two blockchains, if possible, at a national level. The first captures the information on the geographical location of a project, while in the second, the projected CO_2 reduction and its current owner are recorded. Whenever trading of virtual goods is performed, anti-money laundering (AML) becomes a severe issue. Therefore, it will be necessary to introduce some know-your-customer (KYC) processes, together with adequate technology, to mitigate this problem. In the context of blockchains, the word 'approval' is used in the sense that all parties involved need to endorse the addition of a new element to the chain by their signature. To enable this, all participants that need to verify that the blockchain is still unbroken must be able to perform a related integrity assessment.

7.4.1 *Setting Up Trading Infrastructure*

We begin with a short overview regarding the general concept:

- Either a national or a supranational authority controls and approves each operation.
- Institutions need to register.
- Projects get assigned to a real part of the land and need to provide evidence of their CO_2 reduction.
- A non-fungible token carbon credit, which can subsequently be sold, is attached to each of these projects.

Upon describing the details of the proposed infrastructure, we need to distinguish these components and processes that already need to be available in the setup phase of the related system and those that need to be added before the system has reached a steady state in which it is intended to operate permanently. We mark information that relates to the setup phase with the word 'start,' whereas conditions prevailing in the steady state are labelled as 'final.' In cases where our explanations relate to both the setup period and the steady state, this is indicated by the label 'start/final.'

Supranational trustee (start): The supranational trustee (ST) needs to be initiated from the start. It provides the major part of the signing infrastructure. Furthermore, it acts as a proxy for national trustees as long they are not set up.

National trustee (final): A national trustee (NT) is granted by the ST the right to sign on its behalf. In the case of a federalist state structure, the task of the NT might be jointly distributed among the federal states of the related country, yet we assume that from an outside perspective, the NT is seen as acting as one coherent body. In a later stage, the role of the ST as the authority to sign blocks in the absence of national trustees will be dealt with in greater detail. If, however, nations agree that this degree of centralisation would lead to an unintended large concentration of power at the ST, one could alternatively implement a scheme in which a majority vote on the part of the NTs is required to agree on the validity of a block in a blockchain. Under the assumption that the NTs do not act like profit-oriented private players, no proof of work is necessary. Hence, such a 'democratic' solution could be implemented without major energy consumption. However, the question remains open whether such a scheme can really lead to improved results.

Institution (start/final): An institution is almost always associated with a country. This implies that each subsidiary of a multinational corporation will be required to register with its specific country of residence. Unless this condition is met, it will be impossible to keep track of national CO_2 emissions, savings, and capture and sequestration amounts and hence to measure different degrees of achievement for the goals of the Paris Climate Agreement.

Unverified institution (start): As long as there is no NT, an institution can register as an unverified institution (UI) at the ST. The ST does not perform any additional checks apart from the most elementary ones.

The institution is entered into a database that is private to the ST. The ST grants the UI the right to sign contracts within the framework of the proposed solution.

Verified institution (final): An institution registers at the NT, which then performs all the necessary KYC checks. More specifically, it checks whether the institution is actually registered with the country, whether the tax identifiers are correct, whether the statements about the beneficial owners (if required) are accurate, etc. These checks are performed in accordance with the respective national laws. Its completion makes the institution a verified institution (VI) which is subject to the specific set of laws and regulations applicable in its country of residence. The security level should be the same as for any other state-provided service within this country. The institution is entered into a database that is private to the NT. The NT grants the VI the right to sign contracts within our framework. When setting up the NT, all unverified institutions will be checked and transferred from the ST register to the NT register. Any disputes that arise in this context need to be resolved, depending on the circumstances of the individual case.

One-time pseudonyms (start/final): Depending on national laws and/or its preferences, an individual institution may prefer to operate either secretly or openly. Therefore, the ST (or, respectively, the NT) will issue a one-time pseudonym (OTP) on request. Such a one-time pseudonym, once granted, can then be used by its owner to sign for one particular set of operations. In those cases where a pseudonym is used, the signature is performed on behalf of the pseudonym and not of the institution hiding behind it because otherwise this would be completely contrary to the purpose of the pseudonym. From this point onwards, whenever an institution is mentioned, the statement made applies analogously to its pseudonym unless the opposite is stated explicitly. An institution is always allowed to publish, verified by the ST/NT, that it is the holder of a one-time pseudonym. This makes sense, for example, in the following context: Let us assume that an institution enters into an auction anonymously. If it loses, nobody will know that it actually needs, or intends, to acquire carbon credit certificates. If, however, the institution under consideration wins the auction, it might want to disclose that it is actually operating, or has taken a step towards operating, on a low- or zero-emission basis. This is also the reason why selling is only allowed with the same pseudonym as buying. Otherwise, one could buy a carbon credit certificate, publish this, and then secretly sell it under another pseudonym, creating a false impression of the organisation's climate footprint.

Cadaster blockchain (start/final): For now, it is assumed that every piece of land on the planet has a unique 'address' and that for each piece of land thus identified, a distinction is introduced between the following three parts: subsurface, surface, and air. In addition, it is possible to assign to each piece of land a termination date of the current period of usage, if the right of use has been granted to the current holder for a limited period of time only, and this is already known. Otherwise, it is assumed that the usage right is unlimited in time. One could, for example, assume that a carbon capture and storage facility (CCS) located on a specific piece of land will occupy just a small portion on its surface but its entire subsoil (for storage purposes), whereas a park of wind turbines will occupy a medium-sized part on the surface and a major part in the air. This cadaster is introduced in order to make fraudulent overuse of carbon credits much harder.

NT not set up (start): The land is split along the system provided by Google plus codes which assign roughly each plot of land sized 13 m × 13 m in length and width a unique address. Then, whenever an UI first reports the use of a given plot of land for the first time, a block is written into the supranational cadaster blockchain (SCB), in which the percentage of usage and the institution itself is recorded. The authority to approve this is with the ST and the UI. If a UI reports the usage of a given plot of land that is already in use, the ST checks if the utilisation factor of this plot is under or over 100%. If the utilisation factor remains less than or equal to 100% after the new form of use has been recorded, everything is fine and the ST and UI approve it. If the utilisation factor exceeds 100% after the new form of use has been recorded, the state of this particular plot of land is set to 'disputed'; the national authorities are informed, and the real names (rather than just the OTP) of the UIs involved are disclosed to them. In this case, the ST can approve (or reject) a proposed change in the cadaster without the consent of the UI. An additional, optional field is provided, where the UI could point voluntarily to the specific land code which is used in the country it operates in.

NT operational (final): The land is split either as proposed by the Google plus codes or according to any other rule set that is common in the respective country. In Germany, for example, this might lead to dividing the land into land parcels ('Flurstücke'), which are numbered differently and can take arbitrary shapes. In this case, the country is obliged to provide the following information items openly and free of charge:

- size of the land with this unique address;
- location (e.g., GPS coordinates).

When the NT comes to life, all property parts are transferred from the ST to the national cadaster blockchain (NCB). The ST discloses, if necessary, the real names of the institutions, and the NT checks the ownership. Disputes need to be resolved. A pointer to the block and its hash in the SCB is provided in each of the starting blocks. When a VI reports the usage of land for the first time, a block is written into the NCB with the percentage of usage and the institution reported. The NT checks that the VI is actually allowed to claim usage to this part of land, e.g., by presenting a document of ownership, or that the land was leased to the institution for a certain time. Similarly, when the part of land is already in the blockchain, the NT checks if the usage does not exceed 100%. If yes and the ownership check was successful, a new block is written to the NCB. Otherwise, the dispute needs to be resolved. The new block is signed both by the NT and the VI. In the case of a dispute which is lasting longer, the NT can sign without the VI but needs to comment on it within the block.

Territorial disputes (final): As indicated above, there is a possibility that the cumulative usage shares of a given resource (here, land) claimed by two or more institutions jointly exceed 100%. This is akin to a territorial dispute among nations. In this case, the concept envisages that the ST takes a completely neutral stance and either does not transfer the oversight (in the case of newly setting up an NT) or retracts the oversight (in the case of an operational NT) and performs the registering process itself. Therefore, if a piece of land is registered with the ST and not marked as transferred, any part in a national register building on this piece of land shall be considered as invalid. This also holds for every operation on such a piece of land.

Approval: From the viewpoint of mere data security, the approval of a UI/VI, i.e., the endorsement of its inclusion in the system, is not strictly necessary as both the ST and the NT can admit an institution on its own. Yet, for practical reasons, we still think that the joint signature (as an equivalent of the 'two-person rule' often applied when momentous decisions are established on a binding basis) makes sense.

Non-fungible tokens (NFTs): With only a minor additional effort, the same result could be obtained by making each part of land an NFT. The choice to do it the way proposed or with NFTs is more an implementation issue and could actually be decided by each NT separately.

Resource blockchain (start/final): In order to trade carbon credit certificates and other 'resources,' some knowledge needs to be provided on how and where the CO_2 reduction is actually achieved. For this purpose, we set up a resource blockchain. This will always contain a limited number of fields, at least including the following:

- the year in which the reduction has been achieved;
- the technology in use, e.g., CCS, reforesting, replacement of energy from fossil fuels by water power, etc.;
- the amount of CO_2 saved;
- a list of pointers to a cadastral blockchain;
- (optional) an NFT pointing to an open or disclosed document with more information on the resource;
- (optional) a lock, i.e., a fixture that gives the originator of the resource the possibility to grant or to refuse the permission to resell a certificate (and hence to decide on whether a specific resource should be rendered tradable).

NT not set up (start): The UI reports the necessary information, including the information on land usage, to the ST. The ST performs the very basic sanity checks, e.g., it examines whether the proclaimed CO_2 storage with trees is possible given the surface area of the plot of land used. The UI and ST then jointly reserve the land in the SCB and store the information on the blocks and their hashes. Then, for each relevant year, one resource block is set up in the supranational resource blockchain (SRB). As indicated above, this block contains information on the year to which it refers, the technology and the location as pointers to the SCB. The hash of the corresponding block now constitutes an NFT with its first owner being the UI.

NT operational (final): The VI reports the necessary information, including the information on the land usage, to the NT, who then performs all checks necessary under the laws of the respective country and, most importantly, determines whether the stated CO_2 reduction could theoretically be achieved in the way proposed. The VI and NT then jointly reserve the land in the NCB and store the blocks and their hashes in the SCB. Then one resource block is set up in the national resource blockchain (NRB) for each year. As above, the minimum informational content of this block consists of the year, the technology in use, and the location as pointers to the NCB. The hash of the corresponding block now constitutes an NFT with its first owner being the VI. When the NT is set up, all resource blocks from the SRB which are pointing to the current or future years have to be transferred in an obvious manner.

Tracking trades between registered institutions (start/final): To facilitate the explanation, we initially assume that we have two VIs and their corresponding NTs. We have the following:

- a resource NFT originated by VI_{origin} under the supervision of NT_{origin};
- a seller VI_{seller} under the supervision of NT_{seller};
- buyer VI_{buyer} under the supervision of NT_{buyer}.

Then, a new block in the register of NT_{origin} is written, confirming the (complete or partial) transfer of the NFT from VI_{seller} to VI_{buyer}. The following signatures are either always required or needed if certain preconditions are met:

- VI_{seller} (always required);
- VI_{origin} (required whenever VI_{origin} has the opportunity to prohibit trading in the resource);
- NT_{seller} (required if the seller's country of residence has the right and the opportunity to prohibit the transfer of [additional] CO_2 reduction credits to other countries, e.g., in the case of impending limit breaches or sanctions imposed on trades with certain other countries);
- NT_{buyer} (required if the buyer's country of residence has the right and the opportunity to prohibit imports of resources from certain other countries or regions);
- NT_{origin} (required if the originator's country of residence has the right and the opportunity to prohibit the transfer of certain resources to others);
- VI_{buyer} (if this is required by law).

The NTs are required to keep their rules on the required signatures up to date at the ST. A predefined time frame needs to be defined, within which a signature (if required) needs to be rendered (or denied).

Tracking trades between a registered institution and an unregistered individual (start/final): We assume that there is a VI who owns a resource on the one hand and an unregistered individual who wants to buy that one (e.g., to voluntarily reduce his or her own environmental footprint) on the other. This means that we have the following:

- a resource NFT originated by $\mathrm{VI}_{\mathrm{origin}}$ under the supervision of $\mathrm{NT}_{\mathrm{origin}}$;
- a seller $\mathrm{VI}_{\mathrm{seller}}$ under the supervision of $\mathrm{NT}_{\mathrm{seller}}$;
- a buyer under the supervision of $\mathrm{NT}_{\mathrm{buyer}}$.

Then, a new block is entered into the register of $\mathrm{NT}_{\mathrm{origin}}$, which confirms the (complete or partial) transfer of the NFT from $\mathrm{VI}_{\mathrm{seller}}$ to $\mathrm{NT}_{\mathrm{buyer}}$. This implies that formally, the $\mathrm{VI}_{\mathrm{buyer}}$ is replaced by the country of the buyer. The country cannot be a seller, which implies that as a consequence of this transaction, the resource becomes non-tradable. All signatures stay the same, with the exception of the one of the buyer for which no provision has been made here. This solution should strictly comply with all provisions made by local privacy-preserving laws like the General Data Protection Regulation (GDPR) of the EU.

OTPs (start/final): Obviously, when someone bought a resource with an OTP, it could just be sold with exactly this OTP.

Years (start/final): In order to keep the blockchains short, it might be advisable not to put all resources into one blockchain marked with the year but to generate one blockchain for each year. By doing so, one could archive past blockchains without damaging the whole process.

Year on year (start/final): The initial owner of a carbon credit certificate originated in a given year is allowed to carry any unused part of it over into the next year, during which he could sell it to any other participant. However, after this one-year grace period has expired, this resource is considered depleted regardless of whether or not it was sold.

Problems to meet the goal (start/final): Due to a variety of reasons, it is possible that the provider of the greenhouse gas reduction resource can find itself in a situation where the emission-reduction targets set upon origination cannot be attained in the relevant one-year reference period. This failure may either be reported by the originator itself or disclosed by, or at the instigation of, a supervisory body in its country of residence. Then there are three possibilities:

- To the extent possible, those parts of the valid carbon credits that were not yet sold are used to cover the loss amount associated with the failure to meet targets. If the entire loss amount can be compensated in this way, no need for further action arises.
- The resource provider buys some carbon credits from another source. In order to keep fraud potential low, this needs to be done openly.
- If the resource provider is unable (or unwilling) to provide compensation for the loss incurred, all buyers get notified by the ST or, respectively, the NT. In most cases, the buyers will be able to take legal measures in line with the laws of the provider's country of residence and receive compensation as a result.

The loss of parts of the NFT is recorded by adding new blocks in the NRB. This operation can only be signed by $\text{NT}_{\text{origin}}$.

Emission blockchain: If required, supranational and national blockchains relating to the emission of CO_2e can be established in exactly the same way as the resources blockchain. In a number of countries, disclosure of such information is mandatory (at least for some groups of companies) anyway, so that corporations need to report related figures after the end of each year, thus directly giving evidence of their efforts directed at achieving CO_2 reductions. Furthermore, this could be used to keep track of mandatory CO_2 certificates which are required in some regions of the world, e.g., the EU.

Auctions: The system is designed to be completely open, which means one can use any channel to trade the NFT's carbon credits. However, we also want to provide one possibility to trade in an evidentially secure and transparent manner. Such an auction works as follows:

- An NFT or a part of it is auctioned. In order to do so, the NFT is fungible.
- The auction request, potentially (but not necessarily) together with the document attached to the NFT, is published on a bulletin board.
- A VI asks the ST for a permission to participate. For individuals, an NT could do this on behalf of an individual.
- The ST checks if there are any 'show-stoppers,' i.e., any points publicly raised by the NTs of the originator, the seller, and the buyer that indicate that the trade must not happen. If this is not the case, an OTP is issued to the VI.
- The VI sends under its pseudonym a sealed bid to the ST.
- After a grace period, when all bids are collected, the VIs compute via multi-party computation the winning bid and the winning OTP. The maths can be designed in such a way that
  - the bid cannot be changed,
  - no bid, with the exception of that of the winner, becomes public,
  - just the OTP of the winner becomes public,
  - everybody can check the validity of the auction.
- The transfer of property is registered in the NRB.

In order to perform the multi-party computation, every participant is required to provide some computational resources in order to solve the underlying cryptographic task.

7.4.2 *Blockchain Use Cases*

In order to facilitate the understanding of our concept, we present some examples that demonstrate its mode of operation and, particularly, the protective measures against misuse.

7.4.2.1 *Reforesting and a Long-Term Contract*

Assume a non-profit organisation M is set up to reforest a piece of barren land in Mexico and a German company G has agreed to buy the carbon credit with a long-term treaty for the next 10 years. In the second year, flooding destroys parts of the land, such that for one year only two-thirds of the CO_2 reduction can be provided. Both M and G have never been in the above system; the national trustees fully operate.

- Company G registers with the German trustee. After checking the tax number and the trade register extract, the status as a verified institution is granted.
- The non-profit organisation M registers with the Mexican trustee. After checking its purpose and its non-profit status, the status verified institution is granted.
- G and M make a non-public treaty on the carbon credit of the reforestation project. They agree that in line with scientific standards, the best possible estimate for the overall emission reduction amount will be 100.000 t per year.
- M registers the property of land (0% subsurface, 90% surface, 0% air), the purpose of reforesting, and the 100.000 t reduction amount per year (together with a corresponding scientific expert opinion) to the Mexican trustee. After a thorough review, the Mexican trustee approves the registration and a carbon credit of 100.000 t for each of the next 10 years is entered openly into the Mexican resource blockchain, with M as the owner.
- As M has already a fixed treaty with G, both announced that they would like to perform a transfer. The German trustee has communicated to the supranational trustee that, in general, there are no objections to any trades with Mexico. Hence, the Mexican trustee and M approve the 10 transfers (each of which relates to one specific year in the future) of the 100.000 t of carbon credit NFT to G.
- In the first year, G can tell its customers that it offsets all of its CO_2 spendings by the new plantation.
- In the second year, flooding destroys a major part of the newly planted trees. M informs the Mexican trustee and they agree that, in line with scientific standards, the best possible estimate for the emission-reduction amount achieved in that year would be 66.000 t and that the emission-reduction amounts expected for the following years at most will remain at their normal level.

- As stated in their private contract, G now announces that it will return 34.000 t of carbon credits to M. The Mexican trustee (who stated that it wants to be asked for every transaction), the German trustee, and G approve this transfer.
- The Mexican trustee asserts that there is no overspending and closes the case.
- G buys from a second source another 34.000 t of carbon credit for this year to fulfil the commitments it made towards its stakeholders.

7.4.2.2 *Building an Additional Wind Park*

The non-profit organisation M decides to grant company W the right to build a wind park on its land, with a view of receiving subsidies from the Mexican government. W promises reliably not to destroy any of the replanted wood. For the corresponding year, W wants to sell a certificate evidencing that 20 GWh of energy was produced with zero CO_2 emissions to a green energy reseller B from Britain. Due to the fact that Mexico is in danger of violating its own CO_2 reduction goals, the application for the trade is rejected, and the certificate is now auctioned within Mexico. Assume that W and B are already verified institutions.

- Company B registers the property of land (0% subsurface, 10% surface, 100% air) together with its purpose, the written contract with M, and the plan on how to protect all the replanted wood, with the Mexican trustee. This approves an NFT for the 20 GWh. Hence, now it is impossible to register any further project which uses more of either surface or air in this piece of land.
- W and B agree on a price for the green current certificate and announce that they want to trade.
- The British authority approves, but the Mexican does not. The trade does not take place and hence is not entered into the resource blockchain.
- To mitigate its losses, W decides to auction the NFT. As Mexico has rejected all foreign bidders, the ST just approves Mexican companies to take part in the auction.

- A winner, who asks the Mexican trustee to be disclosed, and the winning bid are published. All other participants in the auction and their bids stay secret forever.
- The Mexican trustee and W approve the transfer of rights to the winner.

7.4.2.3 *Protection Against Double Counting*

A company C operating a CCS facility in Norway has a private contract with a company X. In addition, it registers at our platform and sells the same CO_2 reduction once more in the form of carbon credits. X, despite not being a member of our platform, controls the cadastral register (which is open to everyone), finds that C has registered a CCS storage site at its land and observes that the resulting CO_2 reduction was sold to another non-disclosed institution. X tries to contact C but is rejected. Therefore, X contacts the Norwegian trustee, which investigates the case and finally nullifies the NFT certificate issued for the site. The non-disclosed institution is informed of the situation. Legal action follows.

7.4.2.4 *Fake Reforesting*

A company applies at its national trustee for the allocation of carbon credits for a reforestation project although the relevant area is already covered by a mature forest but nevertheless succeeds in acquiring credits through bribery. It sells these illegally acquired certificates to a huge number of enthusiasts on another continent and provides a reference to the NFT in order to build trust. One of the buyers compares the land registered in the cadastral register (which is open to everyone!) with recent satellite images and discovers that this cannot be a proper reforestation project. The national trustee is informed and legal action follows.

7.4.2.5 *Determining the Carbon Footprint of a Country*

In the context of the system sketched in the previous sections, the carbon footprint of a country can be determined according to the following sequence of calculations:

total CO_2e emissions from domestic sources
+ CO_2e emissions associated with imported goods and services
– CO_2e emissions associated with exported goods and services
+ the carbon credits which it sold to buyers outside of the country
– the carbon credits which is generated in the country
– the carbon credit which it bought from sellers outside of the country.

From the above, it follows that the proposed system of registers enables interested parties (e.g., competent supranational organisations) to determine the real carbon footprint of individual nations. The built-in protection mechanism against double counting can reasonably be expected to prevent fraudulent actions directed at selling certificates earned for a given amount of emission reductions more than once.

Part III

Carbon Finance — Markets

Part III discusses the effects of carbon risks on financial assets and markets. We start by considering the trading of emission certificates (EUAs) and the impact of EUAs on energy markets. We only touch upon the impact on energy markets briefly, but the few examples we present highlight the profound effect the transition to a low-carbon economy has on energy markets. We then discuss the existence of a green premium (or risk factor) on equity and credit markets. In doing so, we also present various empirical techniques. We devote a chapter of its own to the emerging market of green bonds, which can be seen as a major source of finance for the transition to a low-carbon economy. In the final two chapters, we turn to institutions. In Chapter 12, we discuss risk-management approaches of financial institutions and their exposure to carbon risk. We outline the possible role of central banks and the design of stress tests. We conclude with the classical problems of hedging a risk exposure and optimising portfolios with respect to carbon risk.

Chapter 8

Emission Certificates on Financial and Energy Markets

8.1 Dynamics of EU ETS Certificates

Before we start with a review of stochastic models, we perform a brief econometric analysis of EUA prices. Figure 8.1 shows the development of the price level from 2012 to 2021 and separately for the periods 2012–2018 and 2018–2021. It is clearly visible that prices started to climb substantially from 2018 onwards. Table 8.1 confirms this impression. The mean price during the period from 2018 onwards is much higher. Also, the volatility during this period shows a substantial increase compared to that during the 2012–2018 period. A look at the returns (Figure 8.2) confirms this impression. However, spikes do not have the extent of those during the period 2012–2018. Rather, the variability of returns is higher, which is confirmed by Table 8.2. We also performed the augmented Dickey–Fuller test for a unit root. As expected, for the return, the existence of a unit root is rejected with high significance for the returns, see Table 8.3. A similar analysis for Phase I and Phase II EUA spot and forward prices is available in Chesney *et al.* (2013).

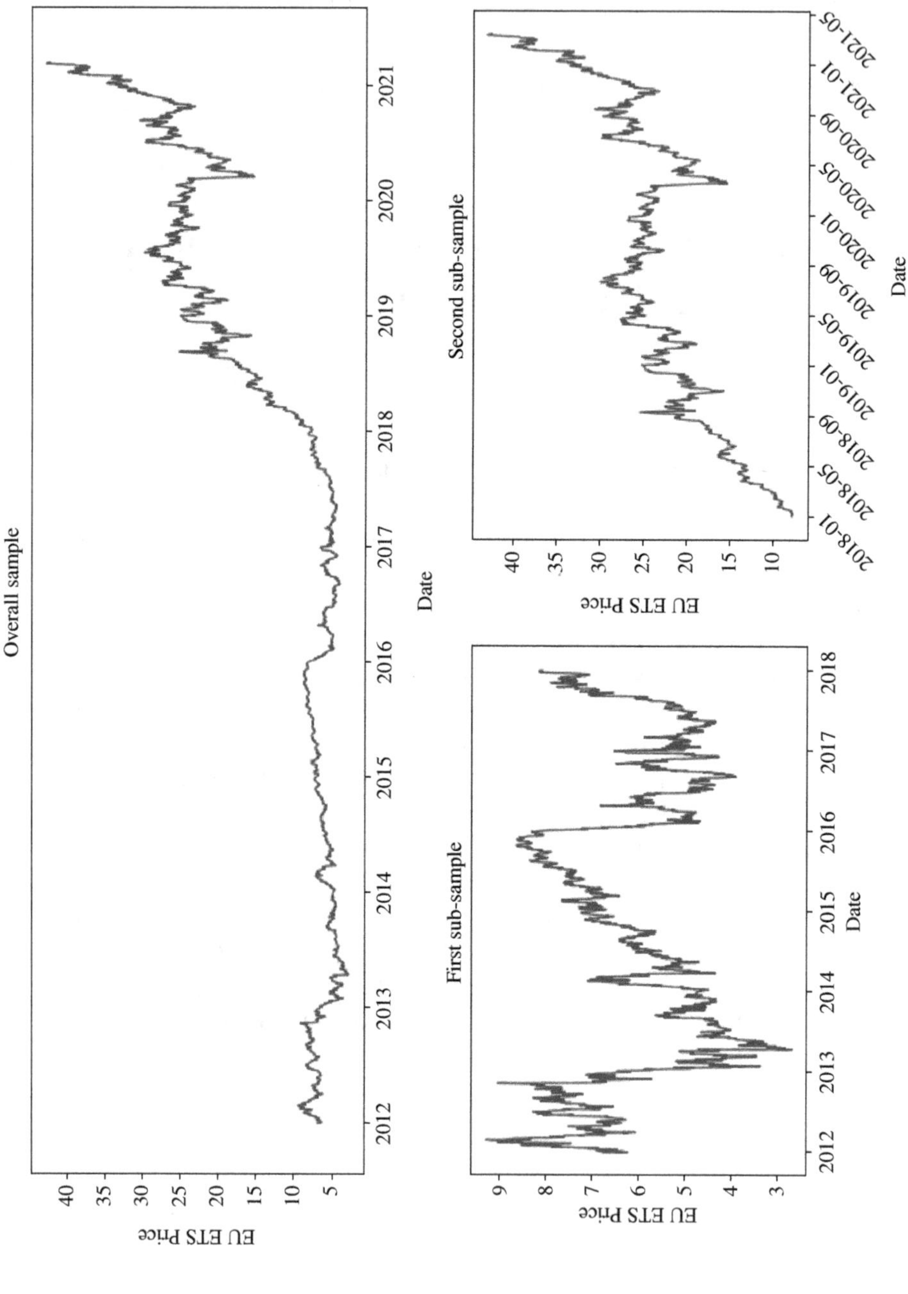

Fig. 8.1. EUA spot prices.

Table 8.1. Descriptive statistics of EUAs for price levels.

	2012–2021	2012–2018	2018–2021
Min	2.68	2.68	7.62
Max	42.77	9.31	42.77
Mean	11.92	6.11	22.73
Median	7.35	6.04	23.87
Standard deviation	8.87	1.35	6.48
Variance	78.63	1.83	42.01
Skewness	1.10	0.064	−0.05
Kurtosis	−0.09	−0.99	0.48
Number of observations	2325	1513	812

Table 8.2. Descriptive statistics of EUA returns.

	2012–2021	2012–2018	2018–2021
Min	−90.76	−90.76	−44.55
Max	59.07	59.07	34.47
Mean	0.34	0.18	0.63
Median	0.00	0.00	0.50
Standard deviation	0.52	0.55	0.47
Variance	0.27	0.30	0.23
Skewness	−0.35	−0.34	−0.33
Kurtosis	10.26	12.12	3.39
Number of observations	2325	1513	812

Table 8.3. Augmented Dickey–Fuller test EUA returns.

	2012–2021	2012–2018	2018–2021
ADF statistic	−36.491482	−30.859889	−29.061631
p-value	0.000000	0.000000	0.000000
Critical value (1%)	−3.433168	−3.434685	−3.438439
Critical value (5%)	−2.862785	−2.863455	−2.865110
Critical value (10%)	−2.567433	−2.567789	−2.568671

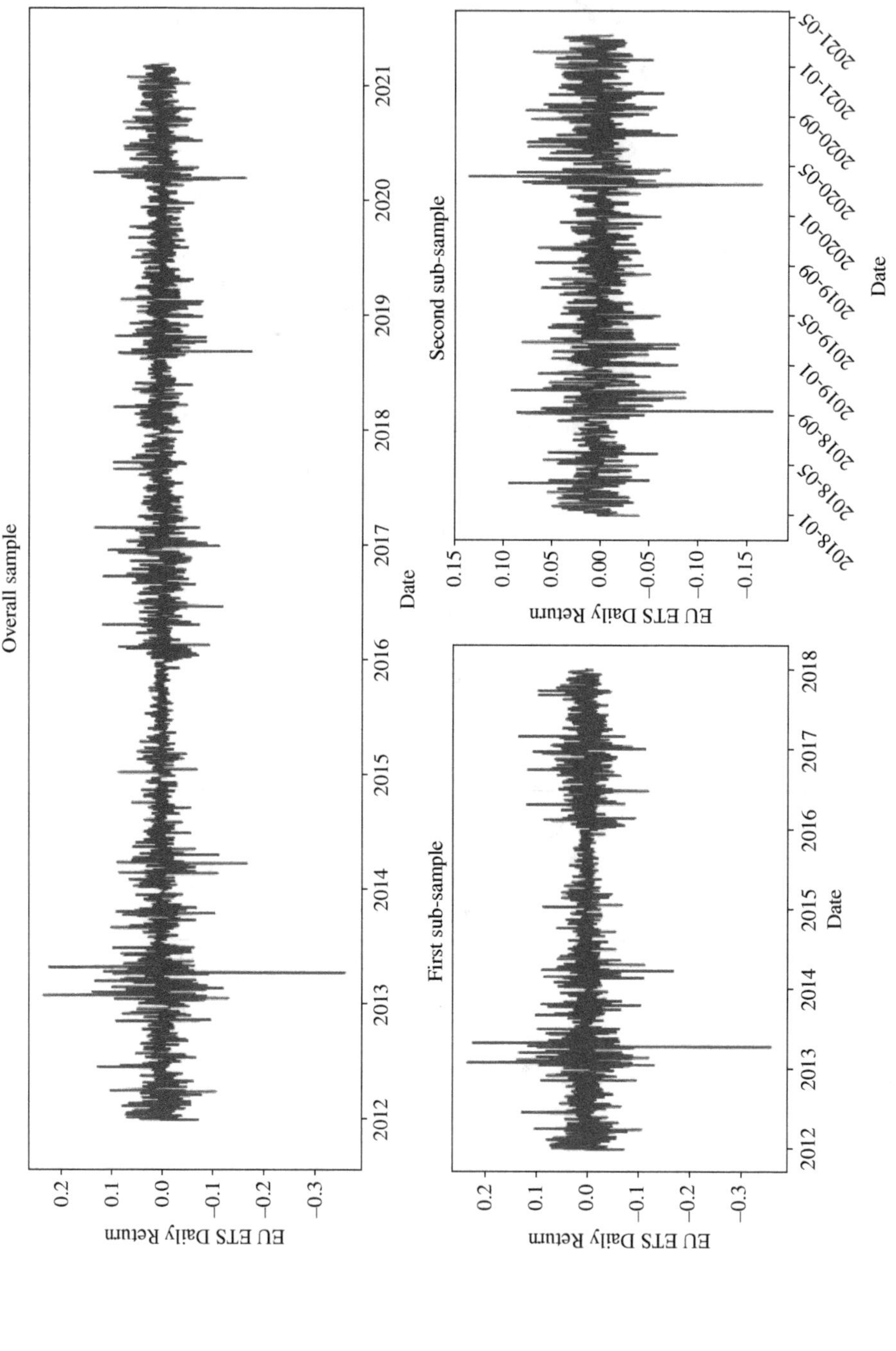

Fig. 8.2. EUA spot prices.

8.2 Stochastic Models for Emission Certificates

We will now provide an outline of a few representative stochastic models for emission allowance prices. As is typical for price models of financial assets, we can distinguish between models which provide an equilibrium argument to determine prices and reduced-form models which basically take a suitable stochastic process to capture the econometric properties of an underlying process. Compared to the models inspired by the asset pricing framework we presented in Section 4.2, the equilibrium models in this section are more parsimonious. However, the purpose of the models discussed in this section is to provide a tractable model for the EUA price dynamics only.

8.2.1 *Equilibrium Models*

Let us start with equilibrium models. Chesney *et al.* (2013) provide a detailed overview of equilibrium models, including early deterministic ones. The underlying idea is to use a representative agent, solve the corresponding cost minimisation problem and show that the individual solution leads to a solution for the joint cost optimum. In the work by Seifert (2008), emission rate dynamics q_t are

$$dq_t = \mu(t, q_t)dt + \sigma(t, q_t)dW_t, \tag{8.1}$$

with W a Brownian motion, $\mu(t, x)$ the drift and $\sigma(t, x)$ the volatility function (satisfying suitable regularity conditions). The central planner decides, at any time instant, on the abatement of emission in order to minimise total expected cost over a trading period $[0, T]$. At the end of the period, actual accumulated emissions and penalty costs are determined.

The total expected emissions over the trading period are denoted by x_t and the rate of abatement chosen by the central planner by u_t; then,

$$x_t = -\int_0^t u_s ds + \mathbb{E}_t\left[\int_0^T y_s ds\right]. \tag{8.2}$$

So, x_t is a controlled stochastic process.

Without abatement, total expected emissions are $\mathbb{E}\left[\int_0^T q_s ds\right]$. The dynamics of the total expected emissions are

$$dx_t = -u_t dt + G(t)dW_t, \tag{8.3}$$

where $G(t)$ is the volatility of the uncontrolled part of x_t and depends both on the drift $\mu(t, q_t)$ and volatility $\sigma(t, q_t)$ of the emission rate. x_T denote the realised emissions that relate to the penalty function.

Assume a constant interest rate r and that the total initial endowment is e_0. Let $C(t, u_t) = -\frac{1}{2}cu_t^2$ be the abatement costs per unit time. As c is constant, the abatement technology does not change in the time period considered. Also, the quadratic form implies linearly increasing marginal abatement costs. The penalty function $P(x_T) = \min[0, p(e_0 - x_T)]$, with p the penalty including all costs.

The central planner faces the optimisation problem

$$\max_{u_t} \mathbb{E}_0 \left[\int_0^T e^{-rt} C(t, u_t)dt + e^{-rT} P(x_T)\right]. \tag{8.4}$$

Seifert (2008) shows that this problem can be solved using the Hamilton–Jacobi–Bellman (HJB) framework (see Appendix A for details). Let $V(t, x_t)$ be the expected value of the optimal policy given x_t. By a standard HJB argument, we arrive at the characteristic Partial Differential Equation (PDE):

$$V_t = -\frac{1}{2}(G(t))^2 V_{xx} - \frac{1}{2c} e^{rt} (V_x)^2 \tag{8.5}$$

with boundary condition

$$V(T, x_T) = e^{-rT} P(x_T)$$

and optimal control

$$u_t = -\frac{1}{c} e^{rt} V_x.$$

The PDE in (8.5) can only be solved analytically for the case in which the emission rate follows a Gaussian process with constant volatility, which is not very realistic. However, as Seifert (2008) shows, the analysis of this particular case provides insights in the general structure of the solution. In case the emission rate is modelled using a better econometric fit equation, (8.5) can be solved numerically.

In an equilibrium framework, the allowance price A must equal the marginal abatement costs; so,

$$A(t, x_t) = cu_t = -e^{rt}V_x(t, x_t). \tag{8.6}$$

Using Itô's formula and the HJB PDE, we find that the discounted permit price is a martingale. Its dynamics are

$$dA(t, x_t) = G(t)A_x(t, x_t)dW_t. \tag{8.7}$$

Hence, the model produces a permit price dynamics and can potentially be calibrated to market data. Seifert (2008) shows that starting from individual (but homogeneous) companies, which face the same cost optimisation problem with the additional possibility to trade permits, the joint optimum is equivalent to the central planner's optimum. Thus, the possibility of trading permits allows one to achieve the best possible solution. However, the assumption of homogeneity and the assumption that all companies face the same source of risk (all dynamics are subject to the same Brownian motion) is somewhat restrictive.

Carmona *et al.* (2009) present a stochastic equilibrium model that captures the essential features of a standard allocation scheme. The structure of a generic cap and trade system is generalised to a discrete-time stochastic framework, where both short-term abatement prices and the total emission volumes evolve randomly. The model considers a multi-firm economy with firms producing electricity from fossil fuel with different costs and trading carbon allowances. A competitive stochastic equilibrium model is formulated and solved in terms of a stochastic control problem. It can be shown that the equilibrium solution is socially optimal, that is, the solution of the individual firm-specific problems (with the possibility to trade carbon allowances) is the solution of the global optimisation problem, where the total pollution is reduced at minimal overall cost. The property of global optimality is used to show the existence of an equilibrium for the individual problem and to calculate the corresponding carbon prices. Importantly, it is shown that the equilibrium carbon price process is a martingale given in terms of the global optimal policy. Their result allows a specification of allowance prices as

$$A(t, x_t) = p \cdot \mathbb{E}\left[\mathbf{1}_{\{x_T - c \geq 0\}} | \mathcal{F}_t\right], \tag{8.8}$$

with x_t the (optimally controlled) emissions, c the cap, and p the penalty.

The results of Carmona *et al.* (2009) also justify rigorously that the equilibrium allowance price equals the marginal abatement costs.

Finally, a stylised model is calibrated to the first phase of the EU ETS. This allows one to identify sensitivities with respect to model parameters and to identify main price drivers for the EUA.

8.2.2 *Reduced-Form Models*

The approaches we consider here use, as the underlying process, cumulative or individual emission rates, and as often in a first stochastic approach, these rates are modelled by a Gaussian process or a geometric Brownian motion. This allows for (semi-) closed-form solutions of the relevant optimisation and valuation problems.

The basic insight is the representation of the allowance price as a digital call on the cumulative emissions. The formal justification is given by the formula (8.8), although the idea was used beforehand.

Let us consider a cap-and-trade emission trading system (such as the EU ETS). The trading period is $[0,T]$, the cap is c, and the penalty for non-compliance is p.

To calculate permit prices, we specify the process for the cumulative emissions as $q_{[0,t]} = \int_0^t Q_s ds$, where the emission rate Q_t follows a geometric Brownian motion. As there is no closed form for the integral available, we use a simple moment matching as in the work of Gruell and Kiesel (2012) with a log-normal random variable as approximation for the exposition (of course, accurate numerical solutions are available). Thus, we choose the parameters of the log-normal distribution in such a way that its first two moments match those of $q_{[0,t]}$. We can then calculate the permit price at time t using (8.8):

$$A_t = \begin{cases} p & \text{if } q_{[0,t]} \geq c, \\ p \cdot \Phi\left(\dfrac{-\ln\left(\frac{c-q_{[0,t]}}{Q_t}\right)+2\ln(\alpha_\tau)-\frac{1}{2}\ln(2\beta_\tau)}{\sqrt{\ln(2\beta_\tau)-2\ln(\alpha_\tau)}}\right) & \text{if } q_{[0,t]} < c, \end{cases}$$

where $\tau = T - t$ is the time to compliance and α_τ, β_τ are obtained by calculating the first and second moments of the integral over a geometric Brownian motion. $\Phi(\cdot)$ denotes the cumulative distribution function of a standard normal random variable. The time needed to exhaust the remaining permits is given by

$$x_t := \frac{c - q_{[0,t]}}{Q_t}.$$

We now calculate the sensitivity (Delta) of the permit price with respect to x_t for $q_{[0,t]} < c$ (that is, the cap is not yet reached):

$$\frac{dA_t}{dx_t}(x_t) := -\frac{pe^{-r\tau}}{\sigma\sqrt{\tau}} \cdot \frac{1}{x_t}\phi\left(\frac{-\ln\left(\frac{1}{\tau}x_t\right) + \left(\mu - \frac{\sigma^2}{2}\right)\tau}{\sigma\sqrt{\tau}}\right) < 0.$$

So, it is easy to see that small changes in x_t move the permit price considerably. This could be observed during the first phase of the EU ETS, when the information that there was an overallocation of allowances pushed the permit price down rapidly, see Figure 8.3. Carmona and Hinz (2010) used the reduced-form approach to price

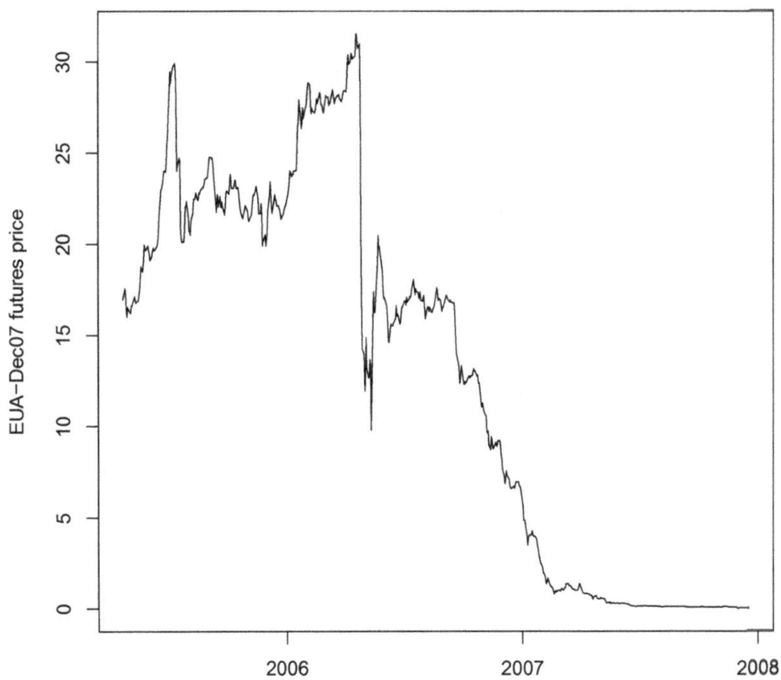

Fig. 8.3. EUA-Dec07 futures price (22 April, 2005–2017 December, 2007).

options on allowances. Instead of starting with an emission rate, they immediately used the process

$$\Gamma_t = \Gamma_0 \exp\left\{\int_0^t \sigma_s dW_s - \frac{1}{2}\int_0^t \sigma_s^2 ds\right\}$$

to model the cumulative emissions. Here, $\Gamma_0 > 0$ and $\sigma(.)$ is a deterministic square-integrable function. From (8.8), the permit price is given as

$$A(t,T) = p\mathbb{Q}\left[\Gamma_T > 1|\mathcal{F}_t\right]$$

(with $\mathbb{Q}$ a pricing measure and $(\mathcal{F}_t)$ the underlying flow of information). Now, we obtain the permit price dynamics from

$$a_t = \mathbb{E}^{\mathbb{Q}}\left[\mathbf{1}_{\{\Gamma_T>1\}}|\mathcal{F}_t\right] = \Phi\left[\frac{\Phi^{-1}(a_0)\sqrt{\int_0^T \sigma_s^2 ds} + \int_0^t \sigma_s dW_s}{\sqrt{\int_t^T \sigma_s^2 ds}}\right]$$

as

$$da_t = \Phi'\left(\Phi^{-1}(a_t)\right)\sqrt{z_t}dW_t, \tag{8.9}$$

with $z_t = \frac{\sigma_t^2}{\int_t^T \sigma_u^2 du}$. A standard model is

$$da_t = \Phi'\left(\Phi^{-1}(a_t)\right)\sqrt{\beta(T-t)^{-\alpha}}dW_t,$$

which specifies a family of volatilities $\sigma_s(\alpha,\beta)$. So, $z_t(\alpha,\beta) = \beta(T-t)^{-\alpha}$ and

$$\begin{aligned}\sigma_t^2(\alpha,\beta) &= z_t(\alpha,\beta)\exp\left\{-\int_0^t z_s(\alpha,\beta)ds\right\}\\ &= \begin{cases}\beta(T-t)^{-\alpha}e^{-\frac{\beta}{1-\alpha}[T^{1-\alpha}-(T-1)^{1-\alpha}]} & \alpha\neq 1,\\ \beta(T-t)^{\beta-1}T^{-\beta} & \alpha = 1.\end{cases}\end{aligned}$$

This specification allows for an explicit formula for a European call with strike K and maturity τ: the option price is

$$C_t = e^{-\int_t^T r_s ds}\int_{-\infty}^{\infty}(P\Phi(x)-K)^+\Phi_{\mu_{t,\tau},\sigma_{t,\tau}}(dx),$$

with

$$\mu_{t,\tau} = \begin{cases} \xi_t \left(\frac{T-t}{T-\tau}\right)^{\frac{\beta}{2}} & \alpha = 1, \\ \xi_t \exp\left\{\frac{\beta}{2(1-\alpha)}[(T-t)^{1-\alpha} - (T-\tau)^{1-\alpha}]\right\} & \alpha \neq 1, \end{cases}$$

and

$$\sigma^2_{t,\tau} = \begin{cases} \left(\frac{T-t}{T-\tau}\right)^{\beta} - 1 & \alpha = 1, \\ \exp\left\{\frac{\beta}{1-\alpha}[(T-t)^{1-\alpha} - (T-\tau)^{1-\alpha}]\right\} - 1 & \alpha \neq 1. \end{cases}$$

Observe that this is, in fact, a compound option (option on an option), as the permit price can be viewed as a binary option. For an extension of the approach to a multi-period setting and a discussion of the properties of a risk premium in allowances between the first two phases of the ETS, see Wen and Kiesel (2016).

8.3 Effects on Financial and Energy Markets

8.3.1 *EUA Certificates and Financial Markets*

8.3.1.1 *Stock Prices and EUAs*

In order to understand the impact of EUA certificate prices on stock prices of utilities, we conduct a small empirical analysis using a sample of 12 European utility companies (ALSTOM, E.ON AG, EDISON S.P.A., EDP - Energias de Portugal, S.A. ELECTRICITE DE FRANCE, EnBW Energie Baden-Wuerttemberg AG, ENDESA, S.A., ENEL S.P.A., Fortum Oyj, IBERDROLA, S.A. NATIONAL GRID PLC, RWE AG.) during the period January 2013 to December 2017.

We used daily stock returns as a dependent variable and additional variables known to effect the return of utilities (in our context, mainly electricity companies). Thus, we include a stock market factor, the EURO STOXX 600, and electricity prices, daily baseload spot prices, as control variables. We did not include any fossil fuel prices as some of the electricity produced already have a substantial portfolio of renewable energy generation. In line with standard procedure, we do our estimation on the daily log-returns.

Table 8.4. Pooled OLS estimation stocks.

		Value	Std. err.	t-stat	p-value
const.	α	–2.79e-05	0.0001	–0.2377	0.8121
Market	β_1	0.7819	0.0122	64.177	0.0000
Elec.	β_2	–0.0006	0.0003	–1.6894	0.0912
EUA	β_3	0.0147	0.0034	4.3037	0.0000

The estimated equation is

$$r_t = \alpha + \beta_1 r_{m,t} + \beta_2 r_{elec,t} + \beta_3 r_{EUA,t} + \epsilon_t, \tag{8.10}$$

with r_t log-return of a utility stock, $r_{m,t}$ the log-return of the EURO STOXX 600, $r_{elec,t}$ the log-return of electricity prices, $r_{EUA,t}$ the log-return of the EUA certificate prices, and ϵ_t a random error term with mean value 0 and a constant variance. We performed a simple pooled ordinary least-squares regression, which produced highly significant overall results according to the F-statistic. Results for individual coefficients are reported in Table 8.4. We find a positive and significant relationship between electricity stock returns and market index and EUA returns. Both variables are significant at 1%. Electricity returns turn out to negatively affect the stock prices and the variable is significant at 10% level.

Our results are in line with estimations from Tian *et al.* (2016), who apply a multi-factor model to address the impact of the EUA prices on the stocks of electricity companies during Phases I and II of the European ETS. They show that stock prices tend to positively respond to EUA price changes for those producers that use predominately green energy in their generation. For carbon-intensive producers, they find an inverse relationship between stock returns and EUA price changes during Phase II. The conditional correlations between EUA returns and electricity stock volatility are found to be significant in Phase II and insignificant in Phase I.

An interesting analysis of abnormal excess returns (alpha) during Phases I and II has been done by Oestreich and Tsiakas (2015). They use 65 German stocks from all sectors included in DAX and MDAX, and divide the companies into three portfolios based on how much EUA certificates they received for free. Thus, the brown portfolio corresponds to a high number of free EUAs, the clean portfolio collects companies with no free EU, and the medium portfolio collects companies in between. In a factor model approach, they calculate the carbon premium, which they define as the excess abnormal return of the 'brown-minus-green' portfolio. They find the premium sizeable and statistically significant. However, as their time horizon includes Phases I and II only, where there was substantial free allocation (grandfathering, compare Section 2.3), this carbon premium may vanish as companies no longer have access to free allocations.

We will return to this type of portfolio construction and analysis in Chapter 9.

8.3.1.2 *Credit Default Swap Spreads and EUAs*

We perform the same type of exploratory analysis on the relation of credit default swap (CDS) spreads of European utilities (electricity producers) and EUA prices. CDS spreads are a widely used indicator of the credit risk of a company. They can be directly related to default probabilities and their term structure. We refer the reader to Chapter 10, where we perform a much more detailed analysis. Here, we perform a pooled OLS on 15 European utilities (in addition to the companies considered above, ENECO Holding N.V., Essent N.V., and Vattenfall are included) and EUA prices. Again, we use the period January 2013 to December 2017, this time however with monthly data. The estimated equation is now

$$cds_t = \alpha + \beta_1 cds_{t-1} + \beta_2 cds_{m,t} + \beta_3 eua_t + \epsilon_t, \tag{8.11}$$

with cds_t the CDS spread which we also include with one month lagged. $cds_{m,t}$ is a CDS benchmark that was derived as a median spread of all non-financial, non-sovereign CDS spreads from Europe with the same contract type as for the sample companies in the total 202 companies. eua_t is the price of EUA certificates and ϵ_t a random error. Again, the results of the regression are highly significant overall. We report the estimates for individual coefficients in Table 8.5. We observe a positive and significant link between CDS spreads and EUA prices.

We take these results as a first indicator that carbon risk has implications on the credit market. In Chapter 10, we show that the impact is not limited to the utility sector only, but affects the whole market.

Table 8.5. Pooled OLS estimation for CDS spreads.

		Value	Std. err.	t-stat	p-value
Const	α	−34.049	3.9465	−8.6279	0.0000
Lagged CDS	β_1	0.9356	0.0080	116.50	0.0000
Market CDS	β_2	0.2971	0.0336	8.8486	0.0000
EUA	β_3	2.6286	0.3319	7.9193	0.0000

8.3.2 *EUA Certificates on Electricity Markets*

In electricity markets, power producers are exposed to the difference of the electricity price and the fuel to run a power plant. Financially, these differences are used to model power plants and are called spreads. Examples are the dark spread between power and coal (model for a coal-fired power plant) and the spark spread between power and gas (model for a gas-fired power plant). Forwards (and futures) on these spreads are used to value power plants, and options provide a risk management tool. The payoff of a typical spread option with underlying S_1, S_2, maturity T and strike K is

$$\max(S_1(T) - S_2(T) - K, 0). \tag{8.12}$$

A closed-form valuation is possible only in the Black–Scholes setting for $K = 0$ (exchange option) due to Margrabe (1978). For $K \neq 0$ and other stochastic models, a simulation approach has to be used.

In countries covered by an emissions trading scheme, plant owners have to consider the cost of CO_2 emission allowances as well. The introduction of emission certificates implies a 3-asset payoff:

$$\max\{S_1(T) - S_2(T) - S_3(T) - K, 0\}, \tag{8.13}$$

with S_1 the price of power, S_2 the price of a (fossil) fuel, and S_3 the price of emission certificates. Obviously, the valuation increases in complexity in this case. In a Black–Scholes type model, Alòs *et al.* (2011) have shown that the payoff (8.13) can be approximated by a classical vanilla option with random strike $S_2 + S_3 + K$ and appropriate volatility:

$$C_{\text{K3}}(S_1(t), S_2(t), S_3(t), K, \tau) \approx C_{\text{BS}}(S_1(t), S_2(t) + S_3(t) + K, \sigma_S, \tau), \tag{8.14}$$

with

$$\sigma_S = \sqrt{\sigma_1^2 + b_2^2\sigma_2^2 + b_3^2\sigma_3^2 - 2\rho_{12}\sigma_1\sigma_2 b_2 - 2\rho_{13}\sigma_1\sigma_3 b_1 + 2\rho_{23}\sigma_2\sigma_3 b_2 b_3},$$

$$b_2 = \frac{S_2(t)}{S_2(t) + S_3(t) + K} \quad \text{and} \quad b_3 = \frac{S_3(t)}{S_2(t) + S_3(t) + K},$$

and ρ_{ij} is the correlation between the underlying i, j. This is a variant of the classical s-asset case Kirk's formula (compare with Carmona and Durrleman (2003)).

For an application of this method, we consider a gas power plant. Financially, a gas power plant is long electricity, short gas, and short carbon. We express this in terms of the clean spark spread as

$$V_t = \max\{P_t - hG_t - c_E E_t - C, 0\}. \tag{8.15}$$

Here, P_t is the price of electricity, G_t the price of gas, E_t the price of emission certificates, and C represents fixed costs (h and c_E are conversion factors). To value the power plant, we calculate the expected value of the sum of the discounted clean spark spreads (as in (8.15)) during the valuation period. This approach has been used by Bannör *et al.* (2016) to analyse the risk of gas fired power plants with respect to various pricing models.

8.3.3 *Green Power Purchase Agreements*

Power purchase agreement (PPA) can be viewed as a support scheme for renewable energy. PPAs can be used to finance facilities for the generation of renewable generation, such as hydro power, wind mills, or photovoltaic farms. Recently, renewable PPPs or green PPPs have gained increasing interest as a mechanism to foster energy generation from renewable sources, see Deutsche Energie Agentur (2021), and as a means of achieving a share of renewable energy in a production portfolio. Figure 8.4 shows the increase in the share of renewable energy corporate use.

These contracts are between owners of renewable assets, who sell electricity to utilities (supply companies), and corporates. As

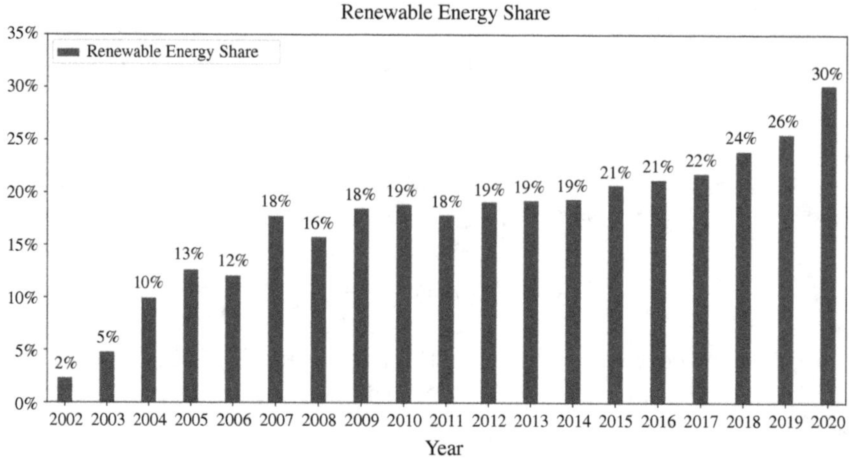

Fig. 8.4. Increase of renewable energy at corporate level.

there is demand from end-users for green energy, utilities can redistribute the green power to their consumers, such as households and businesses.

Larger firms wanting to go green can buy green electricity from a utility using PPAs or combine green certificates or guarantees of origin (GoO) with electricity from the wholesale market. In most cases, do-it-yourself production by building one's own power plant is not feasible due to development, operation and maintenance cost, and availability of appropriate knowledge. PPAs are a way of achieving a share of green generation by outsourcing the operation, while maintaining a direct connection to specific assets. This direct connection is an advantage compared to virtual green certificates, as the firm is directly connected to a tangible asset, which raises its visibility in terms of green projects. It also avoids concerns with respect to greenwashing. To value such a green PPA, a main ingredient is, of course, still the baseload power price. For the contract period under consideration, the forward market is used to develop a sufficiently granular power forward curve for the basic valuation. In addition, there is a premium for the power to be proven green, i.e., for a certification of origin (GoO). By now, several countries have established certification mechanisms such that all power generated from larger facilities obtain such a GoO. In compliance markets with green energy targets, such as a certain percentage of renewable production in total consumption, generators are supplied with a number of green certificates, which in principle can be traded (although due to national restrictions the liquidity is very low). Thus, trading is mostly over-the-counter with high transaction costs and little information on prices. As price levels have been rather low (below 1 €/MWh), the development of the green certificate market has been slow. However, parallel to a revived carbon credit market, there is some optimism towards the growth of this market as well.

Chapter 9

Carbon Risk and Empirical Asset Pricing

9.1 Constructing Factor Models

The capital asset pricing model (CAPM) provides a risk–return relationship featuring just one factor — the (unobservable) market portfolio. As early empirical tests produced ambiguous results, variants of the CAPM extended the simple one-factor models. The question on how multiple factors affected the return resulted in a vast body of empirical literature. As this is the starting point of many of the studies we will discuss in the sequel, we give a brief introduction to the development of the theory and the technical tools for its empirical investigation.

9.1.1 *The Capital Asset Pricing Model and Multi-Factor Models*

A possible model for explaining the expectation of an asset return $R_{i,t}$ is

$$\mathbb{E}(R_{i,t}) = \alpha_i + \beta_i' \mathbb{E}(F_t), \tag{9.1}$$

with F_t a d-dimensional vector of explaining factors and β_i a d-dimensional vector of factor loadings. α_i is the unexplained component. An asset pricing model aims to identify economic or statistical factors that explain the asset prices and eliminate mispricing.

The expected return–beta relationship expression of the CAPM fits into this framework:

$$\mathbb{E}(R_{i,t}) = r_f + \beta(\mathbb{E}(R_{M,t}) - r_f)), \tag{9.2}$$

with r_f the risk-free rate and $R_{M,t}$ the return of the market portfolio at time t. The CAPM theory provides an interpretable formula for β_i:

$$\beta_i = \frac{\mathbb{C}\text{ov}(R_i, R_M)}{\mathbb{V}\text{ar}(R_M^)}.$$

So, β_i is the fraction of the total variance of the market portfolio contributed by stock i. Asset risk is the covariance of the asset return with the market. The risk premium, or the market price of risk, is the expected value of the excess market return. The CAPM is simple and intuitive but has various empirical and theoretical drawbacks. The multi-factor CAPM and the arbitrage pricing theory (APT) offer insight into how multiple systemic risk factors should affect expected returns, but still the relevant factors need to be identified. Furthermore, to perform empirical tests, hedge portfolios for these factors have to be constructed. The most prominent factors and tests are due to the work by Fama and French (1993). They observed historic excess returns of small (based on a market capitalisation) companies over large-sized companies. Likewise, they accounted for the observation that in the long term, companies with a high book-to-market ratio, the so-called value companies, achieve higher returns than firms with a low book-to-market ratio. So, they used as additional factors a spread portfolio long in small firm stocks and short in large firm stocks (SMB) and a spread portfolio long in high book-to-market stocks and short in low book-to-market stocks (HML). The precise construction involves grouping and sorting stocks according to both size and book-to-market values. The empirical analysis showed that the Fama–French model substantially improves the CAPM. In order to evaluate the mutual fund performance (Carhart, 1997), the Fama–French model is extended by inclusion of a momentum factor (WML), which is constructed from the difference of returns of past winners and past losers. One can take different time periods of past returns to construct this factor. This augmented Fama–French (or Fama–French–Carhart model) model has become the standard model to evaluate abnormal returns of stock portfolios. It is also the starting point and benchmark for the analysis of the existence and effect of a carbon risk factor in the following sections. So, let us state the formal relation:

$$\mathbb{E}(R_{i,t}) = \alpha_i + \beta_i^M \mathbb{E}(R_{M,t}) + \beta_i^{SMB} \mathbb{E}(R_{SMB,t}) \\ + \beta_i^{HML} \mathbb{E}(R_{HML,t}) + \beta_i^{WML} \mathbb{E}(R_{WML,t}). \quad (9.3)$$

A great number of additional factors have been proposed and tested for various markets and time periods; see Lewellen (2015) for a review and discussion. The discussion of the CAPM, APT, and multi-factor models is given in the work by Bodie (2020).

9.1.2 *Panel Regression*

We now review the statistical techniques that are in use for the empirical discussion of factors. Let us start with a few general comments on time-series OLS regression; see Wooldridge (2010) or Baltagi (2001) for details. Equation (9.4) provides an example multilinear regression equation[1]:

$$R_{i,t} = \alpha_i + \sum \beta_i' X_{i,t} + \epsilon_{it}, \quad (9.4)$$

with $t = 1, \ldots, T$ reflecting the points in time and $i = 1, \ldots, N$ representing the entities under consideration. R is the dependent, X a set of explanatory variables and ϵ a zero-mean random error term. Typically, financial time series need to be checked for stationarity with the help of a standard test such as the (augmented) Dickey–Fuller test (Pesaran, 2007). In contrast to time-series OLS regression, panel regression not only considers the time-series dimension but also takes into account the cross-sectional dimension. Equation (9.5) displays an example panel regression equation. Here, as in equation (9.4), $R_{i,t}$ represents the dependent variable at time t for entity i, α is the regression's intercept, and $X_{i,t}$ reflects a set of explanatory variables for entity i at time t. One difference in comparison to the multilinear model is that the estimation coefficients do not refer to the single entities but to the whole cross-sectional dimension. Moreover, panel

[1] From now on, we use the statistical notation with random quantities instead of expectations.

models allow one to control for unobserved individual heterogeneity, which if not controlled for could lead to biased estimations (Croissant and Millo, 2018). In equation (9.5), the unobservable variables are $Z_{i,t}$. The usual model transforms equation (9.5) to equation (9.6) and specifies a time-invariant and mostly unobservable characteristic η_i and an unobservable characteristic $\nu_{i,t}$ (Croissant and Millo, 2018):

$$R_{i,t} = \alpha + \beta' X_{i,t} + \gamma' Z_{i,t} + \epsilon_{i,t} \quad (9.5)$$

$$= \alpha + \beta' X_{i,t} + (\eta_i + \nu_{i,t}). \quad (9.6)$$

Depending on the specific panel regression model, equations (9.5) and (9.6) are modified and extended.

The two main classes of panel models are the fixed effects (FE) and random effects (RE) models. The FE model assumes that the unobserved heterogeneity is arbitrarily correlated with the observed explanatory variables (factors), so it can be estimated for each cross-sectional entity. For the RE model, the assumption is no correlation between the unobserved effects and the observed explanatory variables. So, the unobserved heterogeneity acts as a random variable (Wooldridge, 2010). A detailed analysis of the estimators shows that common factors in multi-factor models can capture time-series predictability by firm characteristics as long as the factor is correlated with the lagged characteristic for at least one stock. Likewise, asset pricing factors could explain cross-sectional predictability as long as factor loadings are correlated with firm characteristics for at least one period.

9.2 Stock Returns and Carbon Risk

9.2.1 *Carbon Risk as an Additional Factor in Multi-Factor Models*

A natural idea to analyse carbon risk as a risk factor is to extend the Fama–French–Carhart setting with an additional factor. Goergen *et al.* (2020) follow that avenue by constructing a brown-minus-green (BMG) portfolio. Their first step is to construct a brown green score (BGS) based on individual carbon emission-related measures using ESG databases. Starting from 131 environmental variables that are related to carbon-transition risk, they select 10 variables to describe each of the categories value chain, public perception, and adaptability. Value chain relates to scope 1–3 emissions of a firm, public perception captures how investors, creditors, and customers rate the carbon policy of a firm, and adaptability collects measures of forward-looking climate policies of a firm. This selection covers the range of carbon risks, as discussed in Section 3.1. Naturally, carbon emissions play a prominent role as they are a key ingredient of regulatory measures and in the focus of public discussion. For all variables, firms are ordered individually, and a score is given according to their position (1 above median, 0 otherwise). Finally, scores are added within the three categories, and the final BGS is then calculated as

$$\mathrm{BGS}_{i,t} = 0.70\mathrm{VC}_{i,t} + 0.15\mathrm{PP}_{i,t} + 0.15\mathrm{AD}_{i,t}, \tag{9.7}$$

with VC, PP, and AD standing for value chain, public perception, and adaptability, respectively. Of course, the selection procedure and the weighting scheme needs some justification. The authors refer to discussions with expert panels and extensive statistical analysis and robustness tests.

An application of the panel regression framework leads to the following equation:

$$R_{i,t} = \alpha_i + \beta_{i,1}\mathrm{BGS}_{i,t} + \beta_{i,2}(\mathrm{BGS}_{i,t} - \mathrm{BGS}_{i,t-1}) + \nu_i Z_t. \tag{9.8}$$

As BGS is based on yearly data (see Chapter 5 for data quality and availability), $R_{i,t}$ are the yearly returns and Z captures a range of control variables. The results (the time period is from 2010 to 2017) that Goergen *et al.* (2020) report show that BGS has a significant effect in level and difference. The level (observed carbon risk of a firm) has a positive effect of stock returns, whereas the difference (dynamics of carbon risk) has a negative effect. Thus, 'browner' firms have a higher return and becoming greener (which leads to a negative BGS difference) results in a higher return. These results are in line with the theoretical model of Pastor *et al.* (2020), which we presented in Section 4.3.2. In line with the Fama–French–Carhart (see Section 9.1) approach, Goergen *et al.* (2020) construct a portfolio to investigate the existence and relevance of a factor related to carbon risk. It is constructed by allocating all firms into six portfolios based on their size (market valuation) and BGS score. For the size component, the median and for the BGS portfolio, terciles are used to define the buckets. Then, the value-weighted average monthly returns of the upper and lower BGS terciles together are used to construct the spread portfolio, which is long in brown (SH, BH for small/high BGS, big/high BGS) and short in green (SL, BL for small/low BGS, big/low BGS) firms. Equation (9.9) formalises the construction:

$$\text{BMG}_t - = \frac{1}{2}(\text{SH}_t + \text{BH}_t) - \frac{1}{2}(\text{SL}_t + \text{BL}_t). \tag{9.9}$$

Then, the following factor model is analysed:

$$\begin{aligned} R_{i,t} = \alpha_i + \beta_i^M R_{M,t} + \beta_i^{\text{SMB}} R_{\text{SMB},t} + \beta_i^{\text{HML}} R_{\text{HML},t} \\ + \beta_i^{\text{WML}} R_{\text{WML},t} + \beta_i^{\text{BMG}} R_{\text{BMG},t} + \epsilon_{it}. \end{aligned} \tag{9.10}$$

The results of the estimation show a negative average β^{BMG} and small correlations of BMG to the other factors. Thus, the BMG factor provides additional explanatory power to the Fama–French–Carhart model and is able to reveal carbon risk in equity prices. Goergen *et al.* (2020) support these results with different model specifications and use various asset pricing tests to show the robustness of their results. However, the portfolio approach does not investigate a potential direct association between carbon risk and systematic risk (correlation is often a misleading indicator as it only reveals linear effects). The precise specification of this relation impacts the cost of capital of firms and the allocation of capital between green and brown firms. We will return to this question in Section 9.3.

9.2.2 *Is There a Carbon Risk Premium in Equity Markets?*

A number of articles investigate the question of how carbon risk affects equity markets. In this context, the aim is to identify a risk premium and analyse its sectorial and/or geographical variation. In this context, let us consider an analysis by Bolton and Kacperczyk (2020), who discuss various carbon risk-related hypotheses using data from US equity markets during the period 2005–2017. For instance, they ask whether forward-looking investors may demand a compensation for holding high-carbon firms, which would result in a positive relation between a firm's GHG emissions and its stock return. They label this the carbon risk premium hypothesis. In order to investigate this hypothesis, the following cross-sectional pooled OLS regression model is used:

$$R_{i,t} = \alpha_0 + \beta_1 \log(TE)_{i,t} + \beta_2 CV_{i,t} + \mu_t + \epsilon_{i,t}. \tag{9.11}$$

The dependent variable is the monthly returns of stock i in month t, and the explanatory variables are expressed in generic terms with total emissions (TE), which represent scope 1, 2, or 3 alternatively. Likewise, CV refers to a generic vector which includes firm-specific variables (such as size, book-to-market, momentum), and firm characteristics (such as the value of property, investment over assets) known to explain return. In addition, year/month fixed effects are included. All three scope variables have a positive and statistically significant effect. In addition, the effect is economically significant with one standard deviation increase of any of the scopes leading to annual increase in stock returns by several percentage points. They also show industry effects significantly increase the economic significance by up to 200% relative to the model without industry. The issue of using scope values without normalisation remains problematic, however. Typically, emission intensity (see Chapter 2) is a candidate. As we pointed out in Section 5.2, this may be problematic as time periods may differ. Scope values are mostly backward-looking and may include a substantial amount of past data, while the normalising quantity, e.g., sales, may cover a more recent period. Thus, a look-ahead bias may be included. In addition, the normalisation variable may be correlated with equity, which could introduce another bias. Instead, percentage change of emissions is used in a further model to control for size effects. So, the second regression is

$$R_{i,t} = \alpha_0 + \beta_1 \Delta(TE)_{i,t} + \beta_2 CV_{i,t} + \mu_t + \epsilon_{i,t}. \tag{9.12}$$

The results of this regression reveal similar effects: All scopes produce positive and statistically significant results. However, the inclusion of industry effects results in no magnification of the results.

In summary, the results provide evidence that investors demand a return premium for high-emission stocks. Now, let us turn to the question of whether a systematic carbon risk factor can explain this effect. Consider the regression

$$\beta_{i,t} = \gamma_0 + \gamma' F_t + \epsilon_t, \tag{9.13}$$

with $\beta_{i,t}$ the carbon risk premium estimated in equation (9.11). The vector F collects a range of spread portfolios (including SMB, HML, WML). The coefficient γ_0 should capture the remaining carbon premium after controlling for the other factors. The results in Bolton and Kacperczyk (2020) show that the carbon premium is statistically and economically significant, although of a smaller size than the other factors. Thus, there is evidence for a carbon risk premium in equity markets.

Interestingly, they also document a jump in the carbon premium post 2015, the year of the Paris Agreement (see Chapter 1). As investment funds also started to commit to more carbon-sensitive investment strategies in the aftermath of the Paris Agreement, this may be further evidence that investors became more aware of carbon risk.

In a related study using data from 77 countries, Bolton and Kacperczyk (2021) find a positive and significant carbon premium in most areas of the world, including North America, Europe, and Asia. Emissions are measured in terms of the scopes, but clearly disclosure practices differ around the world. In line with the results just reported, firms associated with higher emissions generate higher stock returns while controlling for the usual firm characteristics.

From the fast-growing list of further investigations, let us mention In *et al.* (2019), who were also looking at a sample of US firms during 2005–2015. They constructed a carbon-efficient minus carbon-inefficient portfolio that started to generate positive abnormal returns from 2010 onwards. Barnett *et al.* (2019) explored the impact of regulatory risk on financial markets. They provide an event study analysis which finds that increases in the likelihood of future climate policy action decreases equity prices for firms with high exposure to climate policy risk. Short-term effects of transition-type carbon risk can be found in option prices. Ilhan *et al.* (2020) show that firms with carbon-intensive business models face higher cost of option protection against extreme downside risks. The reason is that a higher carbon intensity seems to increase the negative skewness in the risk-neutral distribution of a firm's stock return and also its variance risk premium. As the option premium decreases as maturities increase from 1 month to 12 months, the premium should be driven by downside risk. As the regulatory framework becomes increasingly stable, the likelihood of regulatory surprises decreases and these effects should disappear.

Concluding our listing, let us mention applications of machine learning to the carbon premium investigations. Faccini and Matin (2021a) and Engle *et al.* (2020) use state-of-the-art textual analysis machine learning methods to investigate the sensitivity of stock returns to climate news. Both studies find that stocks with lower exposure to climate risk have higher returns during periods with negative news about the effects of climate change.

9.3 Carbon Risk, Cost of Equity Capital, and Cost of Debt

Cost of equity capital (CoE) is defined as the return an investor requires for an investment in a particular asset. To calculate the CoE, either a dividend capitalisation model or the CAPM can be used. For our discussion, we use the CAPM as it is common in practice and supported by empirical evidence; see Da *et al.* (2012) for a discussion. So, the CoE of firm i in year t (which is the time period used in the following) is estimated as

$$\mathrm{CoE}_{it} = r_t + \beta_{it}\mathrm{ERP}_t, \tag{9.14}$$

where β_{it} is the market beta of firm i in year t, r_t a risk-free rate and ERP_t the equity risk premium, which could be based on investor surveys or historical estimates.

Our aim now is to assess whether carbon risk has an effect on the cost of equity capital. To test hypotheses on specific effects, we can use (panel) regression techniques (see Section 9.1) and employ equation (9.1) to obtain values for CoE which will be the dependent variable.

This approach is used by Trinks *et al.* (2020) for a study covering the period 2008–2016 with data from 1897 firms in 55 countries. They investigate the extent to which financial market investors demand a premium for holding assets of high-emitting firms, which in turn will raise the CoE of these firms. Their carbon intensity measure is based on the sum of scope 1 and scope 2 emissions, and they use only firms which report both. They leave out scope 3 data as it is scarce (compare Chapter 5 for data availability) and, additionally, argue that scope 3 emissions are not directly controlled by firms.

The following specification of a panel regression equation is used:

$$\text{CoE}_{it} = \alpha + \beta \text{cind}_{it} + \gamma' X_{it} + \Lambda + u_i + \epsilon_{it} \qquad (9.15)$$

for firm i at time t. cind_{it} is the carbon intensity for which normalisation is performed by using net sales as denominator (see Chapter 3). X_{it} is a vector of observed firm characteristics (size, book-to-market, leverage) with known effects on CoE. Λ is a vector of year-, industry-, and country-fixed effects to control for time trends and heterogeneity, U_i is a vector of firm-specific time-invariant unobserved variables, and ϵ_{it} is an error term. Trinks *et al.* (2020) report a positive and robust impact of carbon intensity on the CoE. They find that for each standard deviation higher carbon intensity, *ceteris paribus*, the CoE increases by six basis points. A sector-relative analysis reveals that an increase of carbon intensity of one standard deviation above sector average raises the CoE by nine basis points. Overall, the carbon risk premium is primarily explained by systematic risk factors: Stock returns of high-emitting firms are significantly more sensitive to macroeconomic fluctuations than those of low-emitting firms. Regional and sectoral differences are reported for EU countries and for high-emitting industries. This gives weight to considering emission reduction as a useful strategy to mitigate risk.

For the time period 2012–2016, focusing on German and Austrian firms (in total 91), Fichtner (2018) performed a similar analysis. He used the regression equation

$$\text{CoE}_{it} = \alpha + \beta \text{cind}_{it} + \beta^I I_{it} + \beta^R R_{it} + \gamma' X_{it} + \Lambda + \epsilon_{it}. \qquad (9.16)$$

Here, I is a dummy variable for inclusion in a sustainability index (German or Austrian) and R a dummy variable for firms in a highly regulated sector. Furthermore, two versions of carbon intensity, one as (scope 1 + scope 2)/sales and the second as (scope 1 + scope 2)/ assets, are used. Results show that for both definitions, carbon intensity and the cost of equity capital are positively related. Also, sustainability report disclosure and membership of a strongly regulated sector reduce the cost of equity capital, which can be explained by greater transparency of the firms.

Let us also mention Kim *et al.* (2015) who consider Korean companies. They define carbon intensity as carbon dioxide (CO_2) emissions per unit of sales and show a positive relationship with the cost of equity capital. They also find that this effect decreases for companies in highly GHG-emitting sectors. However, publishing a sustainability report has no positive effect on the cost of equity capital. The discussion of cost of equity can be seen as an equivalent in terms of investor risk to the social cost of carbon which relates to macroeconomic effects of emission reduction on aggregate consumption risk (Dietz *et al.*, 2018). Investment behaviour is more directly driven by the discount rate applied to the cash flows of individual firms and projects, i.e., the rate of return demanded by investors to compensate for investment risk or — from the perspective of firms — the cost of capital. It is therefore relevant and important to investigate the impact of firms' carbon emissions on financial risk and required returns (CoE).

That higher transparency is rewarded is also reported by Kleimeier and Viehs (2018), who show using a dataset of North American companies that higher transparency with respect to carbon emissions leads to more favourable loan conditions. This is particularly true for firms with high levels of information uncertainty. Opaque firms which answer the annual Carbon Disclosure Project (CDP) questionnaire and voluntarily reveal their carbon emissions pay significantly lower loan spreads compared to firms which do not disclose their emission data. These findings are confirmed by Jung *et al.* (2018), who link the cost of debt to companies' carbon emissions as well as their disclosure behaviour.

9.4 Carbon Risk and Machine Learning

ML techniques have found their way into empirical asset pricing in the last few years. Gu *et al.* (2020) perform a comparative analysis of ML techniques for the factor analysis to measure asset risk premiums. ML allows one to handle the large collection of hundreds of possible factors discussed in the literature and allows one to be flexible about the functional form of the relationship in which the factor affects the risk premium. For the task at hand, methods for supervised learning establishing a relationship between input and output variables are investigated. It turns out that trees and neural networks are the best performing methods. Of course, these types of analysis can be applied in a straightforward manner with a carbon risk factor, say, a carbon intensity, as an additional explanatory variable. Alternatively, the algorithm can be applied to search among the various ESG factors for those with the highest explanatory power. For our discussion here, we focus on a different type of ML technique, namely textual analysis tools, which also have a (short) history in financial applications and have already been applied to assess carbon risk in the stock market (see Engle *et al.* (2020) and Faccini and Matin (2021b)). Let us give a brief description of textual analysis before we proceed (we follow Fischer (2020), Chapter 4 and Wesslen (2018)). Topic models involve an unsupervised machine learning approach that tries to identify and measure latent topics within a corpus of text documents. The underlying assumption is that texts consist of different topics which differ in their form of representation and the specific words being used. Specifically, topic modelling relies on the bag of words assumption, which states that the frequency of words in a document defines the meaning of the text. Topic models use latent Dirichlet allocation (LDA), a Bayesian two-tiered mixture model which specifies topics by identifying co-occurrences of words as patterns. LDA produces topic assignments, which list the most frequently associated words per topic and topic proportions, which are the probabilities for a document of the corpus to be assigned to each of the possible topics. A visualisation is done in terms of a word cloud in which the size of a word (term) is proportional to its frequency. As an illustration, we present word clouds related to the topic of (scientific) climate change, which were generated separately from German (Frankfurter Allgemeine Zeitung (FAZ), Die Welt, Die Tageszeitung (taz)) and US newspapers (*New York Times* and the *Washington Post*) during the period 1990–2015. For a detailed description of the data-gathering process and selection criteria in this particular application as well as for an enlightening study of German and US differences in risk perception, we refer the reader to Fischer (2020). Let us only mention here that unlike other topics, climate change produces rather similar word clouds as seen in Table 9.1.

Engle *et al.* (2020), Figure 1, show a similar word cloud of climate change vocabulary from a corpus of 74 climate change white papers and glossaries from international and national scientific associations linked to climate change research and regulation (such as the IPCC, the Environmental Protection Agency (EPA) and NASA)

Table 9.1. Word clouds on climate change: USA and Germany.

Word cloud USA

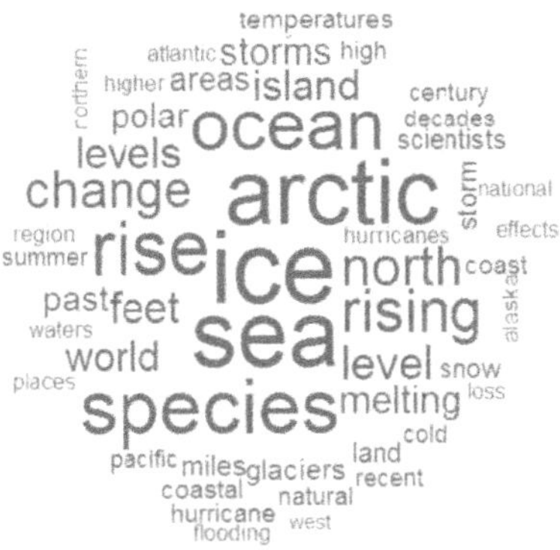

Word cloud Germany

which identifies word frequencies similar to the left-hand panel in Table 9.1.

Let us now turn to the question of how to incorporate news information in order to identify a carbon risk premium in asset prices. Faccini and Matin (2021b) use textual analysis on a corpus of more than 13 million articles from Thomson Reuters news archive covering the period from January 2000 to December 2018. To construct factors related to carbon risk, they use US climate policy, international summits, natural disasters, and global warming from the topics identified based on their relevance to US equity markets and their straightforward interpretability. The risk factors are subsequently constructed as the topic shares of each of these topics for each day from the total news coverage related to climate change. Their regression equation is then

$$R^e_{i,t} = \alpha_i + \beta_i F_t + \gamma' CV_t + \epsilon_t, \tag{9.17}$$

with $R_{i,t}$ the excess return of stock i on day t and F_t one of the textual factors. As usual, CV is a generic vector which includes standard control variables and ϵ_t is an i.i.d. error term with zero mean. The assumption that an increase in news coverage is an indication for an increase in risk implies that a negative β identifies assets that are exposed to carbon risk through the channel of the particular factor. From these results, Faccini and Matin (2021b) construct monthly updated long–short spread portfolios for each of the four factors according to the betas of stocks. Using model (9.17), now with variants of the Fama–French–Carthard factors as control, they then estimate portfolio alphas. They find that the US climate policy factor is positive and statistically significant in most of their model specifications, while the statistical significance of the other factors is mixed at best. Splitting the sample reveals that the climate policy factor gained importance starting from 2012 onwards. So, Faccini and Matin (2021b) can conclude that carbon risks from the political debate are priced and that the most risky assets pay a substantially higher rate than the least risky ones. However, longer-term risks covered by international regulation and highlighted by scientific evidence have not found their way into the risk assessment of investors yet. As political debate relates to mitigation and adaption policy plans, which in turn target carbon emissions, we can use these results in support of the findings presented in Section 9.2.

Chapter 10

Carbon Risk and Default Risk

In this chapter, we investigate how carbon risk affects the pricing of default-risky assets. We focus on credit CDS and (corporate) bonds, with an emphasis on the former as CDS spreads are a liquid and forward-looking indicator for the credit quality of a firm. Furthermore, CDS contracts are standardised with maturities up to 30 years and thus suitable to explore term structure effects of carbon risk. The risk premium that CDS spreads exhibits is purer than that of corporate bonds as there are no liquidity or structural effects.

10.1 Modelling Default Risk

10.1.1 *Merton's Structural Model*

Let us start by considering corporate bonds first to introduce a fundamental way to think about credit (default) risk of a firm. We write $p^d(0,T)$ for the time-zero price of a zero-coupon bond with maturity T and nominal $F = 1$. We assume a constant risk-free rate $r > 0$ and use $\exp(-rt)$ as discount factor for t years. Default probabilities are given by $\mathbb{P}(\tau \leq t), \quad \forall t \in [0,T]$, for each year t, where $\mathbb{P}$ is a given valuation measure. The recovery rate in case of default (as a fraction of the outstanding notational) δ is assumed to be known; recovery payments are done at time of default τ. The general valuation formula for a corporate bond is[1]

$$p^d(0,T) = \mathbb{E}\left[e^{-rT}\mathbf{1}_{\{\tau>T\}} + e^{-\tau}\delta\mathbf{1}_{\{\tau\leq T\}}\right]. \tag{10.1}$$

This is

$$\begin{aligned} p^d(0,T) &= e^{-rT}\mathbb{P}(\tau > T) + \mathbb{E}\left[e^{-r\tau}\delta\mathbf{1}_{\{0\leq\tau\leq T\}}\right] \\ &= e^{-rT}\mathbb{P}(\tau > T) + \delta\int_0^T e^{-rt}d\mathbb{P}(\tau \leq t). \end{aligned} \tag{10.2}$$

Thus, in order to value such a bond, we need a model which allows one to specify (compute) $\mathbb{P}(\tau \leq t)$.

A standard and widely used approach is the firm value approach pioneered by Merton (1974) (also called the structural model). In this setting, it is assumed that a firm is financed by equity and a single zero-coupon bond with notational amount (face value) F and maturity T. Such a firm defaults if the value of its assets falls below the value of its liabilities. In the work by Merton (1974), the firm's value process is given by

$$dV(t) = (r-\gamma)V(t)dt + \sigma V(t)dW(t), \quad V(0) = V_0, \tag{10.3}$$

with W a Brownian motion and a constant payout (dividend) rate γ, which may be negative (i.e., pay-in). Default is only possible at maturity. So, either $V_T \geq F$ and the notational is paid back, i.e., $p^d(T,T) = F$ or $V_T < F$ and the firm value is paid to the bond owners, i.e., $p^d(T,T) = V_T$ (this defines the recovery rate). For equity owners, the payoff is the remaining value $S_T = \max\{V_T - F, 0\}$. Thus, stocks can be viewed as call options on the value of the firm and with $\bar{V}_t = e^{-\gamma(T-t)}V_t$, their value is

$$S_t = C_E(\bar{V}_t, F) = e^{-\gamma(T-t)}V_t\Phi(d_1) - Fe^{-r(T-t)}\Phi(d_2),$$

with Φ the cumulative standard normal distribution function and

$$\begin{aligned} d_1(t, V_t) &= \frac{\log(V_t/F) + (r-\gamma+\sigma^2/2)(T-t)}{\sigma\sqrt{T-t}}, \\ d_2(t, V_t) &= d_1(t, V_t) - \sigma\sqrt{T-t}. \end{aligned}$$

[1]Here, $\mathbf{1}_A$ is the indicator function, which is equal to 1 if the event A has happened and equal to 0 otherwise.

For bond owners, the payoff is

$$p^d(T,T) = F - \max\{F - V_T, 0\},$$

which can be viewed as the difference of a risk-free payment and a put option on the value of the firm. So, after a little calculation, we find

$$p^d(t,T) = V_t e^{-\gamma(T-t)}\Phi(-d_1(t,V_t)) + Fe^{-r(T-t)}\Phi(d_2(V_t,t)). \quad (10.4)$$

Merton's model also allows one to calculate the probability of default of a firm. An oft-used indicator in this context is the distance-to-default (DD), which indicates how far the value of the firm is above the default boundary. Assuming that there are no dividend payments, the DD is defined as[2]

$$\mathrm{DD}(t) = \frac{\log\left(\frac{V_t}{F}\right) + (r + \frac{1}{2}\sigma^2)(T-t)}{\sigma\sqrt{T-t}}. \quad (10.5)$$

We can use the distance-to-default to express the default probability (conditional on the current value of V_t)

$$\mathbb{P}(V_T < F|V_t) = \Phi(-DD(t)). \quad (10.6)$$

Typically, we do not observe the value of a firm but a stock price process S with volatility σ_s. Thus, in order to calculate the parameters, i.e., V_0 and σ, relevant for the dynamics of the firm's value, we have to use the identities (see Bingham and Kiesel (2004) for details)

$$S_0 = V_0\Phi(d_1(0,V_0)) - Fe^{-rT}\Phi(d_2(0,V_0)),$$

$$\sigma_s = \frac{\Phi(d_1(0,V_0))V_0\sigma}{S_0}$$

to obtain risk-neutral default probabilities.

Merton's model also implies, for the corresponding (bond) spreads at time $t = 0$,

$$s(\gamma) = -\frac{1}{T}\log\{V_0 e^{-\gamma T}\Phi(-d_1) + Fe^{-rT}\Phi(d_2)\}. \quad (10.7)$$

For short times to maturity, $t \to T$, the spreads will tend to zero, i.e., indicating no default risk any more as long as the firm value is above

[2]We set $\gamma = 0$ for these calculations.

the face value of the bond. The reason for this is that the stochasticity in Merton's model is driven by a continuous-path stochastic process, so no unexpected events, e.g., a sudden default, can be captured. A possible extension[3] is to allow the firm value process to have jumps; see Bingham and Kiesel (2004), Section 9.3.2. So, for a possible specification, assume that the firm value process is the exponential of a jump diffusion:

$$V_t = V_0 \exp(X_t), \quad X_t = \mu t + \sigma W_t + \sum_{i=1}^{N_t} Y_i, \tag{10.8}$$

where $\mu, \sigma > 0$ are constants and $W(t)$ is a standard Brownian motion. The jumps are generated by a Poisson process N_t with intensity λ, and the jump sizes are independent random variables (Y_i) with distribution F. A common specification for F is also a normal distribution or a double-exponential distribution, which still allows semi-analytic results.

Now, the model allows extreme events to happen and the resulting short-term spreads have positive limits (as empirically observed). However, as the distribution of first-passage times, which are needed to obtain the default times, is not available analytically, bond prices and CDS spreads are not available in closed form.

Merton's model (and its variants) gives a convenient framework to think of the impact of different parameters of the model on changes in default risk. We will use this framework frequently in the following.

10.1.2 *Credit Default Swaps*

A CDS is an exchange of a periodic payment (coupon) against a one-off contingent payment if some credit event occurs on a reference asset. Typically, the price of a CDS is quoted in terms of CDS spreads which are, following the standard approach for swaps, calculated so that the contract has zero value at initiation.

[3] Various other models define more realistic firm value processes and mechanisms which trigger default in a structural framework, see Bielecki and Rutkowski (2002).

Let us specify the coupon dates $0 \leq t_1 \leq \cdots \leq t_n = T$ for $i = 1, \ldots, n$. In case default has not happened at coupon date t_i, the protection buyer has to pay the spread s (in mathematical notation, the payment is $s\mathbf{1}_{\{\tau > t_i\}}$). The payment for the protection seller at time of default τ is $(1-\delta)\mathbf{1}_{\{\tau \leq T\}}$. Equating the payment streams $\mathbb{E}(e^{-r\tau}(1-\delta)\mathbf{1}_{\{\tau \leq T\}}) = \sum_{i=1}^{n} e^{-rt_i} s\mathbb{E}(\mathbf{1}_{\{\tau > t_i\}})$, we can solve for the CDS spreads:

$$s = \frac{\mathbb{E}\left(e^{-r\tau}(1-\delta)\mathbf{1}_{\{\tau \leq T\}}\right)}{\sum_{i=1}^{n} e^{-rt_i}\mathbb{E}\left(\mathbf{1}_{\{\tau > t_i\}}\right)}. \tag{10.9}$$

10.1.3 *The Importance of CDS Spreads for (Bank) Risk Management*

Banks have to allocate capital against credit risk. Besides the probability of a firm defaulting (ProbDef), the exposure at default (ExpDef), i.e., the exposure towards the firm at the time of default and the loss given default (LossDef) are the ingredients needed to calculate the expected loss (ExpLoss). It is defined as

$$\text{ExpLoss} = \text{ExpDef} \times \text{LossDef} \times \text{ProbDef}. \tag{10.10}$$

Observe that the loss given default is $(1-\delta)$ times the exposure at default. Typically, for the exposure at default, historical data provided by rating agencies are used as benchmarks. The probability of default and the loss given default can be inferred from market data. Jarrow (2010) points out that CDS spreads in the first approximation reflect ProbDef × LossDef. So, the expected loss can be estimated as

$$\text{ExpLoss} = \text{ExpDef} \times \text{CDS}.$$

10.1.4 *Determinants of CDS Spreads*

The determinants of CDS spreads have been frequently analysed in the literature (see Ericsson *et al.* (2009) or Collin-Dufresne *et al.* (2001)). We use, as the point of departure, the study of Galil *et al.* (2014). They investigate a representative sample of US firms during the period 2002–2013. Among a range of accounting, macroeconomic, and stock market factors, they find stock return, stock volatility, and the overall condition of the credit market as the most influential. The influence of these factors is in line with the expectation-based Merton's model (Merton, 1974). As the probability of default decreases with increasing market value of equity, spreads will decrease with increasing stock value. On the other hand, a rising stock volatility implies a higher firm value volatility (see Bingham and Kiesel (2004) for the formal argument), and thus, it is more likely that the asset value crosses the default threshold. The market condition is related to the expected recovery rate as well as the probability of default (see Galil *et al.* (2014)), so it negatively affects CDS spreads. As CDS spreads are not stationary, the analysis is done in terms of first differences with the same effects of the factors (stock return negative, stock volatility positive, and the median CDS spread change negative).

We have already seen that CDS spreads reflect carbon risk as part of our preliminary analysis with EUAs. However, as EUAs also have an influence on stock prices (at least for utilities and energy firms), we need to construct a different independent factor.

10.2 CDS Spreads and Carbon Risk

10.2.1 *ESG Factors*

We present a short descriptive analysis of CDS spreads and carbon risk following Blasberg and Kiesel (2021).

We use daily CDS spreads of more than 100 major European firms with maturities of 1, 3, 5, and 10 years covering the period 2013–2018. Each firm also has a credit rating. To asses the carbon risk of the firms, we use Refinitiv's environmental, social, and governance (ESG) data, in particular the subpillar E. We split the universe of firms into six portfolios based on the terciles of the E pillar score and the median of the credit rating. Then green (brown) firms are identified as all firms within the high (low) E-score portfolios. Figures 10.1–10.4 compare the (empirical) distributions of daily mean CDS spreads for green and brown for maturities 1, 3, 5, and 10 years.

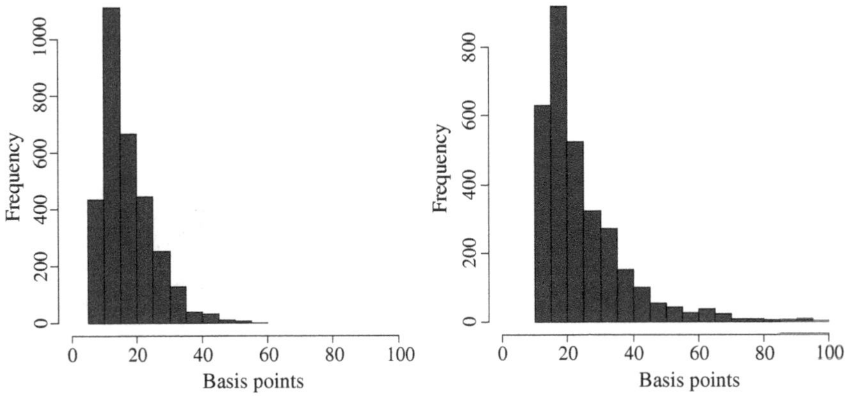

Fig. 10.1. Histogram of daily average CDS spreads one year for green (left) and brown (right) firms.

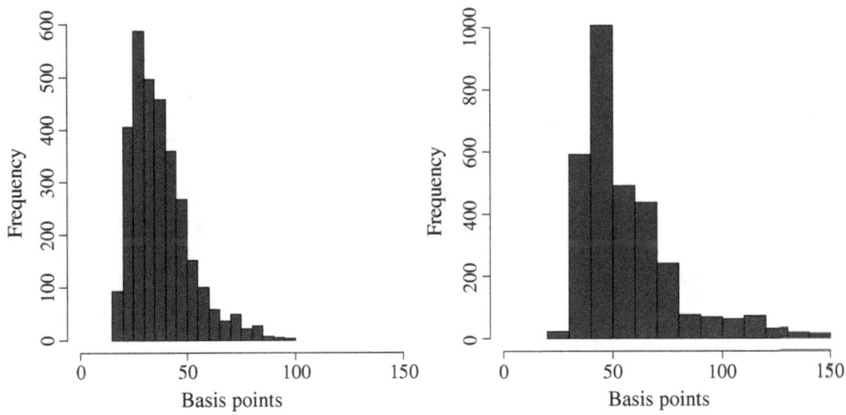

Fig. 10.2. Histogram of daily average CDS spreads three years maturity for green (left) and brown (right) firms.

Across all maturities, we recognise a shift of the distribution to the right for brown firms, indicating that environmentally low-performing firms have a higher CDS spread. Also, the effect becomes more pronounced for longer maturities.

These observations indicate that there is a carbon risk component in CDS spreads which increases in importance with longer maturities. Of course, the maturity effect is expected due to the long-term consequences of climate change. In the following section, we test for this effect on a formal basis.

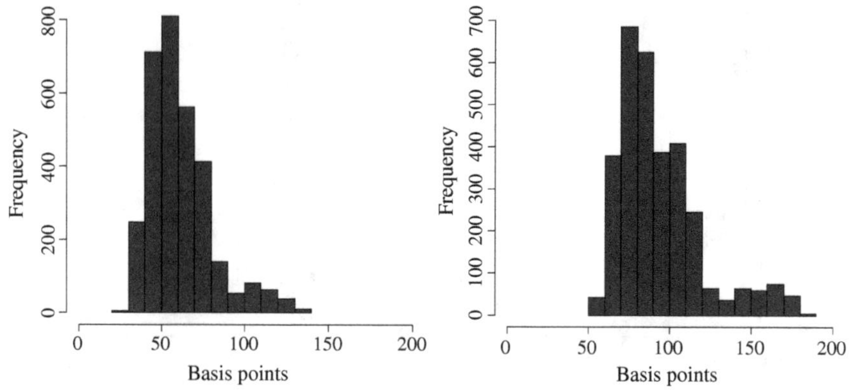

Fig. 10.3. Histogram of daily average CDS spreads five years for green (left) and brown (right) firms.

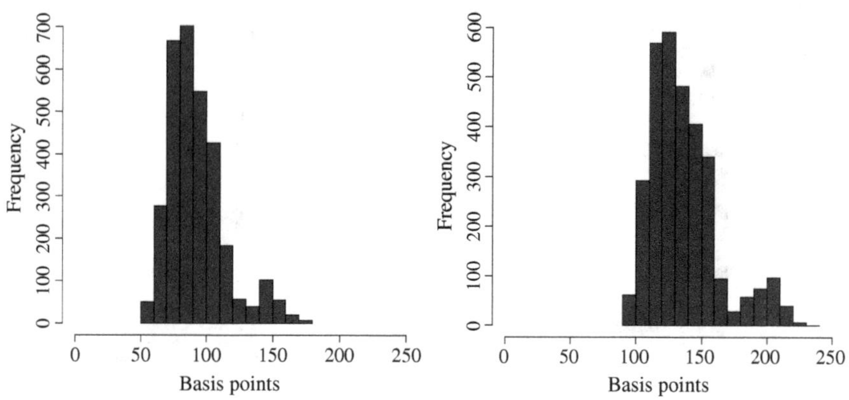

Fig. 10.4. Histogram of daily average CDS spreads 10 years for green (left) and brown (right) firms.

10.2.2 *ESG-Based Carbon Indicator*

For each portfolio, we now compute an equally weighted mean of the CDS spreads and define an E-score-based carbon index (ECI) as the difference between the two best (green) and worst (brown) portfolios. That is, we split the universe of companies into six groups based on the terciles of the E pillar score and the median of the credit rating (unconditional quantile sorting). Afterwards, we compute an equally weighted mean of the CDS spreads of green (two best groups) and brown (two worst groups) firms, respectively. ECI is then defined as the spread between these two means.[4]

We use the setting of the Galil *et al.* (2014) model and extend it with the E-score-based carbon index to explain CDS spreads. Thus, we perform a panel regression and estimate

$$\Delta \mathrm{CDS}_{i,t} = \beta_i + \beta_{1,i} r_{i,t} + \beta_{2,i} \Delta v_{i,t} + \beta_{3,i} \Delta \mathrm{mri}_{i,t} + \beta_{4,i} \Delta \mathrm{ECI}_t + \epsilon_{i,t}, \tag{10.11}$$

where $\Delta\mathrm{CDS}_{i,t}$ refers to the change in CDS spreads for company i at time t, β_i is the company-specific intercept, $r_{i,t}$ is the log return of the stock price of company i at time t, $\Delta v_{i,t}$ represents the change in volatility (annualised variance based on the previous 300 trading days) of company i at time t, $\mathrm{mri}_{i,t}$ measures the change in the median rated index (median CDS spread of all firms in the same rating group; rating groups considered here are AAA/AA, A, BBB, and BB+ or lower) of company i and time t, and finally, $\Delta\mathrm{ECI}_{it}$ is the change in the carbon index. The resulting estimates are averaged across all firms, i.e., $\widetilde{\beta}_j = \frac{1}{N}\sum_{i=1}^{N}\widehat{\beta}_{i,j}$ for all $j = 0, \ldots, 4$. Table 10.1 provides the results.[5]

The coefficients of the standard variables are in line with the predictions of Merton's model and results from the literature. An increased log return will decrease the CDS spread, so we expect a negative sign. A higher volatility results in a higher CDS spread, so the positive sign appears. However, in terms of significance, we have mixed results as often reported in the literature (Koutmos, 2019). The index for the market condition is a positive, highly significant sign, as the individual spreads go along with the market. The results on the carbon index reflect the visual indications from Figures 10.1–10.4 as the significance of the coefficient increases with higher maturities. Also, the sign is expected as the index has a negative value. Thus, an increase in the index means it is smaller in absolute value, which reflects a decrease in the CDS spreads of brown and green firms, which in turn increases the overall level of CDS spreads.

---

[4]A similar construction is done in Barth *et al.* (2020), pp. 22–23.

[5]The t-statistics are computed from the cross-sectional of the individual regression coefficients.

Table 10.1. Regression results (pooling) for maturities 1Y, 3Y, 5Y, and 10Y.

	1Y	3Y	5Y	10Y
Intercept	−0.01	−0.01	−0.02*	−0.02*
	(0.01)	(0.01)	(0.01)	(0.01)
Stock return	−0.17***	−0.24***	−0.28***	−0.29***
	(0.03)	(0.03)	(0.03)	(0.03)
ΔVolatility	0.50*	0.76**	1.29***	1.29***
	(0.20)	(0.25)	(0.25)	(0.24)
ΔMRI	0.71***	0.57***	0.44***	0.46***
	(0.05)	(0.04)	(0.03)	(0.03)
ΔECI	−0.16•	−0.20**	−0.23***	−0.22***
	(0.09)	(0.06)	(0.06)	(0.05)
R^2	0.22	0.27	0.25	0.25
Adj. R^2	0.22	0.26	0.25	0.24

Notes: $^{***}p < 0.001$, $^{**}p < 0.01$, $^{*}p < 0.05$, $^{\bullet}p < 0.1$.

However, as an E-score reflects a variety of indicators, we will later on look at an index generated by emissions directly.

Barth *et al.* (2020) perform an analysis which links the whole universe of ESG scores to CDS spreads. However, the literature splits on the effect of ESG practices on firm value. One strand of literature argues that high ESG standards translate to higher and less volatile cash flows as such firms might be less exposed to natural disasters or changes in regulatory environment, and so, the firm value increases. An alternative line of argument is that implementation of ESG standards leads to a waste of resources in terms of fixed costs due to maintenance of the relationship with stakeholders or signalling of high ESG standards to potential employees, which reduces the firm value. For their analysis, they consider CDS spreads for US and European firms from January 2007 to March 2019. Their results support the first view as they find that higher levels of ESG result in lower CDS spreads. They also find regional differences as the effect is more pronounced for European firms.

Also, von Avenarius (2019) investigated the impact of EU ETS emission prices on CDS spreads using a sample of European companies. However, as EUA prices relate to stock prices (and returns), no strong relationship could be established.

10.3 Heterogeneity of Carbon Risk Effect

We now want to study the impact of carbon risk factors on the whole distribution of the CDS spreads (the response variable in our context). For this kind of analysis, quantile regression has proved to be a very useful method.

10.3.1 *Quantile (Panel-) Regression*

While in ordinary regression our aim is to find the mean of the response variable (distribution), we want to estimate a q percentile such as 1%, 5%, 10%, the median, 90%, 95%, 99% in quantile regression (QR). In fact, we could estimate a whole set of the percentiles to effectively describe the whole distribution. In doing so, we can identify different factors prominent for different quantile levels. QR has found many applications when it is important to study the impact of explanatory variables on the whole distribution of the response variable. Often, heterogeneity of the factors could be identified and differences in responses across quantiles could be revealed.

Let us briefly explain the method. The qth quantile of a random variable Y is given by the quantile function

$$Q_Y(q) = F_Y^{-1}(q) = \inf\{y : F_Y(y) \geq q\}, \tag{10.12}$$

with $0 < q < 1$ and F_Y the cumulative distribution function of Y. In case we have a strictly increasing cumulative distribution function, as in the case of the normal distribution, we can use the inverse function to calculate the quantile. For a discussion on the properties of quantile regression, see Davino *et al.* (2014) or Yu *et al.* (2003). Among the various advantages of QR, let us point out that the empirical results are more robust and assumptions on the structure of the underlying data-generating distribution are not necessary.

The basic framework with unobserved individual effects $\alpha_{q,i}$ is

$$Q_{Y_{i,t}}(q|X_{i,t}) = \alpha_{q,i} + \beta_q' X_{it}, \tag{10.13}$$

where $Y_{i,t}$ and $X_{i,t}$ represent the response and the corresponding driving factors for $i = 1, \ldots, N$ and $t = 1, \ldots, T$ the measurement time points. β_q denotes the vector of estimated parameters which vary with the percentile q.

To obtain estimates for the vector β_q, QR can be put into the least-squares framework. The method to solve for the estimator uses a $L1$-norm penalty term and is called the shrinkage method (see Davino *et al.* (2014)).

10.3.2 *Quantile Analysis of CDS Spreads*

The first application of QR to CDS spreads is carried out by Pires *et al.* (2015), who analyse monthly CDS spreads across 260 firms from European and US markets during the period 2002–2007. In addition to the standard set of explanatory variables, they also include absolute bid–ask spreads as a measure for liquidity. Their analysis reveals that the sensitivity of CDS spreads to explanatory variables is stronger for firms with high CDS spreads and that the estimates for these firms are similar to the standard linear regression. Thus, they conclude that standard regression is only successful in the empirical determinants of CDS spreads for high-risk firms.

Koutmos (2019) uses quantile regression to explain changes in daily CDS spreads of 20 global systemically important banks (G-SIBs) for a dataset covering 2002–2017. Besides the variables of the standard framework, they use macroeconomic factors and the five global Fama–French (Fama and French, 2015) factors. They also find heterogeneity in the explanatory variables. In particular, they show that volatility risk is negatively related to CDS spreads in low quantiles and positively related to CDS spreads in the upper quantiles. This may help explain why some empirical studies on CDS spreads had to remain inconclusive regarding the volatility risk (Collin-Dufresne *et al.*, 2001).

We now perform a QR regression on the same dataset and with the same variables as above. Table 10.2 provides the results.

Except for the volatility in lower percentiles, all explanatory variables are highly significant. Comparing Tables 10.1 and 10.2, we see a similarity to the Pires *et al.* (2015) results in that the coefficients of the higher quantiles (in particular, the volatility) agree with the standard regression. We also observe the changing sign in volatility as in Koutmos (2019). Furthermore, the carbon index also displays heterogeneity across quantiles in that the impact is lower in the centre of the distribution. Figure 10.5 visualises the effect. We refer to Blasberg and Kiesel (2021) for further details.

Table 10.2. Panel quantile regression (5Y); in 1e−04.

	1	2	3	4	5	6	7	8	9
Return	-1525^{***}	-1259^{***}	-988^{***}	-765^{***}	-537^{***}	-682^{***}	-903^{***}	-1173^{***}	-1561^{***}
	(1.97)	(2.60)	(1.41)	(1.15)	(0.51)	(0.70)	(0.93)	(1.71)	(1.44)
ΔVola	-4593^{***}	476	2107^{***}	1554^{***}	898^{***}	1717^{***}	1790^{***}	4191^{***}	8613^{***}
	(687.98)	(634.65)	(406.04)	(316.22)	(161.92)	(150.46)	(290.92)	(519.60)	(454.76)
ΔMRI	3608^{***}	3662^{***}	3589^{***}	3578^{***}	3568^{***}	3558^{***}	3632^{***}	3813^{***}	3985^{***}
	(2.44)	(2.13)	(2.85)	(2.77)	(2.76)	(2.70)	(2.59)	(0.81)	(1.11)
ΔECI	-1122^{***}	-935^{***}	-844^{***}	-703^{***}	-577^{***}	-677^{***}	-760^{***}	-838^{***}	-916^{***}
	(1.34)	(1.69)	(1.35)	(1.39)	(1.68)	(2.78)	(1.60)	(2.73)	(3.17)

Note: $^{***}p < 0.001$.

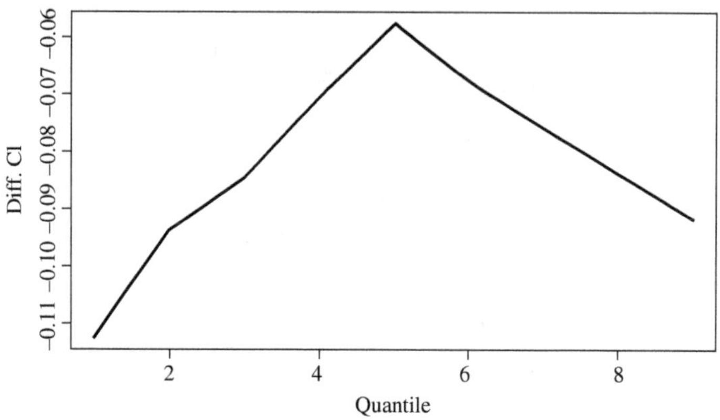

Fig. 10.5. Different ECI estimates for 5Y CDS spread.

As in the discussion of carbon risk in asset market, let us now return to a carbon metric based on emissions (rather than on an ESG score). We have already seen how the market price of carbon, e.g., the price of EUAs, affects CDS spreads of European utility and energy firms (see Chapter 8). One can extend that and construct a factor that is based on a carbon metric to capture firms which are not directly exposed to an emission certificate price. In fact, Blasberg *et al.* (2021) follow this avenue and construct a factor based on the carbon intensity. In addition, rather than following the usual short vs. long portfolio approach, they construct a factor which is based on the whole empirical distributions of CDS spreads of green (low carbon intensity) and brown (high carbon intensity) firms. For that, the distance of the distributions is measured using the Wasserstein metric (see Rachev (1991) and Kiesel *et al.* (2016) for a discussion and details regarding the applications of the Wasserstein metric). They provide a detailed analysis of the sectorial and term-structure effects of carbon risk on the CDS spreads of a large sample of US companies.

10.4 Carbon Risk and Bonds

The bond market is by far the most import securities market in terms of volume. Figure 10.6 shows an ever-growing market volume with the increase flattening a little during the financial crisis,

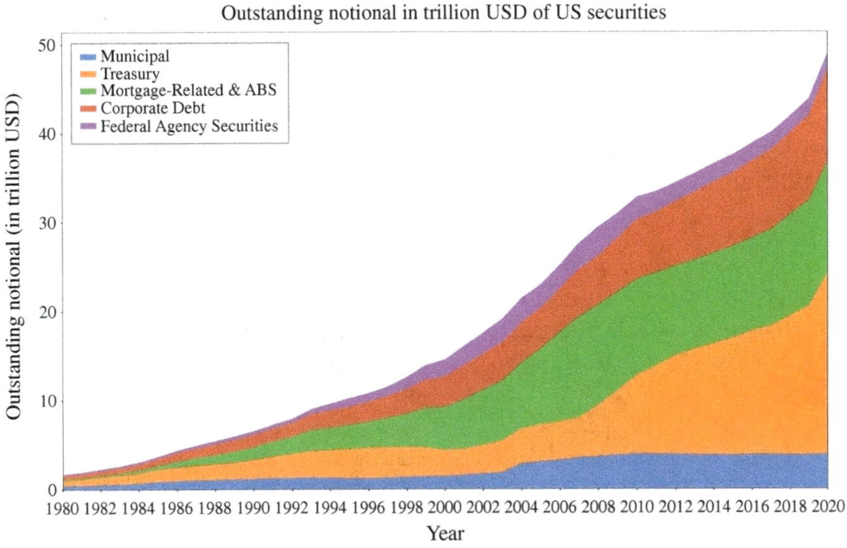

Fig. 10.6. The bond market.

but accelerating again recently. As bond holders have little upside available, it is crucial for them to analyse and assess all the downside risks, including carbon risk.

10.4.1 *Bond Prices and Carbon Risk*

A straightforward way to incorporate carbon risk in bond prices is presented by Bouchet and Le Guenedal (2020) (although their purpose is to generate a scenario analysis for credit risk). They build a credit risk model based on Merton's firm value approach which directly takes carbon prices (in their case tax) into account. The underlying model assumes the usual firm value specification as in (10.3) with firm value $V(i)$, volatility $\sigma(i)$, and outstanding debt $F(i)$. So, they include the scope 1 $sc(i,j,t)$ emissions of firm i in a given region j (which allows for different carbon price regimes) at time t. Now, for each region j and date t, there is a carbon price $\mathrm{CP}(j,t)$ and a firm i that is active in M_i regions has total carbon costs CC at time t of

$$\mathrm{CC}(i,t) = \sum_{j \in M_i} sc(i,j,t)\mathrm{CP}(j,t). \qquad (10.14)$$

From the carbon costs, they calculate a carbon regulation impact on the firm value given by the variable $\xi(i,t) \in [0,1]$. For the definition of the impact variable and the size of the shock, the relation of carbon costs and the EBITDA[6] of a firm is used; see Bouchet and Le Guenedal (2020) for details. So, the firm value under carbon regulation is

$$V(i,t) = (1 - \xi(i,t))V(i,0). \tag{10.15}$$

Observe that only the starting value of the firm value is used. Now, the distance-to-default and the default probability PD can be computed as in (10.5) and (10.6), with the adjusted firm value as

$$\mathrm{DD}(i,t) = \frac{\log\left(\frac{(1-\xi(i,t))V(i,0)}{F(i)}\right) + (r + \frac{1}{2}\sigma(i)^2)(T-t)}{\sigma(i)\sqrt{T-t}} \tag{10.16}$$

and

$$\mathrm{PD}(i,t) = \Phi(-\mathrm{DD}(i,t)). \tag{10.17}$$

The default probability can now be used in the bond price formula (10.2) to obtain a carbon risk-adjusted bond pricing formula.

Similarly, Capasso *et al.* (2020) develop a carbon risk-adjusted version of Merton's model. They, however, operate with emission metrics directly and do not develop a stochastic model for the distance-to-default. Rather, they use the carbon footprint as the amount of CO_2 emitted and a carbon intensity, with firm's revenues as denominator, as explanatory variable in a regression model. In particular, the estimation equation for the distance-to-default of firm i in year t is

$$\mathrm{DD}_{it} = \alpha + \beta X_{it} + \gamma' Y_{it} + \epsilon_{it}, \tag{10.18}$$

with X_{it} either the carbon footprint or the carbon intensity and Y_{it} a vector of firm-level, industry- and country-specific variables. Capasso *et al.* (2020) find negative and highly significant beta values for both measures of emissions. Thus, firms with a higher emission have a

[6]EBITDA, or earnings before interest, taxes, depreciation, and amortisation, is a measure of a company's overall financial performance and is often used to to judge the size of organic cash flow of a firm.

lower distance-to-default and are perceived as more likely to default. Indeed, after the Paris Agreement, the distance-to-default shortened for high-emission companies.

10.4.2 *Further Bond Market Studies*

Let us conclude this chapter with a small survey of further studies relating climate risk to the bond market. The study of Huynh and Xia (2020) uses the climate change news index (CCI) generated by Engle *et al.* (2020) to analyse the impact of changing climate change news on corporate bond returns. Their study uses bond prices during the period July 2002–December 2016 for which they estimate the climate change news beta β^{CCN} from a monthly rolling regression of bond excess returns over a 60-month window. Their regression equation reads as

$$R^e_{i,t} = \alpha_{i,t} + \beta^{\text{CCN}}\text{CCN}_t + \gamma'\text{CV}_t + \epsilon_{i,t}, \tag{10.19}$$

with $R^e_{i,t}$ the excess return of bond i in month t and CCN are the innovations in monthly climate change news. CV is a vector of variables that controls for equity excess market return, bond market illiquidity, the term spread, the default spread, and the TED spread.[7] As usual, ϵ_t is an i.i.d. error term with zero mean. Now, β^{CCN} allows one to measure the bond covariance with the climate change index. A positive covariance identifies bonds that are weakly or even negatively exposed to carbon risk.

Consistent with our findings for equity markets, Huynh and Xia (2020) find that positive-covariance bonds have lower returns. Furthermore, a term-structure effect exists in that the effect of climate change news risk on long-term corporate bonds is about twice the effect on short-term bonds. The findings are robust in terms of rating as subsamples of investment and non-investment grade bonds provide comparable results. In addition, bonds for issuers with a higher environmental score have a significantly higher β^{CCN} during times of a higher frequency in climate change news.

[7]The TED spread is the difference between the three-month London interbank offered rate (LIBOR), based on USD, and the three-month Treasury bill rate.

A further documentation of carbon risk in bond markets is given by Seltzer *et al.* (2020), who show that bond credit ratings and yield spreads are affected by the environmental performance of a firm. This is particularly evident for firms located in a state with more stringent environmental regulations.

An interesting market to study the effects of physical climate risk (which we also consider here) is the municipal bond market. Obviously, municipalities are not able to relocate to avoid the impact of, say, sea level rises or extreme weather events. Structurally, municipal bonds are issued by state or local governments often to finance infrastructure projects and are paid back either from tax revenue or other sources of revenue specified beforehand (revenue bonds tied to electricity, water facilities, or similar projects). Creditworthiness of municipalities is vulnerable to climate change as debt levels are prone to rise due to the cost of cleanups after extreme weather, funding of mitigation projects, and higher insurance premiums. In contrast to the municipalities, corporates and people can leave exposed areas, so the tax basis will shrink due to business and population relocation and diminished economic activity. With highly granular climate data and machine learning methods to generate scenarios, Schulten *et al.* (2019) analyse the US municipal bond market for the impact of physical climate risks. They cover the whole range of physical climate change risks from the impact hurricanes and rising sea levels to (coastal) infrastructure to extreme heat or cold to power plants. A case in point for the latter is the power outage in Texas due to the extreme cold weather in February 2021 (Meyer, 2021). They show that the share of US metropolitan statistical areas (MSAs) affected by climate risk will rise sharply. Within the next 10 years, the share of MSAs in risk of economic losses between 0.5% and 1% of GDP within S&P National Municipal Bond Index will be higher than 15% (by market value). Extending the forecast up to 2100 (under the assumption of no climate policy action), Miami, Houston, and Dallas face the highest risk with GDP losses up to 4.5%. However, according to the authors, the municipal market has yet to price the impact of climate risk.

The findings of Painter (2020) differ. This study uses counties (such as New Orleans, Miami, or Tampa) that are exposed to sea level rises. The climate risk of a sea level rise is also measured in terms of an expected mean annual loss in GDP, which then affects the ability to pay back debt. The results show that increased risk of rising sea levels is associated with a statistically significant increase of issuance costs of long-term maturity (greater than 25 years) bonds. For shorter-term bonds-related climate risk, there is no statistical evidence for the pricing of climate risk. The results also show the lower-rated bonds are more affected than the higher-rated bonds.

Finally, let us refer the readers to Volz *et al.* (2020) for an in-depth and very comprehensive assessment of the interplay of climate change and sovereign risk.

Chapter 11

Green Bonds

11.1 Green Bond Markets

Green bonds are fixed-income securities issued to finance projects that are meant to positively impact the environment and climate, energy, transport, water, land use, and building construction sectors. Thus, the decisive difference between a conventional (plain vanilla) bond and a green bond is the special use of funds aiming to finance or refinance climate-resilient green projects and promote the path towards a low-carbon transition (International Capital Market Association, 2018). The market for green bonds has seen a rapid increase during the last years (see Figure 11.1) and its increase is likely to accelerate in the decade to come.

Green bonds are issued by various issuers, such as governments, municipalities, government-backed institutions, financial institutions, and non-financial corporates. Recent examples include the German Development Bank, KfW (EUR 3 billion, 8 year maturity), the Dutch grid operator, TenneT (EUR 1.4 billion, two trances with maturities 12 and 20 years), and China Construction Bank (USD 500 million, 8 years and USD 700 million USD, 5 years); see Climate Bonds Initiative (2020). We provide an overview in Figure 11.2.

As green bonds provide an attractive financing option, they are sought after for green infrastructure projects. Thus, projects financed by green bonds cover especially low-carbon infrastructure projects in construction and transport. Noteworthy examples are Société du Grand Paris, which was set up by the French Government to construct the Grand Paris Express transport network completely

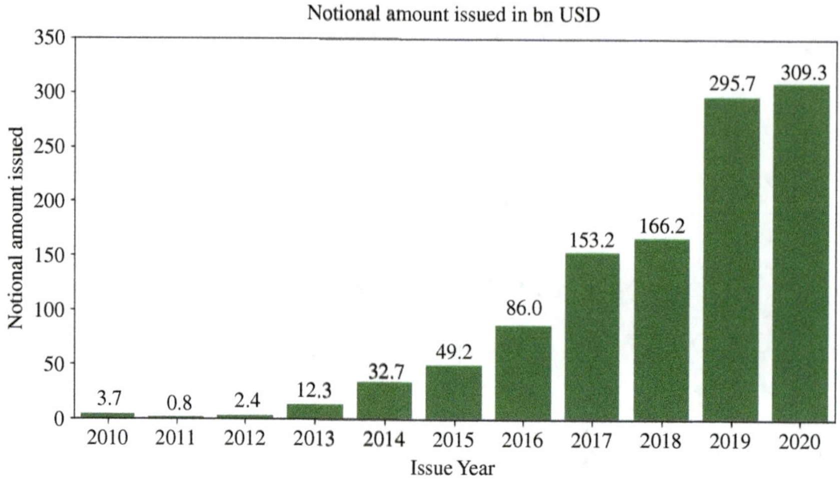

Fig. 11.1. Green bonds development.

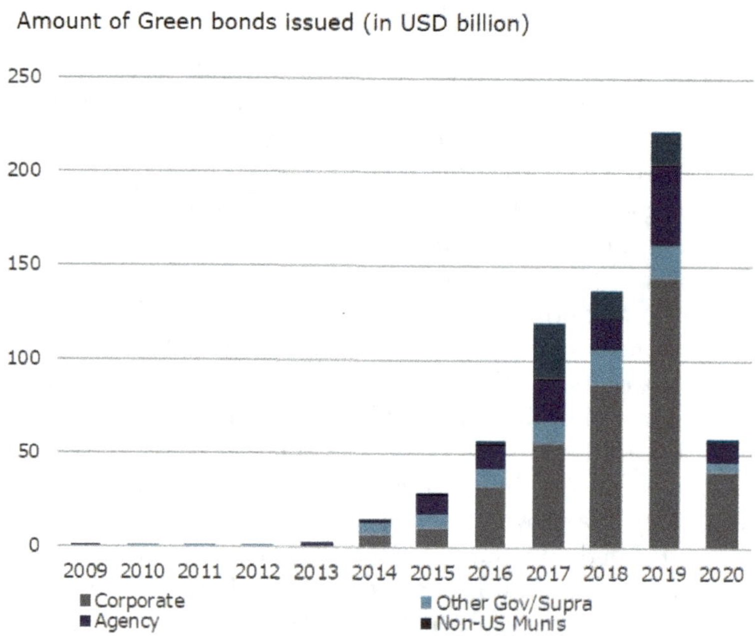

Fig. 11.2. Issuers of green bonds.

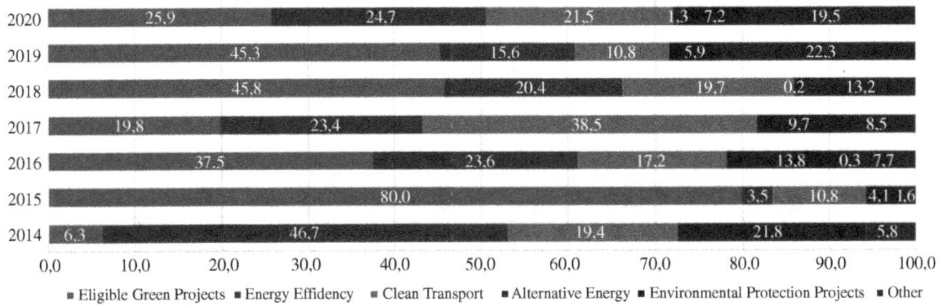

Fig. 11.3. Usage of green bonds.

powered by electricity, and the German carmaker Volkswagen, with two bonds (EUR 1.25 billion, 8 years and EUR 750 million, 12 years) for the development of a modular electrification toolkit and e-charging infrastructure, see Climate Bonds Initiative (2020). Besides there are also energy efficiency and directly environment-related projects, such as water, waste, and land use. Figure 11.3 collects the most common use-of-proceeds categories and their variations over time.

There was a significant change in the term structure of green bonds — away from shorter terms and towards longer ones. In Figure 11.4, we exhibit the term structure of green bonds from 2015 to 2020. Although the mid-term range remained dominant, the share of larger-term bonds is steadily increasing (especially in the 20+ years segment). Again, Figure 11.4 shows the volumes increasing across all tenor ranges.

Green bonds come as corporate bonds, project bonds, and asset-backed securities. As corporate bonds, they are use-of-proceeds bonds, which are issued by a corporate entity with recourse to the issuer in the case of default on interest payments or default on return of principal. Project bonds are backed by a single project or multiple projects. The investor has direct exposure to the risk of the project with or without recourse to the bond issuer. Finally, as an asset-backed security, the bond is collateralised by one or more specific projects. It provides recourse only to the assets except in the case of covered bonds. In the case of a covered bond, in the event of default of the issuer, the primary recourse is to the issuing entity and the secondary recourse is to an underlying cover pool of assets.

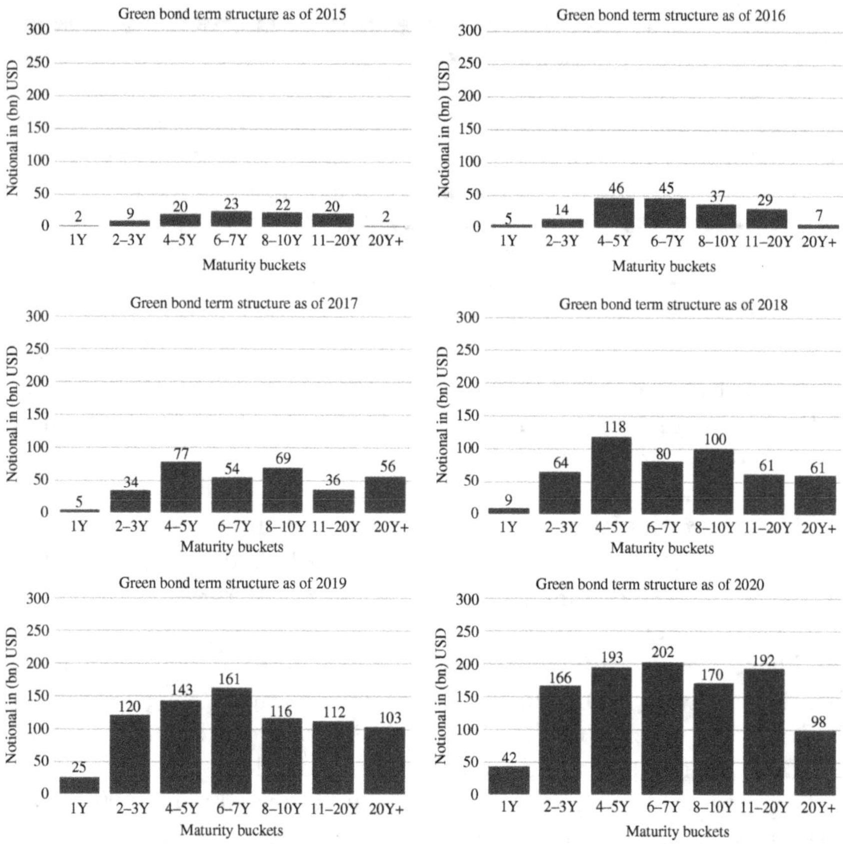

Fig. 11.4. Green bond term structure.

For issuers, green bonds offer several advantages. They highlight the issuers' green business and are beneficial for a green reputation. Strong investor demand can lead to oversubscription and to an increase of issuance size, which has happened for various issuers recently (see Climate Bonds Initiative (2020)). The investor base is diversified and exposure to bond demand fluctuation is reduced. Further, issuers see the issuance of green bonds as an advantage in integrating their previous sustainability work into their overall activities or as an opportunity to promote the implementation of sustainability aspects in their companies' strategic orientations (Maltais and Nykvist, 2020). However, a green bond issue comes with additional transaction costs in terms of reporting on the use of proceeds and certifications. Additionally, there is a reputational risk in case the bond's green credentials are challenged.

Investors, on the other hand, can meet commitments as signatories of Principles for Responsible Investments (PRI) and Institutional Investors Group on Climate Change (IIGCC) with green bonds. They can satisfy ESG investment criteria from asset managers and pension funds and improve their climate impact of fixed income investments. In doing so, they need to balance risk-adjusted financial returns with environmental benefits. On the downside is still the reduced liquidity of the green bond market with small volumes. The lack of unified standards can raise confusion and the possibility for reputational risk if the green integrity of the bond is questioned. In addition, there is limited scope for legal enforcement of green integrity. The lack of standardisation can lead to complexities in research and a need for extra due diligence that may not always be fulfilled.

Green bonds play an important role in refinancing. Currently, investments in global project and infrastructure debt raised are through bank lending, making risk expertise during the planning phase of projects necessary. However, green bonds can be issued after the high-risk construction phase of projects to allow banks to recycle their funds faster into new projects. Institutional investors could then take on the post-construction (lower) risk with more stable returns. Banks can use asset-backed securities to move their longer-term project loan portfolios to long-term investors and, indeed, have an incentive to create an increased pipeline for these types of loans.

Already, there are exchange traded funds (ETFs) devoted to green bonds. The largest — and longest established — green bond ETF is the Lyxor Green Bond DR UCITS, which more than tripled in size in 2020. Among the smaller funds, growth was even higher (up to fivefold). The increasing demand in the secondary market can partly be attributed to the sharp growth in green bond ETFs (Climate Bonds Initiative, 2020).

In sum, the global green bond market has developed rapidly over the last decade regarding diversification and market volume. This trend is expected to continue, driven by further issuance and likely political support measures. For instance, the German government, as a benchmark issuer, plans to create a yield curve for green bonds to strengthen the market for sustainable financial products (Bundesministerium der Finanzen, 2020). However, the rapid growth in the green bond market over the past few years has been met with questions around the environmental claims of these bonds. In the absence of clear and widely accepted definitions around what is green, many investors have raised concerns about greenwashing, where bond proceeds are allocated to assets that have little or uncertain environmental value. This can both shake confidence in the market and hamper efforts to finance a transition to a low-carbon economy. We will turn to these aspects in the following sections.

11.2 Green Bond Standards

While there is a broad agreement on the general framework (environmental protection, CO_2 reduction, sustainability) of green bonds, discussion of the exact definition of the term continues to cause a level of concern among market participants. Since the environmental benefit is the crucial aspect of a green bond, a clear definition and general understanding of green projects and the communication and disclosure of the use of proceeds is the foundation of the green bond market. For this reason, various national and international standards have been developed. Globally, the most accepted standard developed by key market participants and the International Capital Market Association (ICMA) is the Green Bond Principles (GBP) (International Capital Market Association, 2018). These have been formulated by the ICMA in June 2018 and are voluntary guidelines suggested by a private sector entity. They aim to generate transparency and clarification on standards for the green bonds. Issuers as well as investors can use these principles for credibility when selling or buying a green bond.

The GBP list four categories to identify a green bond issuance, namely the use of proceeds, the process for evaluating and selecting environmentally sustainable projects, the management of proceeds, and annual reporting on the use of the proceeds. Activities in all four categories should be laid out in legal documents, be subject to a high-level transparency, and should be externally certified (if possible).

Furthermore, as the EU Green Deal needs green financing standards, the EU proposed EU Green Bond Standard. A first impact assessment has identified the lack of a general definition of green bonds, the complexity of current auditing procedures, and the lack of investable projects and assets as current critical issues in the market. This lack of uniformity leads to increased costs for issuing green bonds (European Commission, 2020). So, with the EU sustainable finance taxonomy (EU TEG, 2019), an EU green bond standard has been proposed (see Technical Expert Group on Sustainable Finance (2020)). The proposed EU standards are similar to the GBP based on the use of proceeds but are much more detailed on criteria for eligibility and third-party supervision. Although they are also voluntary, it can easily be envisaged that their high standards on consistency and credibility combined with the backing of the EU will make them the *de facto* market standard. The taxonomy's primary goal is to provide all market participants, such as investors, issuers, financial institutions, and companies, with information on investments and projects' environmental sustainability and thus facilitate decision-making. The taxonomy has come into force and is to be applied from the beginning of 2021.

Since the environmental benefit is the crucial aspect of a green bond, a clear definition and general understanding of green projects and the communication and disclosure of the use of proceeds form the foundation of the green bond market. Investors need to clearly understand what a green bond label can and cannot deliver in order not to mistake green bond issuance as a signal for firms with low or decreasing carbon emissions. A key question for investors in green bonds and similar instruments is how to verify that the promised environmental benefits are, in fact, delivered (Beschloss and Mashayeki (2019)). Savvy investors can perform due diligence and evaluate the (expected) environmental benefits of the underlying projects. Major investment managers can engage with issuers to provide impact reports — as they increasingly do (Climate Action 100+ (2019)). But not all investors have the capabilities and resources to follow suit (see subsection 'Greenwashing' for discussion).

Current green bond standards use the project-based approach and relate to standalone projects and not the firm's overall activities. Thus, the overall emissions of firms could increase despite projects promising carbon reductions. However, the project-based approach provides an incentive for firms to develop new technologies or business approaches which will generate environmental benefits in the future. Thus, standards should also relate to the forward-looking character of these projects.

In fact, current labels give little indication that issuers have a lower or decreasing carbon intensity (nominator is revenues), so greenwashing, i.e., the effort to promote an environmentally responsible public image without taking substantive actions, remains an issue. As Ehlers *et al.* (2020) point out, companies with the highest carbon intensity represent an equal share of green bond issuers to lower intensity firms. The majority of these firms consists of power producers, so even if bond proceeds are used for green projects (e.g., renewable energy) the majority of activities of a firm may still be carbon-intensive (e.g., use of coal power plants). Also, an assessment of whether the issue of a green bond is associated with a reduction of the carbon intensity of a firm over time reveals that no strong evidence can be found. The results of Ehlers *et al.* (2020) show that the median changes in carbon intensity across firms before and after green bond issuance are minimal and statistically insignificant. So, these results indicate that green bond issuance is no indicator of reduced carbon emissions of firms. Thus, in order to provide a clearer signal on greenness of a firm, the authors propose a firm-level rating system for which they present a stylised example. In an alternative study, Flammer (2020) finds evidence for a decrease of emission and also an increase in the filing of green patents. So, evidence on the effect of the overall reduction of emission (intensity) remains mixed. However, the issuance of a green bond should not be used as the only indicator of the carbon-reduction efforts of a firm.

11.3 Green Bond Premium

A question widely discussed in the academic literature and investor studies is the existence and size of a green bond premium (greenium). That is, can one find a yield differential between a green bond and an otherwise identical conventional bond on the secondary market? Then the characteristics, such as sector and level, of a green bond that may determine the level of the premium need to be investigated. The empirical method primarily used to analyse bond spreads, as we have already seen frequently in the previous chapters, consists in

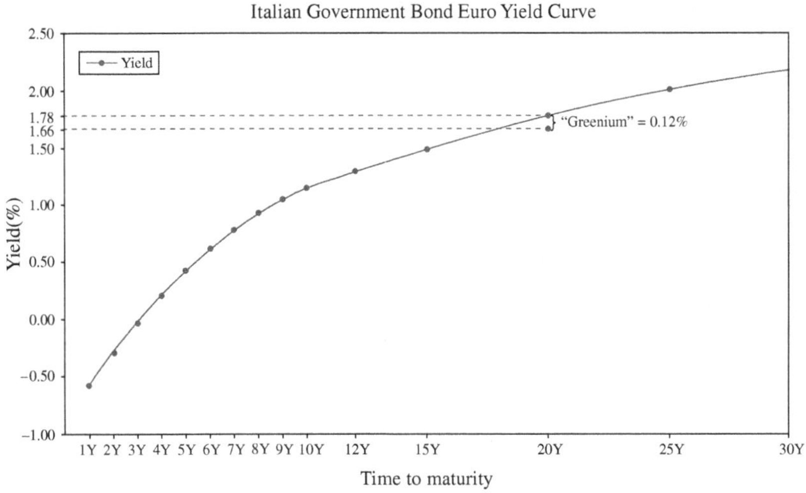

Fig. 11.5. Italian government bond 2021.

performing a regression-based estimation and controlling for standard factors. Thus, the financial and economical variables likely to explain the intrinsic value of a bond spread have to be identified in a first step.

Several recent cases suggested that the yield of green bonds might be lower than that of conventional bonds. Figure 11.5 shows the green premium of an Italian environment-focused government bond with maturity in 2045, which raised more than EUR 8 billion in March 2021. According to the information gathered in Oliver (2021), it was the biggest debut sovereign green bond from a European issuer. The yield of the bond was set at 1.547%; however, it came with a premium against the Italian government bond term structure of 0.12% points. Climate Bonds Initiative (2019) reports greeniums for 26 of 33 green bonds issued in the second half of 2020.

Let us look at the work of Zerbib (2018) for an example of the analysis of a green premium. The study starts with 1065 bonds and considered the time period 2013–2017. In the first step, a matching method is used to estimate the yield of an equivalent synthetic conventional bond. The matching method requires conventional bonds issued closely around (less than two years) the green bond on the time axis. In addition, differences in liquidity and maturity are constrained. This approach reduces the number of green bonds in the sample to 110. On this sample, a fixed effect panel regression is done on the time average difference in yields $\Delta y_{i,t}$ to estimate the green premium p_i as the fixed effect. So, the regression is

$$\Delta y_{i,t} = p_i + \beta \Delta L_{i,t} + \epsilon_{i,t}, \quad (11.1)$$

with $\Delta L_{i,t}$ a variable controlling for residual difference in liquidity between green and synthetic bond and $\epsilon_{i,t}$ the usual error term. The results suggest a small but statistically significant premium of several basis points. In addition to the green premium, Zerbib (2018) also identifies the characteristics that have an impact on it using cross-sectional regressions. The variables considered are the rating, sector, currency, maturity and issue amount of the green bond. Of these, sector and rating turned out to be significant drivers of the green bond premium.

Ehlers and Packer (2017) performed a similar study using a cross-section of 21 green bonds issued between 2014 and 2017, and found that green bond issuers on average have borrowed at lower spreads than they have through conventional bonds.

Hyun *et al.* (2019) provide a further empirical analysis and, as the mean size of green bonds is smaller, they put a special emphasis on controlling the impact of liquidity when calculating the green bond premium. They find that the issued amount negatively affects the green premium, an effect that was not present in the other studies.

The negative green bond premium may be due to the buying pressure in the case of green bonds. Due to the characteristic of green bonds, investor demand is high compared to the volume of bond issuances. So, issuers may prioritise green projects instead of a conventional project due to a lower cost of capital, which would be a desirable environmental effect. However, the greenium also indicates a structural lack of green projects and reduces institutional investor demand for investors who have no binding quota on green investments.

A study extending the analysis to the secondary market is performed by Kapraun and Scheins (2019). They considered a sample of 1500 green bonds globally and compared their yields with similar conventional bonds on both primary and secondary markets. For the primary market, the existence of a negative green premium was confirmed, but the secondary market analysis revealed a positive green

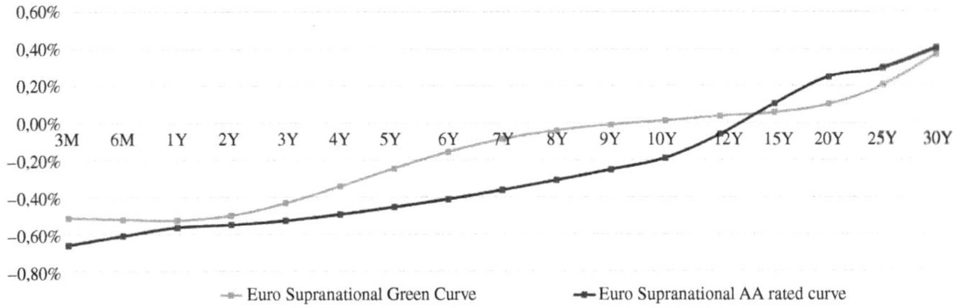

Fig. 11.6. Green vs. Corporate bonds.

bond premium (higher yields for green bonds). Figure 11.6 partly confirms that result. We compared the yields of green and conventional bonds of supranational entities with similar characteristics. We observe a positive green bond premium until about a maturity of 14 years which then turns negative.

Chapter 12

Carbon Risk and Financial Institutions

Carbon risk impacts systematic risk because the transition away from high-carbon production systems will have economy-wide effects (see Battiston *et al.* (2017) and Dietz *et al.* (2018)). While the magnitude of climate-related financial risks is highly uncertain, there is consensus that carbon risk already impacts financial institutions and will continue to do so. Thus, risk-management approaches have to be developed to extend standard risk-management practice to cope with carbon risk. We present a brief introduction to this topic, review the role of central banks in this context, and describe stress tests, which are a major tool to assess carbon risk.

12.1 Standard Risk-Management Considerations

Risk-management approaches for banks and insurance companies have been formed and standardised within the frameworks of Basel II/III and Solvency II. These frameworks evolve around three pillars, which are concerned with capital requirements and the types of capital eligible (I), the supervisory review process (II), and the disclosure of risk-management information to the market (III) (see Hull (2018)). The regulatory measures aim at improving the banking and insurance sector's ability to absorb shocks arising from financial and economic stress, whatever the source is. Likewise, they put emphasis on risk management and governance, i.e., the internal enterprise risk-management process, and encourage institutions to provide transparency to the markets. As carbon risk impacts on all traditional risk types (see Section 3.3), these criteria have to be extended and adjusted. The Network on Greening the Financial System (NGFS) provides guidance. The NGFS reiterates (Network for Greening the Financial System, 2019) that climate-related risks are a source of financial risk and lists several recommendations which can be seen as an extension of the Basel III and Solvency II regulations. They propose to integrate climate-related risks into financial stability monitoring and micro-supervision, which asks for the discussion of carbon risks at board level. A major point is building awareness and intellectual capacity and encouraging technical assistance and knowledge sharing. So, central banks, supervisors, and financial institutions should build in-house capacity and collaborate within their institutions with each other and with wider stakeholders to improve their understanding of how climate-related factors translate into financial risks and opportunities. Again, developing an appropriate database is an issue. The NGFS asks for a robust and internationally consistent climate and environment-related disclosure. So, all companies issuing public debt or equity as well as financial sector institutions are encouraged to disclose in line with the recommendations from the Task Force on Climate-related Financial Disclosures (TCFD, 2020b). These recommended disclosures include a company's governance around climate-related risks and opportunities. Also, the identification, assessment, and management of carbon risks should be made public. The climate-related (emission) targets should be disclosed together with the metric for measurement. We already reviewed the disclosure of firms in Section 5.2. According to TCFD (2020b), the banking and insurance sectors (of which 286 and 138 were included in the TCFD survey) were not frontrunners with scores around 25% of disclosing institutions.

The reason for the lack of disclosure may be the reluctance to reveal sensitive information on strategy or sensitive data to competitors. In Sections 6.3 and 7.3, we discussed federated machine learning techniques which may also be helpful in facilitating disclosure.

Concerning the role of the Network of Central Banks and Supervisors for Greening the Financial System (NGFS), which by definition is a group of central banks and supervisors, there is a vivid discussion in place about the role of central banks in the fight against climate change. We turn to the role of central banks in the following section.

12.2 The Role of Central Banks

The discussion of the role of central backs in addressing climate changes has captured academics, regulators, and the financial industry in recent years. The basic questions are whether central banks have the mandate and the means above their traditional duties. We can only raise a few points in this text and recommend, with emphasis, to the readers the excellent *Green Swan* (Bolton *et al.*, 2020) for an in-depth analysis. Besides making banks aware of climate risks and economic analysis, taking climate change into account in economic forecasts and macroeconomic models and analysing the dangers of climate change to financial stability, central banks could combine monetary policy with climate targets. Due to the urgency of the fight against climate change and the implementation of recent quantitative easing strategies by central banks, the idea of a so-called green quantitative easing (green QE) initiated by the European Central bank (ECB) has been discussed. By favouring green bonds (see Chapter 11), the ECB could easily implement such a strategy under its asset purchase programs (APPs). The strategy behind a green QE is to target investments in green bonds and thus rechannel financial flows strategically to green activities as part of its APPs. The ECB could purchase green bonds issued by national and local governments, development banks, and corporations in a targeted manner, thus providing better financing conditions for these issuers. Various studies, e.g., Dafermos *et al.* (2018) or Matikainen *et al.* (2017), support the feasibility of green QE. In addition, recent research has shown that current purchases favour bonds from high-carbon issuers (Campiglio *et al.*, 2018). So, already, balancing central bank portfolios would be a step towards a green QE. The exclusion of carbon-intensive bonds would be an indirect way to increase the share of green bonds on the ECB balance sheet.

In addition, a green QE will likely lead to an increase in green bond issuance and lower yields, resulting in lower borrowing costs for green projects. This cost advantage makes the issuance of green bonds more attractive, especially compared to conventional bond issuance. With regard to the corporate sector purchase programme (CSPP) of the ECB, Santis *et al.* (2018) have documented increased maturities and a significant shift to euro-dominated bonds. Both phenomena have only been observed for non-financial corporates, which are eligible for purchase in the CSPP. In contrast, for banks ineligible for purchases under the CSPP, no changes in issue volume, maturity, or currency have been observed.

However, higher prices and declining yields triggered by higher demand could result in a shift of investors' capital to other segments, also causing higher prices and lower yields for these bonds. Thus, portfolio rebalancing effects could lead to improved conditions for other bonds as well. Schoenmaker (2019) follows this line of argument to conclude that favouring green corporate bonds would reduce the cost of capital of bonds issued by high-carbon companies as well as low-carbon companies.

In sum, the evidence from the academic literature has shown that the large-scale purchases by the ECB have led to better financing conditions for European corporate bond issuers, especially for bond issuers meeting the eligibility criteria. However, the question whether a green QE will also lead to lower yields on green bonds and thus to better financing conditions for green projects is still open. Furthermore, a strict and binding EU taxonomy for green bonds (see Chapter 11) is a prerequisite for the introduction of a green QE. In any case, the introduction of EU taxonomy alone should generate a further boost in EU green bond issuance. A green QE based on these standards is likely to enhance this impact, causing more transparency and clarity in the European (and global) green bond market.

The formal legitimation of a green QE is an additional obstacle. The ECB mandate is set in article 127, TFEU, and defines price stability as the primary objective. However, the EU sees sustainable finance as a way 'to support economic growth while reducing pressures on the environment,' and further 'aims at supporting the delivery on the objectives of the European Green Deal by channelling private investment into the transition to a climate-neutral, climate-resilient, resource-efficient, and just economy, as a complement to public money' (European Commission, 2020). So, as central bank mandates are not set in stone and examples of adjustments exist, green QE may come into formal existence in the coming years.

12.3 Stress Tests

12.3.1 *Design of Stress Tests*

We now return to the supervisory role of central banks and their role in introducing climate-related stress tests to the supervisory process. This role became evident ever since Mark Carney, then Governor of the Bank of England, announced the introduction of climate-related stress tests in an interview with the *Financial Times* in December 2018.[1] The importance of the related risk factors for the practice of managing bank portfolios as well as for the stability of the financial sector as a whole has attracted a great deal of attention by academics, supervisory authorities, and market participants.[2] Supervisors and financial institutions are developing internal and regulatory climate stress tests by which the risks resulting from the advancing climate change are to be identified and assessed. In an investigation[3] by the Basel Committee on Banking Supervision in 2020, 24 out of 27 respondents stated that they were using both qualitative and quantitative approaches to analyse climate-related risks. We have discussed physical and, in particular, transition climate risks in detail in Chapter 3 and now turn to the question of how to assess them as a financial supervisor. Since the most recent global financial crisis, in addition to classical methods of portfolio analysis, stress tests have played an increasingly important role for assessing the resilience of financial institutions and the entire financial system to extreme adverse shocks. More recently, it was the current COVID-19 crisis that further underscored the importance of the shock absorption capacities of individual institutions. Unlike the abrupt outbreak of the COVID-19 crisis, however, the likely consequences of climate change occur more gradually and call for far-reaching long-term measures. In this context, the possibility that some of the actions taken

[1] *Financial Times*, December 17, 2018.

[2] See, e.g., Fed-Governor Lael Brainard: Why climate change matters for monetary policy and financial stability, Speech at The Economics of Climate Change, November 8, 2019 and Sabine Maurer, Executive Board Deutsche Bundesbank: Central Banks have a part to play in the fight against climate change, *Financial Times*, February 27, 2020.

[3] Climate-related financial risks: A survey on current initiatives, 2020.

at short notice may fail to deliver the desired effects, have highly problematic side effects or overstrain the adaptive capacities of the institutions and persons involved, thus increasing the transition risks even further, must be reckoned with. It thus follows that stress tests for climate-related risks are extremely complex and must account for a large variety of mutually interrelated parameters. Moreover, the NGFS (2019), has emphasised that central banks and supervisory authorities need to integrate climate risks into the analytical framework for mitigating systemic risk. This gives rise to a number of significant operational challenges in terms of data and the likely distribution of stochastic variables capturing risks in models, again see Chapter 3. Moreover, the possibility of tipping points, i.e., abrupt and irreversible shifts of climate patterns, need to be taken into consideration and the long-term time horizon requires additional attention. Moreover, there is a high degree of uncertainty regarding the physical mechanisms of climate change and their interactions. In addition, the possible transition paths of the global economy are diffuse and may differ at a national level. In particular, different regulatory provisions (e.g., relating to emission trading or taxation) as well as technologies (hydrogen, renewable energies, nuclear power) may be preferred in different countries.

The uncertainty prevailing with respect to the projected climate risks and their possible consequences needs to be dealt with in combination with the uncertainty with regard to the mitigation and adaptation efforts in the various regional, economic, and political fields of action. This gives rise to a set of complex analytical problems that, under current conditions, can best be analysed by considering multiple scenarios and a large variety of interrelated sources of stress. The related carbon risks, e.g., physical, transition risks, and their various combinations, need to be modelled carefully. As pointed out in Chapter 3, carbon risk factors affect all risks captured by the commonly used classification schemes. For example, stranded assets very likely affect credit and counterparty risks. Moreover, changes in investment guidelines of mutual funds, special funds, and pension schemes are likely to change the market risk profiles of securities portfolios, and the withdrawal of investments credit lines from certain firms in response to great societal pressure may result in substantial liquidity risks. Hence, regulators and supervisory authorities should account for the influence of carbon risks on the risk-management practices of financial institutions. This necessitates the specification and assessment of requirements concerning the integration of carbon risks into the risk identification, measurement, reporting, and control processes, see Section 12.1. An important aspect of this assessment process arises from the design and implementation of stress tests, which we address in the following.

The TCFD has advanced the introduction of stress tests in the context of regulatory assessments since the year 2017 and most recently in TCFD (2020b). To this end, the following proposals have been made:

- *A paradigm shift has to take place*: Climate risks need to be considered as a source of substantial financial risks rather than being considered a driver of reputational risk only. An immediate consequence of this decision will be the integration of climate risks into the practice of financial risk management.
- Disclosure of related strategies, governance rules, risk-management practices, metrics and objectives.
- *Scenario analysis*: Qualitative and quantitative assessments of the effects of transitional and physical climate scenarios.
- Development of climate scenarios and related quantitative methods (particularly for simulating adverse shocks in stress tests).

The first step that immediately follows from the above is the generation of climate scenarios. A climate scenario consists of a narrative and the projection of a large number of climate-related and macro-financial data. Related proposals on which individual modelling exercises could be based have been proposed by the IPCC in the form of representative concentration pathways (RCPs) as well as the NGFS formed by central banks and regulators. More specifically, three representative scenarios by the NGFS named in the following can lay a foundation for further, more detailed, and comprehensive specifications:

- **The orderly scenario:** This scenario rests upon the assumption that ambitious measures for the transition to a climate-friendly economy are taken at an early stage and that as a consequence, global warming will most probably be capped at below 2°C.

- **The disorderly scenario:** In this scenario, decisive measures are taken later in time (i.e., after 2030) and are disruptive, uncoordinated, surprising, and unpredictable. The measures that will then have to be taken are significantly more drastic than in the orderly scenario and hence lead to a higher transition risk.
- **Hothouse world:** Insufficient measures lead to a substantial warming of the globe and induce a dramatic rise in the resulting physical risks. Irreversible changes, e.g., a strong increase in sea levels, occur as a consequence.

Variations of these scenarios imply similar final stages of the global warming process and its consequences but assume different emissions pathways based on different technological assumptions (with respect to power generation and carbon removal technologies), all of which relate to the global warming process as well as to the adjustment to climate change. The economic developments implied by the three scenarios differ substantially, see Figures 12.1 and 12.2.

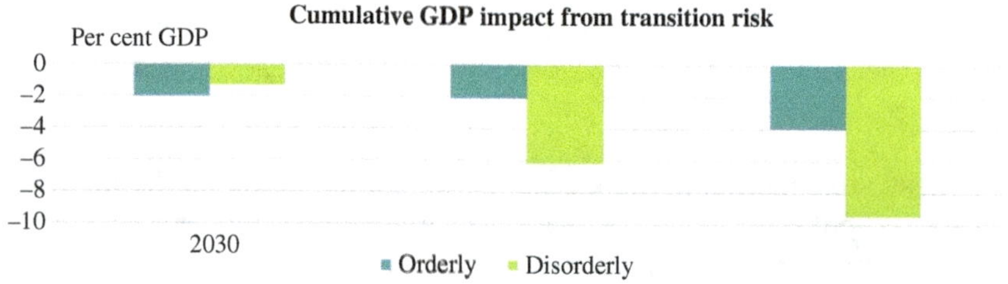

Fig. 12.1. GDP impact.

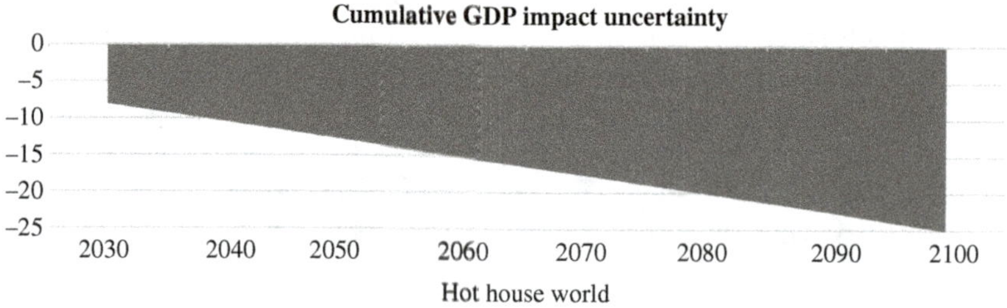

Fig. 12.2. GDP range.

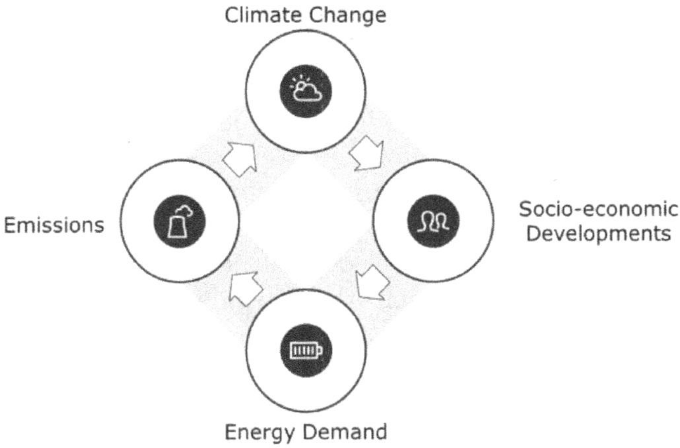

Fig. 12.3. Complexity.

In addition, the substantial uncertainty prevailing with regard to the impact of transitional and physical risks are by no means negligible. The complexity of the scenario, at least in part, is a consequence of the interactions between the physical and the socioeconomic factors. Figure 12.3 illustrates the existing interdependencies.

We now illustrate an approach for analysing the impact of carbon risks on credit portfolio analyses. To this end, a suitable information base must be created first. Once a scenario has been chosen, this amounts to generating the relevant time series of indicators from a combination of historical and projected data. The underlying narrative can be further enhanced by one's own projections of additional macro-financial variables (which also require a combination of historical and projected series). Typical classes of data fields include energy mix (fossil fuels and renewables), prices of emission allowances, CO_2 capture and sequestration (CCS), atmospheric GHG concentration, stock and bond market indices, gross domestic product, consumption, population growth and concentration, as well as land use and agricultural output.

After the completion of the data preparation and preprocessing steps, statistical methods of time-series analysis are used to calculate projections of data series into the future.

In each of these individual scenarios, separate projections for winners and losers of the implied physical change and transition processes need to be derived. A necessary prerequisite for this kind of analysis is, of course, the scenario-specific identification of winners and losers. Linear models, in which the conditional expectation of the dependent variable is essentially modelled as a linear function of the assumed factors of influence, will often not be capable of capturing the true complexity of the stochastic relationships under investigation. In order to avoid incorrect inferences and undue generalisations, flexible functional forms that can approximate nonlinear and non-additive forms of statistical dependence need to be applied. In such an empirical investigation, the dependent variable Y used for measuring the climate friendliness of a firm can be the CO_2 intensity, which is defined as the quotient of total CO_2e emissions with an appropriate denominator (e.g., to total revenue). A general model formulation can then be expressed as follows:

$$Y = f(X, Z, W) + \epsilon, \tag{12.1}$$

where X is a vector of company-specific fundamental data, which may include, e.g., indicators of the capital and labour intensity of production, profitability measures, or investment spending as a percentage of total revenue. Z stands for indicators of a firm's sectoral and regional affiliations, e.g., in the form of segment-specific revenue shares, the geographical location of the company's headquarters, or the GDP per capita of the country of residence USD, adjusted for purchasing power differences. Finally, W is a placeholder for variables capturing key characteristics of a company's economic environment, e.g., information on supply chains and product ranges, and ϵ is a random, zero-mean error term that is stochastically independent of X, Z, and W.

The processes of data gathering and preprocessing as well as their statistical analysis often require the performance of highly computer-intensive tasks in a high-dimensional sample space. Often, analytical techniques summarised under the collective term 'machine learning' (see Chapter 5) have proved extremely useful in this context. Once the above tasks have been performed, credit portfolios can then be analysed for different future points in time on the grounds of projected, scenario-specific data points.

12.3.2 *Applications of Stress Tests*

In the course of its 2021 Biennial Exploratory Scenario (BES), the Bank of England (BoE) intends to examine the resilience of the business models of banks, insurers, and the financial system as a whole to the physical and transitional risks of climate change (Bank of England, 2019). In doing so, the BoE aims at both quantifying the magnitude of these risks and the scope of the necessary adjustment measures. Hence, the focus of the planned research is explorative in nature and is not centred around regulatory capital resources and old or new related requirements. The test is intended to help firms discover data gaps and remedy the shortcomings that caused them. In addition, the development of innovative risk-management techniques is to be promoted. In a more general sense, another main objective is to increase the awareness of the financial risks of climate change among banks and insurers. However, such an approach constitutes a novelty for the banks and companies involved and differs from the usual practice of stress testing in a variety of aspects, such as the following:

- **Multiple scenarios:** The BoE uses three scenarios that essentially match the ones discussed above.
- **Extended participant group:** The test is conducted by large banks and insurers and aims at testing the resilience of the financial system as a whole.
- **Extended modelling horizon:** The time horizon for the related projections and impact evaluations will be set to 30 years. In doing so, the time frame of climate change is taken into adequate consideration; however, this also poses a major challenge for the design, calibration, and implementation of the underlying dynamic models. In this context, however, the BoE allows a static treatment of the balance sheets because the research emphasis is more on the sustainability of the business models in general.
- **Integration of macroeconomic and financial variables:** For each of the scenarios, the BoE provides development trajectories for temperatures, emission amounts, and key climate policy indicators. Separate information sets on the assumed impact of these variables on key indicators of physical and transition-related risks as well as the relevant macroeconomic and financial variables are also provided for each scenario.
- **Modelling of clients and counterparties:** In this context, the BoE expects the impact of climate change on the business

models of clients and counterparties (e.g., as a consequence of 'stranded' assets) to be included in the analysis.

On the basis of the scenarios and their predefined trajectories for climate, macroeconomic, and financial variables, banks and insurers are required to analyse both their own business models and those of their clients and counterparties. To this end, an analysis of the balance sheet impacts of the scenarios will be conducted. More specifically, balance sheets will be frozen at the starting date of the analysis and left unchanged for a period of 30 years. In intervals of five years each, a re-evaluation of the balance sheets is then conducted.

The conduct of this analysis requires a number of complex analytical operations, which the BoE has illustrated using the example of a corporate bond issued by an energy supplier with coal and gas power plants in Poland and the United Kingdom. Figure 12.4 summarises the high-level analytical steps.

The above exposition gives an idea of the requirements regarding the data and analytical tools associated with such a set of scenario analyses. Even in a static setting, high-dimensional and data-intensive valuation problems need to be solved.

While the BoE approach focuses on classical scenarios with gradual transition processes, a working paper by Vermeulen (2019) presents the possible scenarios of a disruptive transition to a low-carbon economy. These stress scenarios are aligned with specific dimensions of climate policy on the one hand and energy technology on the other and are used to analyse climate risks in portfolios of more than 80 Dutch banks. The related narratives focus on climate policy and possible technological breakthroughs. With respect to the design of climate policy, the analysis focuses exclusively on the aspect of reducing GHG emissions by adequately pricing emission allowances.

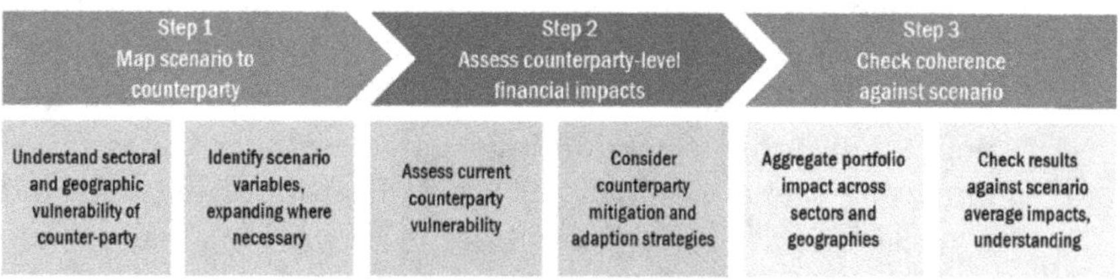

Fig. 12.4. Transition.

As far as technology is concerned, the split of energy generation between fossil and green sources receives most attention. The different scenarios thus generated are then analysed in the framework of a multi-national macroeconomic model. The sectoral relevance (e.g., crude oil refineries vs. providers of telecommunication services) of the scenario-specific, projected macroeconomic developments is then evaluated with the help of a transition vulnerability factor (TVF). This TVF, in turn, is determined using normalised GHG emission amounts in the production process of the company under investigation. In doing so, both the direct emissions (scope 1) and the indirect emissions resulting from the use of primary products, commodities, and services are taken into account (scope 2 and scope 3). The TVF then plays a decisive role in the scenario-specific risk assessments of individual companies. In line with common practice in conventional stress testing, market and credit risks are considered. One of the main results is that potential losses in the portfolios of insurers and pension funds may reach up to 11% of the current net asset values, whereas potential losses in typical bank portfolios are expected to be somewhat lower (2–4%).

Similarly, the study of Bouchet and Le Guenedal (2020) (see Section 10.4) uses various carbon price scenarios (that is, in fact, transition scenarios) to assess the credit risk of firms and bank portfolios. Let us also mention Klusak *et al.* (2021), who use a random forest model to predict sovereign credit ratings on S&P rating data from 2015 to 2020 and simulate the effect of climate change on sovereign credit ratings for 108 countries. Then, they forecast climate-related sovereign rating adjustments under various global warming scenarios. They find that as early as 2030, downgrades will start and will increase in intensity and across more countries over the remaining part of the century.

Chapter 13

Carbon Risk and Investors

In the same vein as societies develop adaptation and mitigation strategies in response to climate change, investors also face similar choices. They can adapt by improving the evaluation of risks and the financial system such that more capital is allocated to low-carbon industries and firms. Or they can mitigate the risk by constructing portfolios that are more robust against carbon risk.

In his letter to CEOs, Larry Fink of BlackRock (Fink, 2021) asks all companies to actively mitigate climate risk and initiate measure on a path to net-zero emission. He also puts emphasis on the disclosure of climate-related risk according to the recommendations of the TCFD. Thus, BlackRock can serve as a prominent example of an investor putting effort in adaptation and mitigation.

We will start now by sketching a more general picture of institutional investor strategies concerning carbon risks. Then, we will discuss approaches for constructing low-carbon portfolios. We will close with the construction of a low-carbon portfolio.

13.1 Carbon Risk and Investment Portfolios

13.1.1 *The Current State of Play*

Starting from the initiation of the Principles for Responsible Investment (PRI) in 2006, institutional investors recognised the relevance of environmental, social, and corporate governance issues to investment practices. The PRI has grown from 20 initial members in 2006 to more than 2700 members representing more than USD 110 trillion of assets under management. However, until only recently, climate change was just a subcategory within the E pillar of ESG. Now, investors recognise the importance on climate change as a financial risk. Academic evidence for carbon risk as a (long-run) factor in asset portfolios is provided in Chapters 8–10.

So, institutional investors have begun to consider climate risk in their investment decisions. For instance, the Institutional Investors Group on Climate Change (IIGCC), an European membership body for investor collaboration on climate change, with more than 250 members and over EUR 33 trillion in assets under management, started an initiative in 2019 to align portfolios of investors to the goals of the Paris Agreement (Paris Aligned Investment Initiative, PAII). The initiative focuses on decarbonising investment portfolios consistent with achieving the net-zero GHG emission goal by 2050. Furthermore, investment in low-carbon industries, such as renewable energy and energy-efficient technologies should be fostered (The Institutional Investors Group on Climate Change (IIGCC), 2020). However, as InfluenceMap (2021) reports, currently, portfolios managed by the leading institutional investors are not aligned with Paris climate goals in the key sectors of transport, electric power, and fossil fuels. The deviations from Paris-aligned targets are between 8% and 27%. Furthermore, there is still a substantial investment in companies in sectors with a high risk of stranded assets.

A survey conducted by Philipp (2019) of more than 400 institutional investors, of which 48 have more than USD 100 billion under management, documents at least a growing awareness. According to this survey, institutional investors believe that climate risks have financial implications for their portfolio firms and that these risks, particularly regulatory risks, are already beginning to materialise. Many of the long-term, larger, and ESG-oriented investors prefer risk management and engagement over divestment to address carbon risks.

As many institutional investors stopped investing in carbon-intensive industries (e.g., Norway state pension funds stopped investing in more than 40 companies and will sell more (*Financial Times*, 2020), we may observe a shift in investor strategy from divestment to more sophisticated risk-management strategies.

In sum, the current literature provides ample evidence that investors actively decarbonise their portfolios. Of course, this requires targets and metrics, which we will discuss in the following section.

13.1.2 *Carbon Accounting for Equity Portfolios*

In Section 3.2, we introduced carbon intensity (or footprint) as a metric for measuring the individual CO_2e emissions of a company. We now extend this metric to portfolios following the guidance of the TCFD (2020b).

The TFCD recommended metric is the weighted average carbon intensity (using company revenue) calculated as

$$\sum_{i=1}^{n} \text{Portfolio weight}_i \times \frac{\text{Issuer's emissions}_i}{\text{Issuer's sales}_i} = \text{CI in } \frac{\text{tonnes CO}_2}{\text{\$M revenue}}. \tag{13.1}$$

So, for the weighted average carbon intensity, each company's emissions are divided by its revenues to obtain the carbon intensity of each holding. The results are averaged using company weights in the portfolio to obtain an overall carbon intensity of the portfolio. Alternatively, the portfolio carbon footprint (based on company revenue and market value) is suggested. The definition is

$$\frac{\sum_{i=1}^{n} \frac{\text{\$investment}_i}{\text{Issuer's full mcap}_i} \times \text{Issuer's emissions}_i}{\sum_{i=1}^{n} \frac{\text{\$investment}_i}{\text{Issuer's full mcap}_i} \times \text{Issuer's sales}_i} = \text{CI in } \frac{\text{tonnes CO}_2}{\text{\$M revenue}}. \tag{13.2}$$

Now, the emission and revenues of companies in a portfolio are allocated based on the share of market value owned by an investor. The portfolio carbon footprint is also referred to as financed emissions/financed revenue. If an investor owns $X\%$ of a company, and the company emits Y tonnes of CO_2 annually, then the investor has financed

$$X\% \times Y = \text{tonnes of CO}_2.$$

By adding emissions across all companies in the portfolio, we obtain

$$\sum_{i=1}^{n} \frac{\$\text{investment}_i}{\text{Issuer's full mcap}_i} \times \text{Issuer's emissions}_i$$
$$= \text{portfolio emissions in tonnes CO}_2. \qquad (13.3)$$

Division by the portfolio value to express carbon footprint in CO_2 per $M AUM defines the exposure to carbon-related assets.

According to TCFD (2020b), these three are the most widely used carbon metrics among the PRI signatories with the portfolio carbon footprint being the most popular one.

Other metrics in use are the total carbon emissions, defined as the absolute GHG emissions associated with a portfolio, expressed in tonnes of CO_2e, and the carbon intensity, which is the volume of carbon emissions per million dollars of revenue (carbon efficiency of a portfolio), expressed in tonnes CO_2e/USD million revenue.

Typically, these metrics will be used to define constraints in an optimisation setting. Because of the backward-looking character of these metrics and the issue of unreliable emission data (see Section 6.2), modern approaches take additional more forward-looking metrics into account.

13.2 Hedging Climate Risk

13.2.1 *A News-Based Climate Risk Indicator*

Engle *et al.* (2020) use textual analysis to construct an aggregate climate change risk measure. Figure 13.1 shows the reaction of the news index to significant global news on climate change. Now, the idea is to construct spread portfolio long stocks that rise in value on bad news and short stocks that fall in value on bad news. Such a portfolio will generate profits on negative climate change news and provide a hedge against carbon risk. In the work by Engle *et al.* (2020), it is shown how such a portfolio can be constructed (it is actually long only for a weighted average of funds) and be continually updated. The out-of-sample correlation between the return of the

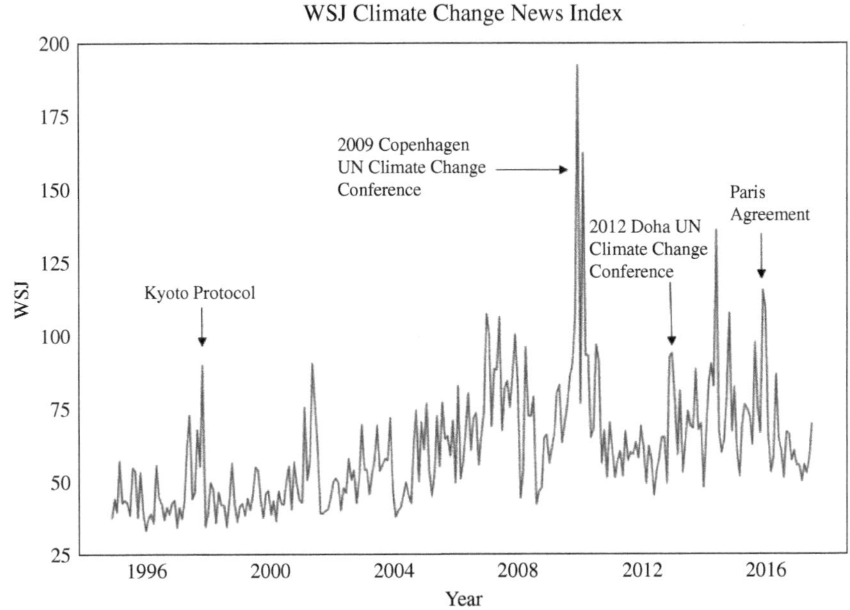

Fig. 13.1. Climate change news index (generated with data from Engle *et al.* (2020)).

hedge portfolio and the innovations of the climate change index is in the range of 20–30%. Thus, such a hedge portfolio, based on a rigorous methodology of constriction, is a valuable tool in hedging carbon risk.

13.2.2 *Portfolio Approaches*

Are climate risks hedgeable? The first study to discuss this question from a portfolio point of view was performed by Andersson *et al.* (2016). Their approach goes beyond a divestment of high-carbon or/and risk-of-stranded-asset industries because it does not aim at just a simple exclusion of companies. It tries to deliver a dynamic investment strategy that hedges climate risk without sacrificing any financial returns.

To explain the Andersson *et al.* (2016) approach, let us look at a benchmark index with N constituent stocks. The weight of each stock in the benchmark index is given by

$$w_i^b = \frac{\text{Mkt cap}(i)}{\text{Total mkt cap}} \quad \text{with} \quad i \in \{1, \ldots, N\}. \tag{13.4}$$

Further, each constituent company is ranked in decreasing order of carbon intensity, q_l^i, with company $l = 1$ having the highest carbon intensity and company $l = N$ the lowest.

We can distinguish between two different optimisation problems in order to construct a decarbonised index. In the first case, the new weights w_i^g are the result of the following minimisation problem:

$$\begin{aligned} &\min \text{TE} = sd(R^g - R^b), \\ &\text{subject to} \quad \begin{cases} w_l^g = 0 & \text{for all} \quad l = 1, \ldots, k, \\ 0 < w_l^g & \text{for all} \quad l = k+1, \ldots, N, \end{cases} \end{aligned} \tag{13.5}$$

where TE is the tracking error, sd the standard deviation, and $R^{g,b}$ the return of the index with weights w^g and w^b. So, the worst k performers in terms of carbon intensity are excluded and the remaining stocks reweighted to minimise the tracking error. In the second case, we allow the new index to simply underweight high-carbon-footprint stocks without completely excluding them. However, the aggregated portfolio carbon intensity must be below some given threshold Q:

$$\begin{aligned} &\min \text{TE} = sd(R^g - R^b), \\ &\text{subject to} \quad \begin{cases} \sum_{l=1,\ldots,N} q_l w_l^g \leq Q \\ w_l^g \geq 0 \end{cases} \qquad \text{for all } l = 1, \ldots, N. \end{aligned} \tag{13.6}$$

The framework is set in the standard mean–variance setting of portfolio optimisation (Bodie, 2020) and yields mathematically simple optimisation problems. However, for large portfolio sizes N, the estimation and calculation of covariance matrices become tricky. To asses the quality of the approach, the tracking error (TE) is used. Portfolio managers use two different measures of tracking error. The *ex-post* TE is the measure of the volatility of the realised active return deviations from the benchmark, while the *ex-ante* TE is an estimation based on the estimated multi-factor model used for the optimisation.

Andersson *et al.* (2016) use the *ex-ante* tracking error with the following minimisation problem:

$$\min\left[\sqrt{(W^P - W^b)'(\beta\Omega_f\beta' + \Delta)(W^P - W^b)}\right], \tag{13.7}$$

with $(W^P - W^b)$ the vector of active weights of the portfolio with regard to the benchmark, Ω the covariance matrix, β the matrix of factor exposures, and Δ the diagonal matrix of specific risk variances.

Several examples of decarbonised indices are discussed in detail by Andersson *et al.* (2016). One is the Fourth Swedish Pension Fund (AP4), which applied a similar approach to hedge the carbon exposure of its global equity portfolio. It excluded 20% of the worst performers in terms of carbon intensity (CO_2/sales), which reduced its overall carbon footprint by roughly 50%. Strikingly, the tracking error never exceeded 0.5%, which shows the effectiveness of the methodology.

An important issue is how the filtering of companies should be done. A filtering across the benchmark implies a sector-blind filtering out of high-carbon-footprint sectors, which might lead to an unbalanced decarbonised index. Most of the fossil energy sector, electric utilities, and mining and materials companies would be excluded. Filtering sector by sector might result in a significantly reduced carbon footprint while still maintaining a sector composition roughly similar to that of the benchmark.

In the work by Cheema-Fox *et al.* (2019), the filtering approach is extended to the construction of decarbonisation strategies, which in principle construct various spread portfolios with respect to combinations of carbon and financial risk factors.

The Paris Aligned Investment Initiative (The Institutional Investors Group on Climate Change (IIGCC), 2020) recommends optimising portfolios for the achievement of net-zero goals also with respect to forward-looking metrics. One could use the carbon intensity percentage allocated to climate solutions or some variant of a climate value at risk. However, they also state that a balanced approach has to be used. The optimal portfolio could be overly exposed to specific risk factors, such as regulatory risk. Furthermore, it should be well diversified across technologies and sectors. Thus, so often, expert judgement has to accompany mathematically advanced techniques.

13.3 Sustainability Optimisation

13.3.1 *Introduction*

The need to reconcile the objectives of offering clients decent returns on their investments, keeping financial risks at an acceptable level, and making a significant contribution to the attainment of a sustainable economy is among the key challenges investment managers face today. This is, in part, due to the fact that the goal of sustainability itself is a multi-faceted concept that comprises environmental targets (e.g., the reduction of GHG emissions), social principles (e.g., the observation of human rights), and aspects of corporate governance (e.g., the alignment of incentive systems with stakeholder interests). Against this background, this section seeks to address two main points. On the one hand, it is intended to demonstrate that thoughtful analysis of comprehensive, high-quality, firm-level sustainability data gathered by specialised providers enables asset managers to turn customer-specified sustainability guidelines into specific, measurable criteria that can then be seamlessly integrated into the practice of constructing, monitoring, and rebalancing asset portfolios (see Section 13.3.2). Since this involves the need to 'filter out' assets with particularly favourable sustainability profiles from the universe of possible and admissible investments, we use the term 'sustainability filters' in this context. On the other hand, we demonstrate that (if some rather elementary preconditions are met) the trade-off prevailing between financial profitability targets, limited risk budgets, and sustainability objectives can be formalised mathematically with the help of a multidimensional criterion function and then resolved using numerical optimisation techniques (Section 13.3.3). In conclusion, our approach is applied to a real-life example.

13.3.2 *Sustainability Filters: Relevant Data and Example Applications*

13.3.2.1 *Available Data: A Selective Overview*

Data-driven portfolio management requires the integration of various data types into a 'smart' platform, i.e., an integrated technology solution that allows data from different sources to be governed, accessed, and delivered to users or applications for business purposes. On the one hand, typical data types used in the asset management process include market data (e.g., equity prices and index levels, bond prices and yields, FX rates, CDS spreads) along with company-specific data (e.g., information from financial statements and financial ratios derived from it as well as data on sectoral and geographical affiliation, exchange listing, and index membership). On the other hand, the use of detailed, high-dimensional data on ESG (i.e., environmental, social, and governance) related characteristics of assets and issuers has gained momentum, giving rise to a substantial growth in the number and variety of investment products (e.g., mutual funds) structured around ESG-related principles. An overview of the relevant data categories is given in Table 13.1.

Firm-level ESG data usually consist of quantitative and qualitative variables. Frequently, data offerings by adequately specialised vendors include proprietary scores or rating grades in which information on different aspects of sustainability has been condensed to summary and easily understandable metrics. Traditionally, most of the quantitative variables relevant for portfolio construction and management relate to the environmental pillar of the ESG data offering. In this subfield, typical examples of variables of interest include (but are not limited to) GHG emissions, energy consumption, renewable energy usage, amounts of waste generated, the number of carbon offsets purchased, or R&D expenditure amounts relating environmental purposes.

Qualitative information included ESG datasets containing data fields with answers to questions like the following:

- Does the company have a policy to protect customer health and safety?
- Does the company have a policy on fair trade?
- Does the company have a succession plan for executive management in the event of unforeseen circumstances?
- Does the company report on its impact or on activities to reduce its impact on biodiversity?

In order to harness such qualitative data for the application of mathematical and statistical techniques of portfolio optimisation, it is usually required to encode the underlying information using binary indicators, i.e., sequences of zeros and ones in which '1' indicates

Table 13.1. Example overview of relevant databases and their coverage.

	Asset 4	Datastream	Worldscope	Fixed income data	Thomson Reuters fundamentals	CDS data
Data type	ESG data Company controversies	Equity prices and indices Futures FX data Commodities Macro-economic data	Company fundamental data Fundamental ratios Segment revenue decomposition	Interest rates Bond prices/yields Bond static data Benchmark curves	Basic company information Company industry information Company fundamental data Segment revenue decomposition	CDS spreads
Coverage	> 10.000 active companies, 424 active items 13 score categories GHG data > 31.000, ESG data > 80.000 company years	Equity prices: >107.000 companies Index data: > 285.000 indices FX data: > 9.000 pairs Commodities: > 105.000 assets Macro-economic data: > 8.9 mil. series	> 55.000 companies > 800 items Segment data linked to SIC code	> 500.000 bonds and convertibles > 20.000 interest rates > 800 benchmark curves	> 45.000 companies > 800 items Segment data linked to NAICS code	> 96.000 instruments
Time-series update frequency	Annual data available Update cycle: biweekly	Daily data available Macro-economic data: monthly/quarterly Update cycle: daily	Quarterly/ Annual data available Update cycle: daily	Daily data available Update cycle: daily	Quarterly/Annual data available Update cycle: daily	Daily data available Update cycle: daily

Application	Quantitative and qualitative ESG filters Emission data: > basis for carbon exposure index calculation ESG scores used to rank companies Strategic asset allocation	FX data: convert data to a common currency Macroeconomic data: used in carbon exposure index Equity and index prices and returns used as input variables for the portfolio calibration and as response variables to test the market significance of the carbon exposure index	Fundamental data and ratios used to estimate carbon exposure index Segment decomposition used to segregate and quantify sector exposure on the company level	The term structure of interest rates Quantification of the effect of carbon exposure index on bond yields	Fundamental data and ratios used to estimate carbon exposure index Segment decomposition used to segregate and quantify sector exposure on the company level	Used as a response variable and as a measure of carbon risk market impact

Data is a key for the integration of carbon risk into the management of financial portfolios.

that a predefined, 'yes-or-no'-type condition has been fulfilled by the organisation to which the record relates, whereas '0' signifies the opposite. This preprocessing step transforms qualitative information into interpretable values of numerical variables and hence enables the simultaneous use of qualitative and quantitative information by accordingly specialised algorithms.

As indicated in the previous paragraphs, the complexity and multidimensionality of the sustainability principle often render the preprocessing and subsequent use of related raw data rather cumbersome. A pragmatic solution to this problem, offered by several specialised agencies as well as most vendors of ESG data, is to aggregate information from a considerable variety of indicators to form one or more comprehensive indicators or scores, according to which assets or company can then be ranked or graded. Often, separate scores are offered for each of the three pillars E, S, and G, and in some cases, such indicators can even be more granular. Refinitiv, for instance, offers separate scores on the topics of resource use, emissions, and environmental innovation in conjunction with the environmental pillar, separate summary indicators of management quality, shareholder orientation and CSR Strategy as part of the governance pillar as well as workforce, human rights, community and product responsibility scores in the social pillar. These scores are then aggregated to the overall ESG score that weights individual scores based on the sector the company belongs to.

13.3.2.2 *Examples of Sustainability-Related Filters and Results of Their Application*

Case 1: Carbon intensity below the industry average
In the first case studied here, the constraints that jointly constitute the filter used to identify appropriate investments were carefully chosen to remove those companies from the set of eligible investees whose carbon intensity was found to be worse than that of their peers.[1] A secondary condition to which the filtering procedure was subject to was the stipulation to retain enough companies from different economic sectors to form a well-diversified portfolio. The filtering procedure actually applied can be interpreted as a stepwise selection

[1]Since carbon emission data are highly skewed, comparison with average will remove only worst-in-class companies.

Table 13.2. Filtering procedure.

Filter variable	Operator	Objective	Remaining companies
Region of incorporation	Equals	Western Europe	598
Operating margin	Greater	10%	537
Interest coverage ratio	Greater	5	371
GHG intensity[a]	Below	Industry average[b]	225
Renewable energy use	Equals	Yes	185
Environmental supply chain selection management	Equals	Yes	160
Crisis management systems	Equals	Yes	110

Notes: [a]We define carbon intensity as total GHG emissions (scope 1 and scope 2) divided by total revenues in a given fiscal year.
[b]We consider 33 industries (TRBC business sectors).

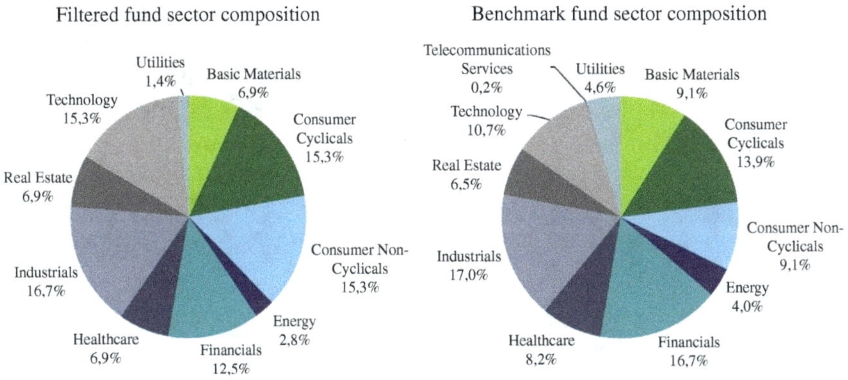

Fig. 13.2. Sector decomposition of filtered portfolio vs. benchmark: Case 1.

process that is summarised in Table 13.2. The set of companies to which this procedure was applied is the group of firms jointly constituting the STOXX 600 index.

An example application of this set of criteria, applied to a subuniverse of 600 companies forming the basis of the STOXX Europe 600 stock index and for the year 2020, yielded a total of 110, each of which complied with all of the stated conditions. In the graph in Figure 13.2, the sectoral composition of a hypothetical fund portfolio built according to the above filter is compared to that of the underlying benchmark. It becomes obvious that the application of the filter described leads to a significant shift in the sector composition of the target portfolio. At the same time, however, all sectors present in the benchmark, with the exception of telecommunications services (which only constitute a tiny fraction of the benchmark), are also present in the filtered portfolio (see Figure 13.2).

The purpose of this example is to show how the application of such a filter enables an investment manager to first compare the climate footprint of each individual firm with the sector mean (and/or median) on the one hand and with the benchmark total on the other, and then to adjust the weights of the individual benchmark components to obtain a new portfolio in which the cumulated greenhouse gas intensity is reduced to a new target value that lies significantly below the original amount, while at the same time inducing only very limited deviations from the original sectoral exposure profile of the benchmark.

The reason why this is achieved and the way in which the climate footprint of the filtered portfolio differs from the benchmark is shown in Figure 13.3. It becomes obvious that in most sectors under consideration, there is a relatively small number of individual firms (here represented by coloured dots) for which the GHG intensity exceeds the sector median (represented by the horizontal line) by far, so that

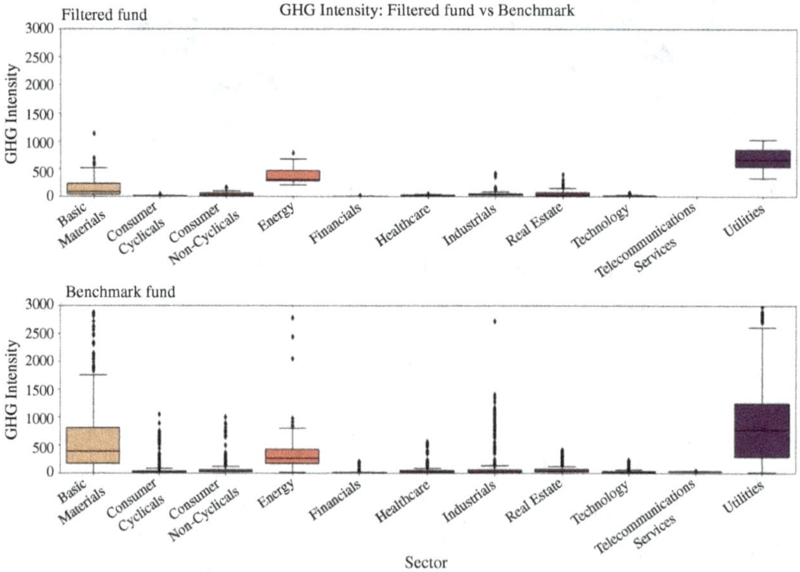

Fig. 13.3. Filtered portfolio vs. benchmark carbon intensity: Case 1.

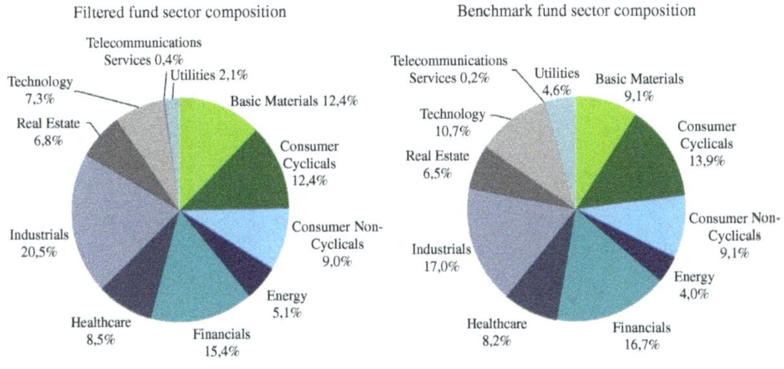

Fig. 13.4. Filtered portfolio vs. benchmark sector decomposition: Case 2.

as a consequence, a removal of these issuers from the portfolio leads to a significant improvement of its climate footprint without the need for any major change in its sectoral structure.

Case 2: ESG categories scores: 'Best-in-class' stock selection
In case 2, the filtering procedure applied was to select the 30 highest ranking companies in each of the 10 ESG categories. Since there were a number of companies who held high-ranking positions in more than one of these categories, the final sample obtained contains 234 companies. Its sectoral decomposition is presented in Figure 13.4. In this regard, we find only small differences between the filtered stock proportion and the benchmark. We further compare the distribution of ESG score in every economic sector for the filtered fund and the benchmark. Results are shown in Figure 13.5. We can observe a clear improvement of the median ESG score across all sectors once the filter has been applied. This result is accompanied by a substantial reduction of the portfolio shares of potentially harmful companies.

In conclusion, this suggests that a careful application of filtering procedures based on ESG criteria facilitates a reconciliation of the two objectives of holding a well-diversified portfolio and achieving a significant improvement of its ESG profile.

Case 3: Environmental innovation
In our third example, the research effort taken by companies to improve their environmental footprint is used as a filtering criterion. More specifically, we start with the same benchmark portfolio above and identify those companies whose environmental R&D expenditures exceed 1% of total revenues. The subgroup we end up with

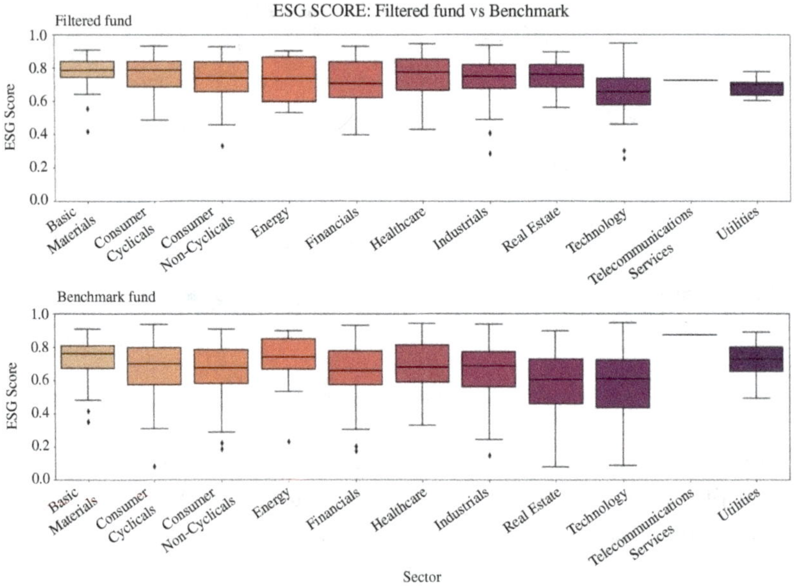

Fig. 13.5. Filtered portfolio vs. benchmark ESG score comparison: Case 2.

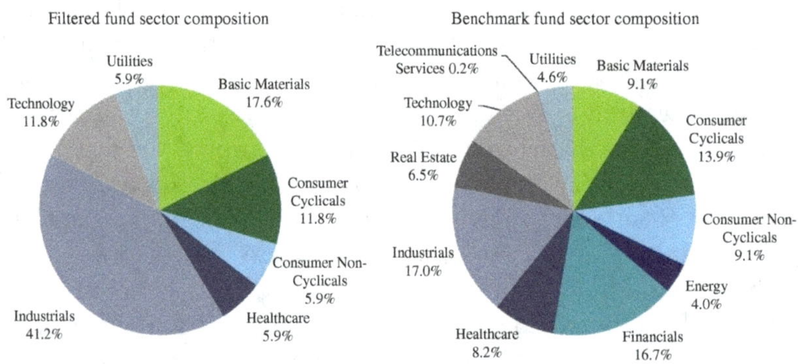

Fig. 13.6. Filtered portfolio vs. benchmark sector decomposition: Case 3.

consists of 17 companies; its sectoral composition is compared to the benchmark in Figure 13.6. Compared to the benchmark, it is significantly overweighted in the industrials and basic materials sectors and far less granular in terms of the single name concentration risk involved.

The purpose of the following section is to show that with the help of a mathematical model and a related optimisation procedure, a multitude of qualitative and quantitative filtering criteria can be combined to formulate a set of inequality constraints (with or without reference to environmental objectives) under which an optimal structure of a target portfolio can be derived.

13.3.3 *Portfolio Optimisation under Sustainability Constraints: A Mathematical Model*

13.3.3.1 *Definitions and Introductory Explanations*

As a starting point, we define a set of investible assets that are considered relevant for the portfolio under consideration and number the elements of this set consecutively from $i = 1$ to N.

We define a portfolio of investible assets as a set of pairs $\{i, w_i\}$, $i = 1$ to N, in which each of the relevant assets i has been assigned a weighting factor w_i in such a way that the sum of the weighting factors adds up to 1.

Moreover, we assume the existence of a benchmark portfolio $\{i, \overline{w}_i\}$, $i = 1$ to N, of which the risk–return profile serves as a comparison scale for any actual or hypothetical real-world portfolio under examination. Such a benchmark portfolio may be based on an externally provided or internally calculated index or may have been built to represent an 'ideal' portfolio structure as it would stand if no side constraints (e.g., on the number of the positions taken) were in place.

13.3.3.2 *Asset Characteristics*

Group affiliations
Each individual asset i may or may not be affiliated with one or more group indexed by $g = 1, \ldots, G$. Such a group can be the asset class that asset i belongs to, its issuer's economic sector or country of residence, or currency the asset is denominated in. The entirety of group affiliations an asset may or may not have is captured by a $(\mathrm{G} \times 1)$ vector Z, each element of which is a binary indicator variable taking values 0 or 1. The gth element of its asset-specific realisation Z_i, denoted by $Z_{i,g}$, is set to 1 if asset i belongs to group g and to 0 otherwise.

Asset returns
The timescale is divided into successive intervals of equal length, each of which is represented by an integer number t. The return on

an asset in time interval t, denoted by $r_{i,t}$, can then be expressed as

$$r_{i,t} := (P_{i,t} + d_{i,t}) / P_{i,t-1},$$

where $P_{i,t}$ is the price of the asset at the end of time interval t, adjusted for the effect of past dividends and capital measures, and $d_{i,t}$ is the dividend per unit paid in time interval t.

Sustainability score
Each asset i is assumed to have a sustainability score S_i, scaled to a range from 0 (worst) to 1 (best) associated with it. Although the sustainability characteristics of an asset may change as time passes, the time index t is suppressed here because the value it takes is treated as constant by the time the portfolio formation decisions are taken.

13.3.3.3 *Criterion Function and Side Constraints*

The objective pursued is to form a portfolio having a financial risk–return profile resembling that of the benchmark as closely as possible while at the same time having a portfolio-wide sustainability score that equals or exceeds a predefined target value S^* that exceeds the sustainability score of the benchmark.

The degree of similarity prevailing between the risk–return profile of the portfolio and the benchmark can, pragmatically, be measured by the tracking error

$$\tau := \sum_{i=1}^{N} (w_i - \overline{w}_i)^2 \sigma_i^2 + 2 \cdot \sum_{i=1}^{N} \sum_{j=1}^{i-1} (w_i - \overline{w}_i)(w_j - \overline{w}_j) \rho_{i,j} \sigma_i \sigma_j. \tag{13.8}$$

Typically, a number of inequality constraints need to be observed when forming a portfolio. For example, it may have been decided that the number of distinct assets inside the portfolio must not exceed a predefined number M:

$$\sum_{i=1}^{N} I(w_i > 0) - M \overset{!}{\leq} 0. \tag{13.9}$$

Here, $I(\cdot)$ stands for an indicator function that is set to 1 if the condition in brackets is fulfilled and to 0 otherwise.

Moreover, the minimum condition relating to the sustainability indicator can be formulated as

$$S^* - \sum_{i=1}^{N} w_i \cdot S_i \overset{!}{\leq} 0. \tag{13.10}$$

Likewise, upper $(Z_g^{(u)})$ and lower $(Z_g^{(l)})$ limits to be imposed on the share of certain groups g of assets in the portfolio can be formally expressed as

$$\sum_{i=1}^{N} w_i \cdot Z_{i,g} - Z_g^{(u)} \overset{!}{\leq} 0 \tag{13.11a}$$

and

$$Z_g^{(l)} - \sum_{i=1}^{N} w_i \cdot Z_{i,g} \overset{!}{\leq} 0. \tag{13.11b}$$

Let

$$h(x) = (\max(x;0))^2. \tag{13.12}$$

Then, an approximate solution to this problem can be sought by minimising the criterion function

$$\begin{aligned}
\Lambda := & \sum_{i=1}^{N} (\tilde{w}_i - \overline{w}_i)^2 \sigma_i^2 \\
& + 2 \cdot \sum_{i=1}^{N} \sum_{j=1}^{i-1} (\tilde{w}_i - \overline{w}_i)(\tilde{w}_j - \overline{w}_j) \rho_{i,j}\sigma_i\sigma_j \\
& + \lambda_1 \cdot h\left(\sum_{i=1}^{N} I(w_i > 0) - M\right) \\
& + \lambda_2 \cdot h\left(S^* - \sum_{i=1}^{N} w_i \cdot S_i\right) \\
& + \lambda_3 \cdot h\left(w_i \cdot Z_{i,g} - Z_g^{(u)}\right) \\
& + \lambda_4 \cdot h\left(Z_g^{(l)} - \sum_{i=1}^{N} w_i \cdot Z_{i,g}\right).
\end{aligned} \tag{13.13}$$

The portfolio weights $\tilde{w}_i$ are expressed as a function of the auxiliary parameters δ_1 to δ_N as follows:

$$\tilde{w}_i = \frac{\exp(\delta_i)}{\sum_{j=1}^{N} \exp(\delta_j)}, \text{ with } \delta_1 = 1 \text{ and } \delta_2, \ldots, \delta_N \text{ being real numbers.} \tag{13.14}$$

A problem with this way of proceeding is that under the condition stated in (13.14), none of the weights can become exactly zero, so that it is impossible to meet condition (13.9). The proposed solution to this problem is to introduce a positive yet very small 'materiality threshold' Θ (in this example, $\Theta = 10^{-8}$) and to treat weights that fall below this threshold as if they were zeros.

Due to the possibility that the criterion function (13.13) has multiple local optima, a global search heuristic needs to be applied. In the case of the example application presented in the following section, a combination 'brute force' random search procedure was used in conjunction with the differential evolution algorithm due to Price (1999).

13.3.3.4 *Example Based on Simulated Data*

The following example demonstrates the feasibility of the approach sketched above in the context of a real-world portfolio. The universe of permissible investments, in this case, was assumed to be the Euro STOXX 50 stock market index. From this universe, in the first step, an unconstrained benchmark portfolio was created by deliberately overweighting past out performers (using the year 2020 as a reference period) relative to the index while, at the same time, keeping the sector allocation inside predefined target intervals in order to maintain a relatively high degree of diversification. The chosen sustainability indicator was the GHG intensity of the individual firm with each individual value entering the calculation with a negative sign because low emissions are associated with a high sustainability contribution. Firm-specific GHG intensity data (reporting year: 2020) are given in Figure 13.7.

The optimisation procedure sketched above was performed under the constraint that the GHG intensity of the target portfolio should be 15% lower than the corresponding value of the unconstrained benchmark.

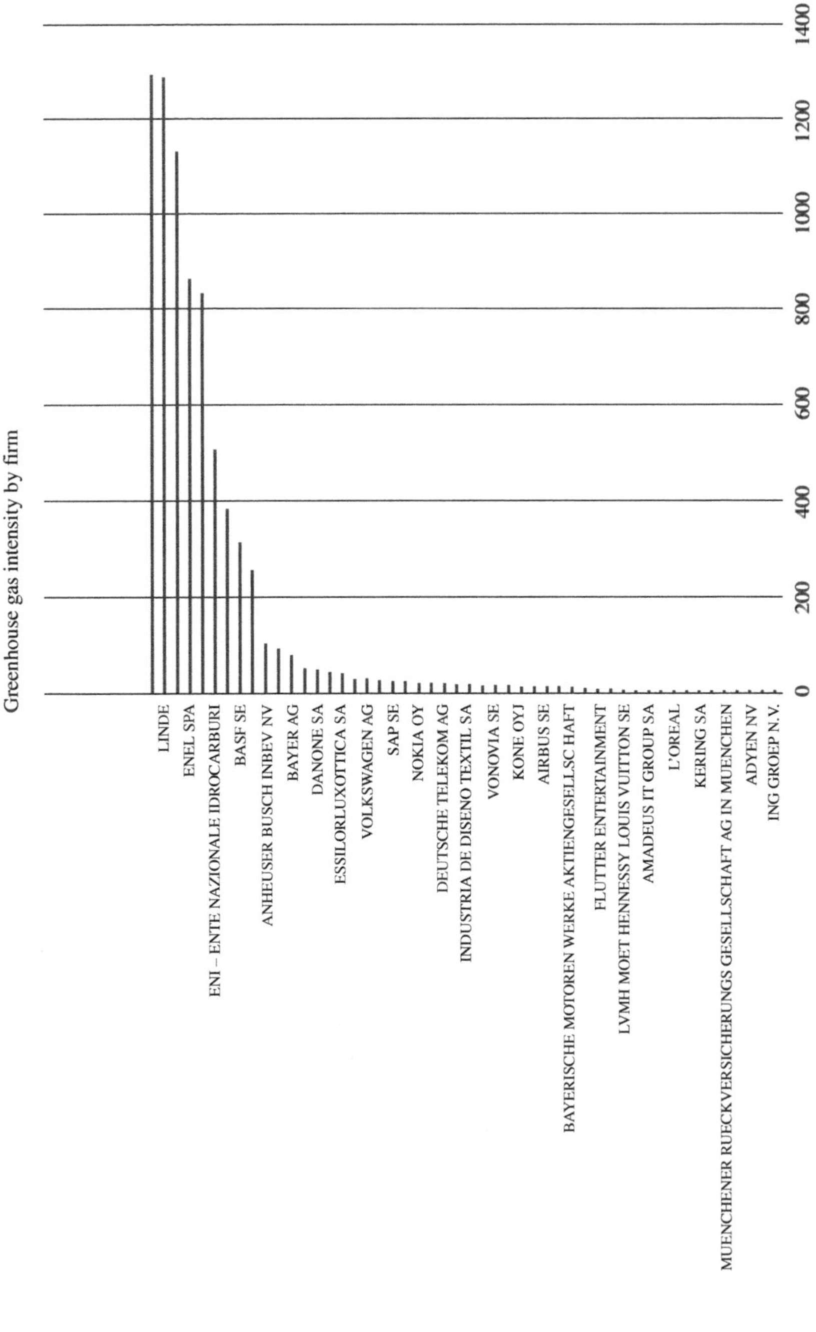

Fig. 13.7. GHG emissions by firm.

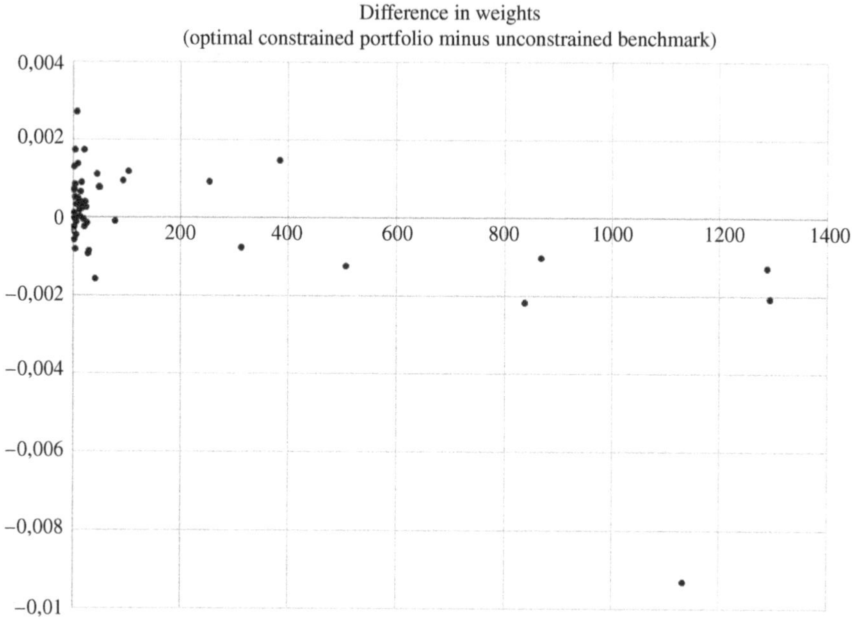

Fig. 13.8. Difference of weights.

The outcome of the calculation procedure is summarised as follows. The tracking error of the optimised portfolio could be limited to 0.15%, which will probably be considered acceptable by most users, particularly given the fact that the difference between the historical one-year returns on the unconstrained benchmark on the one hand and the optimised portfolio on the other turns out to be effectively zero. In Figures 13.8 and 13.9, the firm-specific greenhouse gas intensity is plotted on the horizontal axis, whereas the difference in the weights of the associated stocks in the optimal constrained portfolio vis-à-vis the benchmark is measured on the vertical axis, so that each individual stock is represented by a point in the corresponding scatter plot. As intuition would have led us to expect that the proposed optimisation procedure leads to a portfolio structure where stocks with a high emission intensity are systematically underweighted compared to the unconstrained benchmark.

The availability of company-level micro-data on a great variety of sustainability indicators presents asset managers with great opportunities for developing and implementing ethically responsible

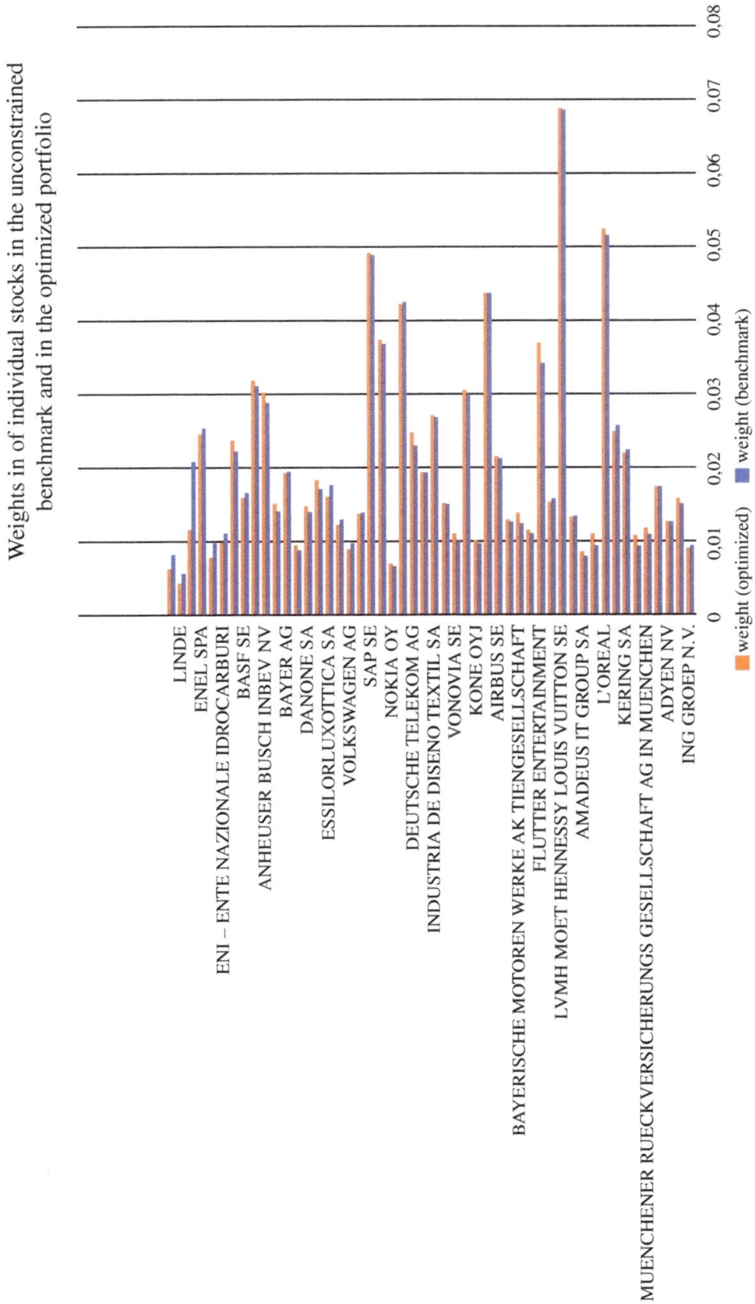

Fig. 13.9. Difference of weights.

and financially rewarding investment products. In order to benefit from this opportunity, however, the relevant indicators and selection criteria must be chosen, weighted, and aggregated carefully. It turns out that the use of mathematical models, in which the objectives pursued and the constraints to be observed are captured by a multidimensional criterion function, can be of great help when it comes to providing a reliable scientific basis for the related decision processes. The practical applicability of the sophisticated numerical optimisation techniques required to solve such problems and the fact that the outcomes produced fit well with economic intuition was demonstrated by an example application to a real-world equity portfolio model. This does not, however, relieve decision makers from the need of setting investment objectives and constraints in a logically consistent and empirically plausible manner.

Appendix A

Basics from Probability Theory and Financial Mathematics

The material of this appendix is based on the work of Bingham and Kiesel (2004) to which we refer for details and proofs.

Measurable space: We denote Ω as a sample space. A collection $\mathcal{A}_0$ of subsets of Ω is an algebra on Ω if

(1) $\Omega \in \mathcal{A}_0$,
(2) $A \in \mathcal{A}_0 \Rightarrow A^c = \Omega \setminus A \in \mathcal{A}_0$, and
(3) $A, B \in \mathcal{A}_0 \Rightarrow A \cup B \in \mathcal{A}_0$.

We call an algebra $\mathcal{A}$ of subsets of Ω σ-algebra on Ω if for a sequence A_n holds:

$$A_n \in \mathcal{A}, n \geq 1 \Rightarrow \bigcup_{n=1}^{\infty} A_n \in \mathcal{A}.$$

Consequently, every σ-algebra is an algebra. We denote the pair $(\Omega, \mathcal{A})$ as a measurable space.

Probability measure: We denote $\mathbb{P}$ as a probability measure on $(\Omega, \mathcal{A})$ if $\mathbb{P}$ fulfils the following axioms:

(1) For every $A \in \mathcal{A}$ exist a real number $\mathbb{P}(A)$ on the closed interval $[0, 1]$, the probability for A.
(2) $\mathbb{P}(\Omega) = 1$.

(3) For the disjunct outcomes, $\{A_n, n \geq 1\}$ hold
$\mathbb{P}\left(\bigcup_{n=1}^{\infty} A_n\right) = \sum_{n=1}^{\infty} \mathbb{P}(A_n)$ (σ-additivity).

Probability space: We call the triple $(\Omega, \mathcal{A}, \mathbb{P})$ a probability space.

- A probability space $(\Omega, \mathcal{F}, \mathbb{P})$ consists of a sample space Ω, a σ-algebra $\mathcal{F}$ (the set of events on Ω we attach a probability of happening to), and a probability measure $\mathbb{P}$.
- A filtered probability space $(\Omega, \mathcal{F}, (\mathcal{F}_t), \mathbb{P})$ allows one to dynamically increase information using a filtration $(\mathcal{F}_t)$ (an increasing family of σ-algebras, representing our knowledge $\mathcal{F}_t$ at time t increasing with t).
- The usual conditions are certain technical conditions which make a filtered probability space behave well.

We always assume that we work on a filtered probability space satisfying the usual conditions.

Stochastic process: We consider a collection $\mathcal{F}$ of subset of Ω, whose probabilities $\mathbb{P}(A)$ are defined and which are complete under the conditions of a σ-algebra. Thus, $\mathcal{F}$ is a σ-algebra on which $\mathbb{P}$ is defined. A random variable X is a $\mathcal{F}$-measurable function $X : \Omega \rightarrow \mathbb{R}$. Thus, for every $\omega \in \Omega$ $X(\omega)$ is a real number.

A stochastic process $\{X(t)\}_{t\in[0,T]}$ is a family of random variables, defined on some common probability space and parametrised by time t, i.e., for each $t \in [0, T]$, $X(t)$ is a random variable.

Martingales: Let $(\Omega, \mathcal{F}, \mathbb{P})$ be a probability space, let T be a fixed positive number, and let $\mathcal{F}(t)$, $0 \leq t \leq T$, be a filtration of sub σ-algebras of $\mathcal{F}$. Consider an adapted stochastic process M_t, $0 \leq t \leq T$.

(1) If

$$\mathbb{E}[M_t|\mathcal{F}_s] = M_s \quad \text{for all } 0 \leq s \leq t \leq T,$$

we say this process is a martingale. It has no tendency to rise or fall.

(2) If

$$\mathbb{E}[M_t|\mathcal{F}_s] \geq (\leq) M_s \quad \text{for all } 0 \leq s \leq t \leq T,$$

we say this process is a submartingale (supermartingale). It has no tendency to fall (rise), it may have a tendency to rise (fall).

Equivalent martingale measure:

- A probability measure $\mathbb{P}^*$ defined on $(\Omega, \mathcal{F}, \mathbb{F})$ is an equivalent martingale measure (EMM) if
    (i) $\mathbb{P}^*$ is equivalent to $\mathbb{P}$[1], and
    (ii) the discounted price process $\tilde{S}$ is a $\mathbb{P}^*$ martingale.
- The relevant facts of the martingale property in our context are as follows:
    - $\tilde{S}$ has a constant $\mathbb{P}^*$-expectation, and
    - the $\mathbb{P}^*$-dynamics of $\tilde{S}$ contain no drift.

EMMs and arbitrage: Assume $\mathbb{P}^*$ is an EMM. Then, the market model contains no arbitrage opportunities.

Complete market: A contingent claim X is a random variable satisfying some mild integrability conditions. A contingent claim X is called attainable if there exists at least one admissible trading strategy such that

$$V_\varphi(T) = X.$$

We call such a trading strategy φ a replicating strategy for X. A financial market model is said to be complete if any contingent claim is attainable.

Options:

- An option is a financial instrument giving one the *right, but not the obligation* to make a specified transaction at or by a specified date at a specified price, the *strike price.*
- *Call* options give one the right to buy an asset. *Put* options give one the right to sell an asset.

[1]Equivalent probability measures allocate zero probability to the same events.

- The date specified in the contract is called the *expiration date* or *maturity date.*
- *European* options can be exercised only on the expiry date. *American* options can be exercised at any time prior to or at expiry.

Payoff and profit:

- The payoff of a call option is

$$\max(S(T)-K,0)=\begin{cases} S(T)-K & \text{if } S(T)>K,\\ 0 & \text{otherwise,}\end{cases}$$

  more briefly written as $(S(T)-K)^{+}$.
- The payoff of a put option is

$$\max(K-S(T),0)=\begin{cases} K-S(T) & \text{if } K>S(T),\\ 0 & \text{otherwise,}\end{cases}$$

  more briefly written as $(K-S(T))^{+}$.
- The profit from an option is payoff minus option premium.

Forwards:

- A *forward contract* is an agreement to buy or sell an asset S at a certain future date T for a certain price K.
- The agent who agrees to buy the underlying asset is said to have a *long* position, the other agent is said to have a *short* position.
- The settlement date is called *delivery date* and the specified price is referred to as *delivery price.*

Payoff of a forward contract:

- The payoff from a long position in a forward contract on one unit of an asset with price $S(T)$ at the maturity of the contract is

$$S(T)-K.$$

- Compared with a call option with the same maturity T and strike price K, we see that the investor now faces a downside risk too. He has the obligation to buy the asset for price K.

Futures:

- Futures can be defined as standardised forward contracts traded at exchanges, where a clearing house acts as a central counterparty for all transactions.
- Usually, an initial margin is paid as a guarantee.
- Each trading day a settlement price is determined and gains or losses are immediately realised at a margin account.
- Thus, credit risk is eliminated, but there is exposure to interest rate risk.

Options vs. Futures/Forwards:

- A futures/forward contract gives the holder the obligation to buy or sell at a certain price.
- An option gives the holder the right (but not the obligation) to buy or sell at a certain price.

Arbitrage:

- Arbitrage means a guaranteed profit without exposure to risk. Given that rational agents are assumed, they would always accept such profit.
- The essence of the technical sense of arbitrage is that it should not be possible to guarantee a profit without exposure to risk. Were it possible to do so, arbitrageurs would do so, in unlimited quantity, using the market as a 'money-pump' to extract arbitrarily large quantities of riskless profit.
- The concept of arbitrage lies at the centre of the *arbitrage pricing technique.*
- *We assume that arbitrage opportunities do not exist!*

Put–call parity:

- We have the following put–call parity between the prices of the underlying asset S and European call and put options on stocks that pay no dividends:

$$S(t) + P(t) - C(t) = Ke^{-r(T-t)}.$$

- This may be shown by considering a portfolio consisting of one stock and one put long and one call short. Write $V(t)$ for the value of this portfolio. Then,

$$V(t) = S(t) + P(t) - C(t)$$

for all $t \in [0, T]$.

- At expiry, we have

$$V(T) = S(T) + (K - S(T))^+ - (S(T) - K)^+ = K.$$

- This portfolio guarantees a payoff of K at time T. Using the principle of no arbitrage, the value of the portfolio must at any time t correspond to the value of a sure payoff K at T that is $V(t) = Ke^{-r(T-t)}$.

Risk-neutral valuation formula: The arbitrage price process of any attainable claim is given by the risk-neutral valuation formula

$$\prod_X(t) = S_0(t)\mathbb{E}_{\mathbb{P}^*}\left[\frac{X}{S_0(T)}\middle|\mathcal{F}_t\right].$$

Black–Scholes model: The classical Black–Scholes model is

$$\begin{aligned} dB(t) &= rB(t)dt, & B(0) &= 1, \\ dS(t) &= S(t)(bdt + \sigma dW(t)), & S(0) &= p, \end{aligned}$$

with constant coefficients $b \in \mathbb{R},\ r, \sigma \in \mathbb{R}_+$.

The Black–Scholes price process of a European call is given by (we write Φ for the standard normal distribution function)

$$\begin{aligned} C(t) = S(t)&\Phi(d_1(S(t), T - t)) \\ &- Ke^{-r(T-t)}\Phi(d_2(S(t), T - t)). \end{aligned}$$

The functions $d_1(s, t)$ and $d_2(s, t)$ are given by

$$d_1(s, t) = \frac{\log(s/K) + (r + \frac{\sigma^2}{2})t}{\sigma\sqrt{t}}$$

and

$$d_2(s, t) = \frac{\log(s/K) + (r - \frac{\sigma^2}{2})t}{\sigma\sqrt{t}}, \text{ respectively.}$$

Simple futures market model:

- Black's model defines the market standard for pricing options on futures (forward) contracts. It models a single futures contract for a given maturity and does not take any dependencies for different maturities into account.
- It assumes the standard geometric Brownian motion model for the futures dynamics (no reference to the maturity T is needed):

$$dF(t) = \mu F(t)dt + \sigma F(t)dW(t).$$

- As it costs nothing to enter a futures position, there are no financing costs for changing the position. So, for pricing, we switch to the risk-neutral setting and the drift $\mu = 0$.

Black's formula:

- We use the usual notation — strike K, expiry T, $\tau = T - t$ for time to maturity as in the spot case, and write Φ for the standard normal distribution function.
- The arbitrage price C of a European futures call option is

$$\begin{aligned} C_{K,T}(t, K) = 7e^{-r\tau}F(t)\Phi(d_1(F(t), \tau)) \\ - e^{-r\tau}K\Phi(d_2(F(t), \tau)), \end{aligned} \tag{A.1}$$

where

$$d_{1,2}(F(t), \tau) := \frac{\log(F(t)/K) \pm \frac{1}{2}\sigma^2\tau}{\sigma\sqrt{\tau}}.$$

Hedging a futures position:

- Observe that the quantities d_1 and d_2 do not depend on the interest rate r.
- This is intuitively clear from the classical Black approach: One sets up a replicating risk-free portfolio consisting of a position in futures options and an offsetting position in the underlying futures contract. The portfolio requires no initial investment and therefore should not earn any interest.

Financial market model:

- We call an $\mathbb{R}^{d+1}$-valued process

$$\varphi(t) = (\varphi_0(t), \ldots, \varphi_d(t)), \quad t \in [0, T]$$

a trading strategy (or dynamic portfolio process).

- Here, $\varphi_i(t)$ denotes the number of shares of asset i held in the portfolio at time t — to be determined on the basis of information available *before* time t, i.e., the investor selects his time t portfolio after observing the prices $S(t-)$.

Portfolio process: The value of the portfolio φ at time t is given by

$$V_\varphi(t) := \varphi(t) \cdot S(t) = \sum_{i=0}^{d} \varphi_i(t) S_i(t).$$

$V_\varphi(t)$ is called the value process, or wealth process, of the trading strategy φ. The gains process $G_\varphi(t)$ is

$$G_\varphi(t) := \sum_{i=0}^{d} \int_0^t \varphi_i(u) dS_i(u).$$

Contingent claims: A contingent claims X is a random variable with existing expected value. A contingent claim X is called attainable if there exists at least one admissible trading strategy such that

$$V_\varphi(T) = X.$$

We call such a trading strategy φ a replicating strategy for X. A financial market model is said to be complete if any contingent claim is attainable. If a contingent claim X is attainable, X can be replicated by a portfolio $\varphi \in \Phi(\mathbb{P}^*)$. This means that holding the portfolio and holding the contingent claim are equivalent from a financial point of view. In the absence of arbitrage, the (arbitrage) price process $\Pi_X(t)$ of the contingent claim must therefore satisfy

$$\prod_X(t) = V_\varphi(t).$$

The arbitrage price process of any attainable claim is given by the risk-neutral valuation formula

$$\prod_X(t) = S_0(t) \mathbb{E}_{\mathbb{P}^*} \left[\frac{X}{S_0(T)} \middle| \mathcal{F}_t \right].$$

Controlled diffusion processes: Consider a control model where the state of the system is governed by a stochastic differential equation (SDE) valued in $\mathbb{R}^n$:

$$dX_s = b(X_s, \alpha_s)ds + \sigma(X_s, \alpha_s)dW_s, \tag{A.2}$$

where W is a d-dimensional Brownian motion on a filtered probability space $(\Omega, \mathcal{F}, (\mathcal{F}_t), \mathbb{P})$ satisfying the usual conditions. Further,

- assume the control $\alpha = (\alpha_s)$ is a (progressively measurable) stochastic process taking value in some set $A \subset \mathbb{R}^m$;
- assume that the functions $b : \mathbb{R}^n \times A \to \mathbb{R}^n$ and $\sigma : \mathbb{R}^n \times A \to \mathbb{R}^{n\times d}$ satisfy regularity conditions such that for any initial condition $(t, x) \in [0, T] \times \mathbb{R}^n$ the SDE (A.2) has a solution x at $s = t$;
- we denote by $\{X_s^{t,x,}, s \in [t, T]\}$ this solution with a.s. continuous paths;
- let $f : [0, T] \times \mathbb{R}^n \times A \to \mathbb{R}$ and $g : \mathbb{R}^n \to \mathbb{R}$ be two functions, which again satisfy suitable technical conditions;
- f and g describe running and terminal revenues, respectively.
- denote, by $\mathcal{A}(t, x)$, the subset of controls α of $\mathcal{A}$ such that

$$\mathbb{E}\left[\int_t^T |f(s, X_s^{t,x}, \alpha_s)|\mathrm{d}s\right] < \infty,$$

  and assume that $\mathcal{A}(t, x)$ is non-empty for all $(t, x) \in [0, T] \times \mathbb{R}^n$.

The gain function and the value function: Define the *gain function* as

$$J(t, x, \alpha) := \mathbb{E}\left[\int_t^T f(s, X_s^{t,x}, \alpha_s)\mathrm{d}s + g(X_T^{t,x})\right]$$

for all $(t, x) \in [0, T] \times \mathbb{R}^n$ and $\alpha \in \mathcal{A}(t, x)$. The objective is to maximise via the control process the function J. To this end, introduce the associated *value function*:

$$v(t, x) := \sup_{\alpha\in\mathcal{A}(t,x)} J(t, x, \alpha).$$

$\hat{\alpha} \in \mathcal{A}(t, x)$ is called an *optimal control* if $J(t, x, \hat{\alpha}) = v(t, x)$.

Continuous-time dynamic programming principle: As in the discrete case, the optimisation problem can be split into two parts: an optimal control on the whole interval $[t, T]$ may be obtained by first searching for an optimal control from time θ given the state value $X_\theta^{t,x}$, i.e., compute $v(\theta, X_\theta^{t,x})$ and then maximising over controls on $[t, \theta]$ the quantity

$$\mathbb{E}\left[\int_t^\theta f(s, X_s^{t,x}, \alpha_s)\mathrm{d}s + v(\theta, X_\theta^{t,x})\right],$$

where

$$\begin{aligned} v(t,x) &= \sup_{\alpha \in \mathcal{A}(t,x)} \sup_{\theta \in \mathcal{T}(t,T)} \mathbb{E}\left[\int_t^\theta f(s, X_s^{t,x}, \alpha_s)\mathrm{d}s + v(\theta, X_\theta^{t,x})\right], \\ &= \sup_{\alpha \in \mathcal{A}(t,x)} \inf_{\theta \in \mathcal{T}(t,T)} \mathbb{E}\left[\int_t^\theta f(s, X_s^{t,x}, \alpha_s)\mathrm{d}s + v(\theta, X_\theta^{t,x})\right]. \end{aligned}$$

The Hamilton–Jacobi–Bellman (HJB) equation: The HJB is the infinitesimal version of the dynamic programming principle. It describes the local behaviour of the value function when θ is close to t.

Consider the time $\theta = t + h$ with $h > 0$ and a control $\alpha \in \mathcal{A}(t, x)$. According to the dynamic programming principle,

$$v(t,x) \geq \mathbb{E}\left[\int_t^{t+h} f(s, X_s^{t,x}, \alpha_s)\mathrm{d}s + v(t+h, X_{t+h}^{t,x})\right]. \tag{A.3}$$

By assuming that v is smooth enough, one may apply Itô's formula:

$$v(t+h, X_{t+h}^{t,x}) = v(t,x) + \int_t^{t+h} \left(\frac{\partial v}{\partial t} + \mathcal{L}^{\alpha_s} v\right)(s, X_s^{t,x})\mathrm{d}s + \text{remainder},$$

where the remainder term is a (local) martingale and the operator $\mathcal{L}^a$ is defined by

$$\mathcal{L}^a v := b(x,a) \cdot D_x v + \frac{1}{2} tr\big(\sigma(x,a)\sigma'(x,a) D_x^2 v\big).$$

Taking expectations on both sides and substituting this into equation (A.3) yields

$$\mathbb{E}\left[\int_t^{t+h} \left(\frac{\partial v}{\partial t} + \mathcal{L}^{\alpha_s} v\right)(s, X_s^{t,x}) + f(s, X_s^{t,x}, \alpha_s)\mathrm{d}s\right] \leq 0.$$

Dividing by h and letting $h \to 0$, one obtains

$$\frac{\partial v}{\partial t}(t,x) + \mathcal{L}^a v(t,x) + f(t,x,a) \leq 0$$

for all $a \in A$. Choosing an optimal control $\alpha^* \in \mathcal{A}(t,x,)$ such that

$$v(t,x) = \mathbb{E}\left[\int_t^{t+h} f(s, X_s^{t,x}, \alpha_s^*)\mathrm{d}s + v(t+h, X_{t+h}^{t,x})\right],$$

one would have obtained

$$\frac{\partial v}{\partial t}(t,x) + \mathcal{L}^{\alpha^*} v(t,x) + f(t,x,\alpha^*) = 0.$$

This suggests that v should satisfy

$$\frac{\partial v}{\partial t}(t,x) + \sup_{a\in A}[\mathcal{L}^a v(t,x) + f(t,x,a)] = 0$$

for all $(t,x) \in [0,T) \times \mathbb{R}^n$. This equation is called the *Hamilton–Jacobi–Bellman equation* (HJB equation). Sometimes, this PDE is written in the form[2]

$$-\frac{\partial v}{\partial t}(t,x) - H(t,x,D_x v(t,x), D_x^2 v(t,x)) = 0 \qquad \text{(A.4)}$$

for all $(t,x) \in [0,T) \times \mathbb{R}^n$, where

$$H(t,x,p,M) = \sup_{a\in A}[b(x,a)\cdot p + \frac{1}{2}tr(\sigma(x,a)\sigma'(x,a)M) + f(t,x,a)].$$

The function H is called the Hamiltonian of the associated control problem.

The solution of (A.4) with terminal condition $v(T,x) = g(x)$ leads to the value function considered at the time horizon T.

Verification theorems: The HJB equation is a necessary but insufficient condition. A crucial step in this classical approach to dynamic programming consists therefore in proving that, given a smooth solution to the HJB equation, this candidate coincides with the value function. A broad range of 'verification theorems' is available but lies beyond the scope of this book.

---

[2] D_x and D_x^2, respectively, denote differentiating once and twice with respect to x.

Appendix B

Federated Learning Algorithm

B.1 The Algorithm

From now on, we abbreviate federated counting by $\mathfrak{C}$.

count: int = $\mathfrak{C}$ (condition_for_1, broadcasted_value)

This can be interpreted as follows. If, e.g.,

condition_for_1 = 'local_value > broad_casted_value',

then every institution needs to answer honestly whether the local value is bigger than the value given by the server (signal 1) or not (signal 0).

Differential privacy is achieved by modifying the local value. The reason is that our goal is not defending the result of the 'bigger than' question but the local number itself.

B.1.1 *Federated Median in the Range [0,1]*

Assume that every institution has secretly generated a value between 0.0 and 1.0, respectively, and has no opinion regarding this value. The goal is the federated determination of the median. We initialise by federatedly determining how many institutions actually have an opinion regarding this particular value. Afterwards, we determine the median via bisection (Press and Flannery, 1992). Therefore, we act as follows: The server shares with the institutions the current best guess for the median via public broadcast. The institutions secretly determine if their own value (modified by differential privacy) is bigger or smaller than this best guess.

(1) 0: no opinion or value smaller than best guess,
(2) 1: value bigger than best guess.

The median has the property of

$$\text{Number of values} > \text{median} = \text{number of values} < \text{median}.$$

Due to the monotonicity, we necessarily have convergence of the algorithm. Hence, we get the following federated algorithm for the median which we abbreviate with $\mathfrak{M}$:

```
def 𝔐():
lower: float = 0.0
upper: float = 1.0
number_companies = ℭ('has rating')
for count in range(MAX_ROUNDS):
median: float = (lower + upper) / 2
median_too_low = ℭ('has rating and rank(rating)
> median', median)
if median_too_low > number_companies / 2:
lower = median
else:
upper = median
return median
```

The server and, potentially, the institutions get to know something about the statistics of the distribution, but not who is actually thinking, that the value is bigger than the median and vice versa. Privately, the institutions get to know if their own value is bigger or smaller than the median obviously. A fraudulent institution has the possibility to change the value of the counting by ± 1. If the rest of the values has a non-pathological distribution, the change in the median is marginal. In order to achieve this goal, we could also have obviously used any other robust aggregation method (Pillutla *et al.*, 2019).

However, if the number of malevolent institutions is in the majority, these can both actively determine the value of the other participants or manipulate the outcome. But the attribution of a value to a certain institution stays secret. There are further algorithms to determine federatedly the median and other robust estimators, e.g., Pillutla *et al.* (2019). The above method was chosen due to its simplicity and resilience with respect to fraudulent participants.

B.1.2 *Rank Statistics*

For an aggregating assessment, it is basically impossible to reproduce proper ratings due to the liberty the institutions have defining their own rating v. However, it is still possible to sensibly determine the truth of the following statement: Company A is better than company B. One can mathematically map this to an equivalent rank statistic.

That is, if it holds for the values $v_{i_0} \leq v_{i_2} \leq \cdots \leq v_{i_n}$, then the corresponding rank is defined as

$$r_{i_k} = \frac{k}{n}.$$

Note that this is not equality and order preserving. If two values are equal, their rank is still different.

B.1.3 *Determining Participating Companies*

Using federated counting, we could determine for each company if at least three institutions have an opinion regarding this company. The higher one sets this threshold, the more secure the assessment gets with respect to possible manipulation attempts. This seems to be the absolute minimum.

It is likely that techniques like 'encrypted entity alignment' (Yang *et al.*, 2020) yield similar results.

To make the above simple algorithm differentially private, each participant needs to deliver instead of its own value (yes/no) with probability p the opposite. Obviously, this requires a readjustment of the threshold such that one has extremely high probability for minimally at least three institutions.

However, as we think that this information is just of moderate importance, we consider the security added by the federated counting as sufficient.

If one thinks that there is at least one malevolent player, we would strongly advice to improve the threshold to five or higher.

B.1.4 *Remarks on Optimisation*

To determine mapping functions from rating to local ranks, we will run into the following problem:

(1) $\mu(\Omega)$: the rank given for company Ω by the server,
(2) $f_{x_0,\ldots,x_n}(\nu(\Omega))$: the function which maps the rating $\nu(\Omega)$ of a company Ω into a rank, and
(3) $x_0, \ldots, x_n \in \mathbb{R}$: parameters which determine the form of the function.

That is, we have an error vector

$$e = \begin{pmatrix} f_{x_0,\ldots,x_n}(\nu(\Omega_1)) - \mu(\Omega_1) \\ \cdots \\ f_{x_0,\ldots,x_n}(\nu(\Omega_{\mathrm{N}})) - \mu(\Omega_N) \end{pmatrix}.$$

Now, we want to optimise $f_{x_0,\ldots,x_n}$ such that it minimises the distance between given ranks from the server to the ranks given by the server for some distance like function $d(\ )$, i.e.,

$$\min_{x_0,\ldots,x_n} d(e).$$

To do this, we need a Jacobian J (respectively a Jacobian-like) matrix of derivatives, i.e., for every $\nu(\Omega)$ and for every x_i, we need the following derivative:

$$\frac{\partial f_{x_0,\ldots,x_n}(\nu(\Omega))}{\partial x_j}.$$

Knowing these, we can determine the direction of search by 'inverting':

$$J^{-1}e.$$

Inverting is in most cases non-trivial because either J does not possess full rank (i.e., we need to add auxiliary known information about f) or J is rectangular, i.e., we have an overdetermined linear system to solve. Furthermore, the inversion of J might be unstable due to an unfavourable distribution of eigenvalues. Therefore, we will use in these cases the regularised Moore–Penrose inverse to determine the direction of the update:

$$\left(J^T J + \varepsilon I\right)^{-1} J^T e,$$

where I is the identity matrix and ε is a regularisation parameter. This regularisation method is known under a variety of names, e.g., Tikhonov regularisation, Tikhonov–Phillips regularisation, or Ridge regression (Engl and Neubauer, 2000). As we deal with extremely small problems, the choice of ε will not affect the solution too much (professional opinion of Bauer and Lukas (2011)). The dimension of the system of equations is hence not the number of companies but the number of x_i. Thus, solving is virtually for free.

We cannot apply naïvely the update to the function as we are in the realm of nonlinear optimisation. Therefore, when we know the direction of the update, we can determine the update itself using a simple line search, which minimises the error (Press and Flannery, 1992). This is nothing but one of the manifold modifications of the steepest descent Newton method for nonlinear optimisation (Press and Flannery, 1992).

B.1.5 *Local Rank Determination*

To simplify, we assume that the rank is projected to the interval $[0, 1]$. Regarding the local rank determination, we consider two different cases. Every time when an institution has no opinion at all, it sends an NaN (not a number = standard indicator for a value which should not be used downstream).

That is, for every company, every institution signals the following, where $r(\Omega, \Xi)$ is the internal rating of Ξ for company Ω, if available:

$$f(\Omega, \Xi) = \begin{cases} f_\Xi(r(\Omega, \Xi)) & \text{if } r(\Omega,\ \Xi) \text{ exists,} \\ \text{NaN} & \text{otherwise.} \end{cases}$$

Hence, we need to elaborate on the determination of f_Ξ. To perform the optimisation steps later on, we need to determine the derivatives of f_Ξ.

Rating categories: For now, we assume that we have n rating categories. For the sake of simplicity, we assume that they are numbered consecutively: 1 for the worst and n for the best one.

As we deal with a sorting into categories, we could signal for each category a rank $r_1, \ldots, r_n$ to the server, where the r_i are monotonous, i.e., $0.0 < r_1 < r_2 < \cdots < r_n < 1.0$.

Forward step: We choose values $x_0, \ldots, x_n \in \mathbb{R}$ and determine r_i:

$$r_k = \frac{\sum_{i=0}^{k-1} |x_i|}{\sum_{i=0}^{n} |x_i|}.$$

Without loss of generality, we could always normalise x_i such that they coincide with the r_i:

$$x_i := \frac{|x_i|}{\sum_{i=0}^{n} |x_i|}.$$

Hence, we can assume in most situations $\sum x_i = 1$, and thus,

$$r_k = \frac{\sum_{i=0}^{k-1} x_i}{\sum_{i=0}^{n} x_i} = \sum_{i=0}^{k-1} x_i.$$

Jacobian: Using the quotient rule, it holds for the derivative for $k \leq j$:

$$\frac{\partial r_k}{\partial x_j} = \frac{\partial}{\partial x_j} \frac{\sum_{i=0}^{k-1} x_i}{\sum_{i=0}^{n} x_i} = \frac{-\sum_{i=0}^{k-1} x_i}{\left(\sum_{i=0}^{n} x_i\right)^2} = -r_k.$$

Respectively, for $k > j$,

$$\frac{\partial r_k}{\partial x_j} = \frac{\partial}{\partial x_j} \frac{\sum_{i=0}^{k-1} x_i}{\sum_{i=0}^{n} x_i} = \frac{\sum_{i=0}^{n} x_i - \sum_{i=0}^{k-1} x_i}{\left(\sum_{i=0}^{n} x_i\right)^2} = 1 - r_k.$$

Hence, we have determined the exact representation of the Jacobian of our mapping. As this one cannot have full rank due to its dimensionality, we need to add the equation $\sum x_i = 1$.

Remark: Fraudulent institutions, also called byzantine in the literature, can send whatever it wants as outcome in the forward step. The calculation of the Jacobian is not necessary as the malevolent institution has no interest in improving its own result.

Continuous rating: For the rank determination, we will use linear splines (Press and Flannery, 1992), otherwise the method is similar to the one with discrete categories.

Forward step: Between minimal and maximal ratings, we put evenly distributed support points $s_1, \ldots, s_n$. Each rating is attributed correspondingly to its neighbouring support points, i.e., if

$$s_k \leq \rho(\Omega, \Xi) \leq s_{k+1},$$

then we attribute to Ω the numbers $\frac{s_{k+1}-\rho(\Omega,\Xi)}{s_{k+1}-s_k}$ and $\frac{\rho(\Omega,\Xi)-s_k}{s_{k+1}-s_k}$, which add to 1.

Each support point is mapped to a rank $0.0 < r_1 < r_2 < \cdots < r_n < 1.0$, i.e.,

$$r_k \frac{s_{k+1} - \rho(\Omega, \Xi)}{s_{k+1} - s_k} + r_{k+1} \frac{\rho(\Omega, \Xi) - s_k}{s_{k+1} - s_k}.$$

Due to the monotonicity of r_i, we have monotonicity in the coefficients. Again, we choose the numbers $x_0, \ldots, x_n \in \mathbb{R}$ such that

$$r_k = \frac{\sum_{i=0}^{k-1} |x_i|}{\sum_{i=0}^{n} |x_i|}.$$

Without loss of generality, we could always normalise x_i such that they coincide with the r_i:

$$x_i := \frac{|x_i|}{\sum_{i=0}^{n} |x_i|}.$$

Hence, we can assume in most situations $\sum x_i = 1$, and thus,

$$r_k = \frac{\sum_{i=0}^{k-1} x_i}{\sum_{i=0}^{n} x_i} = \sum_{i=0}^{k-1} x_i.$$

Denote $\tau = \frac{\rho(\Omega,\Xi)-s_k}{s_{k+1}-s_k}$. Then, the following holds:

$$f(\rho(\Omega, \Xi)) = r_k (1 - \tau) + r_{k+1}\tau = \frac{\sum_{i=0}^{k-1} x_i + \tau x_k}{\sum_{i=0}^{n} x_i} = \sum_{i=0}^{k-1} x_i + \tau x_k.$$

Jacobian: For the derivative, we need to distinguish three cases. First, consider $k < j$:

$$\frac{\partial f}{\partial x_j} = \frac{\partial}{\partial x_j} \frac{\sum_{i=0}^{k-1} x_i + \tau x_k}{\sum_{i=0}^{n} x_i} = \frac{-\sum_{i=0}^{k-1} x_i + \tau x_k}{\left(\sum_{i=0}^{n} x_i\right)^2} = -f.$$

Then, for $k = j$,

$$\frac{\partial f}{\partial x_j} = \frac{\partial}{\partial x_j} \frac{\sum_{i=0}^{k-1} x_i + \tau x_k}{\sum_{i=0}^{n} x_i} = \frac{\tau \sum_{i=0}^{n} x_i - \left(\sum_{i=0}^{k-1} x_i + \tau x_k\right)}{\left(\sum_{i=0}^{n} x_i\right)^2} = \tau - f.$$

Finally, for $k > j$,

$$\frac{\partial f}{\partial x_j} = \frac{\partial}{\partial x_j} \frac{\sum_{i=0}^{k-1} x_i + \tau x_k}{\sum_{i=0}^{n} x_i} = \frac{\sum_{i=0}^{n} x_i - \left(\sum_{i=0}^{k-1} x_i + \tau x_k\right)}{\left(\sum_{i=0}^{n} x_i\right)^2} = 1 - f.$$

B.2 Simulation

The general ideas underlying the simulation can be summarised as follows:

(1) There exists a global number $\aleph(\Omega)$ which reflects the true sustainability performance of a company Ω. This number, however, is 'latent' in the sense that it is not known to any of the participants. We can use these quantities to determine the reliability of the model in use via simulation.

(2) As in real life, sustainability is assumed to have several particular aspects, and a given company will rarely, if ever, perform equally well (or equally badly) in each individual subfield of this domain. For example, two companies that rank equally with respect to their overall sustainability score might still differ in specific areas: One might have a low carbon footprint by using sophisticated carbon capture and storage technologies, while the other one attains the same goal by minimising the consumption of energy from fossil fuels. To capture the multiplicity of aspects that enter an overall sustainability assessment, while at the same time maintaining a parsimonious specification, we restrict ourselves to four random factors, which will average exactly to the true, company-specific, overall sustainability performance indicator. Again, these four factors are latent, i.e., never observable to

any of the participating parties. Choosing a total number of four factors is completely arbitrary; it reflects a compromise between the needs to account for the multiplicity of sustainability factors and the need to maintain parsimony and computational tractability.

(3) In a real-life situation, approximate estimates of the strength or weakness of certain sustainability-related factors of influence can, for example, be obtained by studying related disclosures in companies' annual reports or by examining the information disseminated by adequately specialised data providers or research institutes. In our model, this perception is mirrored by the assumption that the company-specific realisations of the above four factors can be measured with some random error (or 'noise').

(4) Different financial institutions may have different areas of specialisation and serve different client groups in their respective business. In our model, this is captured by the assumption that each institution is completely free to choose which companies it considers and which ones it does not cover. However, simulating this attribution process as purely random might lead to a far greater degree of homogeneity among the observed profiles of the model institutions than we can realistically expect to observe in real life. Therefore, we include a bias term that introduces some degree of statistical dependence between the sustainability performance of a company and the likelihood of being considered by a certain institution.

(5) In real-life situations, the ways in which indicators relating to different aspects of sustainability are aggregated to form a summary sustainability score or rating grade differ considerably among institutions. In our model, this phenomenon is mirrored by the assumption that each institution is completely free to choose how it aggregates the four numbers it gets for a given company into one single rating. We will simulate that by randomly assigning weights to the individual measurements. Most institutions will additionally condense the information thus obtained by assigning firms to rating 'buckets' depending on the specific interval in which the summary rating score lies. In line with experience from real-life situations, we assume that the number of buckets on the rating scale, and the way in which the related intervals being set, differ randomly among institutions.

To incorporate these sources of randomness and uncertainty, we will use a lot of independent random variables. The exact choices made for the underlying parameters (e.g., means, standard deviations, etc.) is of secondary importance and thus made arbitrarily because the main objective pursued here is to capture the heterogeneity of companies, institutions, and rating methodologies that we find in real life in an approximate manner.

What follows is a short glossary:

$\mathcal{N}(m, \sigma)$	Standard-Normal distribution with average m and variance σ
$\mathcal{G}(u, o)$	Uniform distribution with bounds u and o
Hebrew letters $\aleph, \beth, \daleth$	Latent variables, which are unknown to everybody
Greek small letters	Characteristics and their measurement
Greek capital letters	Names or assignments
Numbers with '.'	Floating point numbers. i.e., $\mathcal{G}(0, 1) \in \{0, 1\}$ whereas $\mathcal{G}(0.0, 1.0) \in [0.0, 1.0]$

Sustainability of a company: To simulate a realistic scenario and simultaneously be capable of reliably assessing our ansatz, we have the following assumptions:

(1) Each company Ω is assigned a $\mathcal{N}(0, 1)$ distributed random variable $\aleph(\Omega)$, which describes its real sustainability. This is covert to all participants and will just be used to assess the quality of our ansatz in the simulation.

(2) Each company Ω is assigned four additional $\mathcal{N}(0, 0.2)$ distributed random variables $\beth_1(\Omega)$, $\beth_2(\Omega)$, $\beth_3(\Omega)$, $\beth_4(\Omega)$. Out of these, we compute the outside visible characteristics of the real sustainability using the following formula:

$$\daleth_i(\Omega) = \aleph(\Omega) + \beth_i(\Omega) - \frac{\sum_{i=1}^{4} \beth_i(\Omega)}{4}.$$

Hence,

$$\frac{\sum_{i=1}^{4} \daleth_i(\Omega)}{4} = \aleph\left(\Omega\right).$$

An institution Ξ can measure these characteristics once and retrieves four measurements of these characteristics $\alpha_i(\Omega, \Xi)$. For each i, the following holds:

$$\alpha_i\left(\Omega, \Xi\right) = \daleth_i\left(\Omega\right) + \mathcal{N}\left(0, 0.1\right).$$

In principle, every institution Ξ could freely decide how to aggregate the $\alpha_i\left(\Omega, \Xi\right)$ to a rating $\rho(\Omega, \Xi)$. Besides the possibility of issuing a regular rating, we also consider the possibility of arbitrary or coordinated assessments. These will be presented subsequently.

Fraudulent ratings: We now present different kinds of fraud. Obviously, this collection is not exhaustive.

Wrong or arbitrary rating: Ξ is completely free choosing $\rho(\Omega, \Xi)$. For the sake of simplicity, we assume that 5% of the companies are marked as 'favourites' (rating 1), additional 5% as 'enemies' (rating 0) and 40% of the companies as 'I could not care less' (rating 0.5). The remaining 50% will be marked as unknown.

Collaboration: For the sake of simplicity, we assume that in this case the institution performs a one-to-one copy of the answers of the second institution and hands these in as its own answers.

Replay attack: The institution remembers the latest result of the joint rating computation and passes this as its own rating.

Valid ratings: Honest institutions need to answer the following questions internally:

(1) For which company do we want to issue a rating?
(2) How do we aggregate the known information?
(3) How do we present the aggregated information?

To represent the heterogeneity of the participating institutes, we employ again random elements in our simulation.

Issuing an assessment: Not every institution will know every company and issue an opinion regarding that company. Additionally, institutions typically specialise and just regard fuzzy subsets of companies. Therefore, we approach the task as follows.

For the institution, we draw randomly $\mathcal{G}(1,4)$ an integer $i(\Xi) \in \{1, 2, 3, 4\}$. Additionally, we draw a $\mathcal{N}(0,1)$ distributed random number $\beta(\Xi)$, a kind of 'bias' which represents the institute-specific specialisation. Additionally, we randomise for each company with another $\mathcal{N}(0, 0.5)$ distributed random variable $\varphi(\Omega, \Xi)$. Finally, we draw randomly $\mathcal{G}(0.1, 0.9)$ a coverage percentage $\tau(\Xi)$.

If and only if $\left|\alpha_{i(\Xi)}(\Omega, \Xi) - \beta(\Xi)\right| + \varphi(\Omega, \Xi)$ within the $\tau(\Xi)$ smallest values, then a rating is issued, otherwise not.

Locally continuous assessment: Ξ freely chooses (in our simulation randomly) four parameters $\overline{\beta_i(\Xi)}$ independently distributed $\mathcal{G}(0.0, 1.0)$ and normalises these to weights

$$\beta_i(\Xi) = \frac{\overline{\beta_i(\Xi)}}{\sum_{i=1}^{4} \overline{\beta_i(\Xi)}}.$$

Afterwards, one defines the locally continuous assessment as a weighted sum of the visible characteristics of the sustainability $\aleph(\Omega)$:

$$\overline{\rho(\Omega, \Xi)} = \sum_{i=1}^{4} \beta_i(\Xi)\, \alpha_i(\Omega, \Xi).$$

Continuous ratings: Return $\rho(\Omega, \Xi) = \overline{\rho(\Omega, \Xi)}$.

Rating categories: As described in the continuous case, we will first choose $\beta_i(\Xi)$ to generate a locally continuous assessment $\overline{\rho(\Omega, \Xi)}$. Afterwards, we randomly determine the number of potential rating categories $m(\Xi)$ out of $\mathcal{G}(6, 21)$. Afterwards, we draw the boundaries $\gamma_1(\Xi), \gamma_2(\Xi), \ldots, \gamma_{m(\Xi)-1}(\Xi)$ randomly from $\mathcal{N}(0, 1)$ and sort them in ascending order. Virtually, we add the boundaries $\gamma_0(\Xi) = -\infty$ and $\gamma_{m(\Xi)}(\Xi) = \infty$. To rule out pathological cases, we remove all empty rating levels.
The following holds:

$$\rho(\Omega, \Xi) = k \Longleftrightarrow \gamma_{k-1}(\Xi) < \overline{\rho(\Omega, \Xi)} \leq \gamma_k(\Xi).$$

For every k, there exists at least one attributed company.

Composition: The choice of assumptions, how many institutions are fraudulent, continuous or with discrete rating levels, is completely up to us. However, to reach some minimal stability, we need to simulate a certain minimal number of institutions, keeping the number of fraudulent ones in a small minority.

Additionally, the provisions to keep unconditional secrecy have a negative impact on the overall precision which again needs to be compensated by a higher number of participating institutions.

B.3 Concluding Remarks

It is important to see, before a real implementation, if the general concepts work in principle. Therefore, we set up a Python prototype, which performs the simulation as described. This is just an algorithm test. Testing the stability in a real-life environment, at best with shaky communication lines, needs to be the next step.

Some examples for numbers: To familiarise, we will just display some numbers from an experiment, the variances as indicated in the simulation section:

- Real sustainability (shadowed): [0.4706],
- Sustainability indicators (shadowed): [0.4684, 0.6714, 0.4025, 0.3400],
- Measurements, company 1: [0.4364, 0.5247, 0.3645, 0.1449],
- Measurements, company 2: none because company not included,
- Measurements, company 3: [0.5215, 0.6411, 0.2979, 0.3096],
- ...

Other parameters:

- Companies: 1000
- Malevolent institutions (manipulative value): 2
- Malevolent institutions (copy of another): 1
- Malevolent institutions (replay attack): 1
- Honest institutions (rating categories): 10
- Honest institutions (continuous rating): 7

That is, depending on the way one counts the copied institution, we have slightly below or slightly above 20% of malevolent institutions, which disturb the overall rank determination process.

We hope that this number is by far exaggerated when it comes to real-world applications. Consider the human factor: If someone knows that most likely cheating does not give any positive impact for oneself, but it means work and potentially even harms oneself, then it is by far more likely that the person just would not participate.

Federated computation: We chose as federation method secret sharing. This was performed by three different classes within the same thread. So, we could consider this as a proof of concept but still far away from a viable life implementation. In such a life implementation, we could realise on the one hand heavy speed gains due to the intrinsic parallelisability of the process and on the other hand also significant slowing down due to the necessary client–server traffic.

As all other federated computations, the security overheads make them rather slow. On an up-to-date desktop computer with a non-optimised single-threaded implementation, the overall run time is about three minutes. This is about 2–3 orders of magnitudes slower than simply taking the median without any security precautions.

It is important to note that the algorithm is linear in the number of considered companies and linear in the number of participating institutions. Hence, overall, we judge the algorithm itself application capable.

Results: We heavily work with random numbers. Therefore, the following results could just be seen as indicative. Every implementation might see slightly different results. However, we expect the overall behaviour to be comparable.

If one would arbitrarily rank the companies, one would get an error of 40.3%, i.e., on average, the distance of the real rank and the assigned arbitrary rank is 40% of the field. Even without any calibration, by simply making a federated aggregation of the local rankings, one can reduce the error to 11.4%. Within four steps, this further reduces to 4.0% and more than two-thirds of the institutions are content with the result and hence the iteration stops. In this context, we assumed that the malevolent clients pretended to be always content with the current solution. So, we had about 50% of the regular clients who actually considered the solution to be non-improvable.

As expected, the error if one just looks within the institutions itself is slightly higher, since they work on disturbed data and not like the server on averaged and therefore approximatively undisturbed data. However, the overall trend is similar, the error declines from 13.9% to 5.1% within four iterations.

If one runs artificially more iterations, the overall result does not change too much more. In general, the error stabilises around the given values.

Bibliography

Alt, F. (2021). Der Märchenwald. *Transparenz TV*. Premiered at February 9, 2021. Available at https://www.youtube.com/watch?v=_J34lXxrp_o.

Alòs, E., Eydeland, A., and Laurence, P. (2011). A Kirk's and a Bachelier's formula for three asset spread options, *Energy Risk* **9**, 52–57.

Andersson, M., Bolton, P., and Samama, F. (2016). Hedging climate risk, *Financial Analysts Journal* **72**, 3, 13–32.

Atkins, T. (2014). Deutsche Bank settles Kirch case in milestone deal, *Reuters*.

Bajic, A., Hellmich, M., and Kiesel, R. (2021). Handle with care: Challenges and opportunities of using company-level emissions data for assessing financial risks from climate change, *HEMF Working Paper*.

Baltagi, B. H. (2001). *Econometric Analysis of Panel Data* (New York: Wiley).

Bank of England (2019). The 2021 biennial exploratory scenario on the financial risks from climate change, *BoE Discussion Paper*.

Bannör, K., Kiesel, R., Nazarova, A., and Scherer, M. (2016). Parametric model risk and power plant valuation, *Energy Economics* **59**, C, 423–434.

Barkemeyer, R., Figge, F., Hoepner, A., Holt, D., Kraak, J. M., and Yu, P.-S. (2017). Media coverage of climate change: An international comparison, *Environment and Planning C: Politics and Space* **35**, 1029–1054. doi:https://doi.org/10.1177/0263774X16680818.

Barnett, M., Brock, W. A., and Hansen, L. P. (2019). Pricing Uncertainty Induced by Climate Change, *University of Chicago, Becker Friedman Institute for Economics Working Paper No. 2019-109.* doi:http://dx.doi.org/10.2139/ssrn.3440301.

Barrieu, M. and Fehr, P. (2010). Integrated EUA and CER pricing and application for spread option pricing, *Working Paper.*

Barth, F., Hübel, B., and Scholz, H. (2020). ESG and Corporate Credit Spreads, *SSRN.*

Battiston, S., Mandel, A., and Monasterolo, I. (2017). A climate stress-test of the financial system. *Nature Climate Change* **7**, 283–288.

Bauer, F. and Lukas, M. (2011). Comparing parameter choice methods for regularization of ill-posed problems, *Mathematics and Computers in Simulation* **81**, 1795–1841.

Behncke, N., Bassen, A., and Lopatta, K. (2020). *Klimaberichterstattung bei boersennotierten Unternehmen*, PwC report.

Bernoville, T. (2020). *What are Scopes 1, 2 and 3 of Carbon Emissions? Plan A Academy.* https://plana.earth/academy/what-are-scope-1-2-3-emissions/.

Beschloss, A. and Mashayekhi, M. (2019). A greener future for finance — Green bonds offer lessons for sustainable finance, *IMF Finance and Development* **56**, 4.

Bielecki, T. and Rutkowski, M. (2002). *Credit Risk: Modelling, Valuation and Hedging* (New York: Springer).

Bingham, N. H. and Kiesel, R. (2004). *Risk-Neutral Valuation: Pricing and Hedging of Financial Derivatives*, 2nd ed. (London: Springer-Verlag).

Blasberg, A. and Kiesel, R. (2021). CDS spreads and E-scores, *HEMF Working Paper.*

Blasberg, A., Kiesel, R., and Taschini, L. (2021). Climate default swap — Disentangling the exposure to transition risk through cds, *HEMF Working Paper*.

Bodie, Z., Kane, A., and Marcus, A. J. (2020). *Investments*, 12th ed. (McGraw-Hill Education Ltd.).

Bolton, P., Despres, M., Pereira da Silva, L., Samama, F., and Svartzman, R. (2020). *The Green Swan: Central Banking and Financial Stability in the Age of Climate Change Risk* (Bank for International Settlement).

Bolton, P. and Kacperczyk (2020). Do investors care about carbon risk? *NBER Working Paper.*

Bolton, P. and Kacperczyk, M. T. (2021). Global pricing of carbon-transition risk. doi:http://dx.doi.org/10.2139/ssrn.3550233.

Boscovic, D. (2021). How non fungible tokens work and where they get their value — A cryptocurrency expert explains NFTs, *The Conversation.*

Bouchet, V. and Le Guenedal, T. (2020). Credit risk sensitivity to carbon price. doi:http://dx.doi.org/10.2139/ssrn.3574486.

Boykoff, M. T. (2013). Public Enemy No. 1?: Understanding Media Representations of Outlier Views on Climate Change, *American Behavioral Scientist (ABS)* **57**, 796–817, doi:https://doi.org/10.1177/0002764213476846.

Brainard, L. (2021). The role of financial institutions in tackling the challenges of climate change, Speech at 2021 IIF U.S. Climate Finance Summit.

Bundesministerium der Finanzen (2020). Pressemitteilung.

Burke, M., Hsiang, S. M., and Miguel, E. (2020). Global non-linear effect of temperature on economic production, *Nature* **527**, 235–239. doi:https://doi.org/10.1038/nature15725.

Busch, M., Johnson, T., and Pioch, T. (2018). Consistency of corporate carbon emission data, *University of Hamburg Report WWF Deutschland.*

Caesar, L., McCarthy, G. D., Thornalley, D. J. R., Cahill, N., and Rahmstorf, S. (2021). Current Atlantic Meridional Overturning Circulation weakest in last millennium, *Nature Geoscience* **14**, 118–120, doi:https://doi.org/10.1038/s41561-021-00699-z.

Cai, Y. and Lontzek, T. S. (2019). The social cost of carbon with economic and climate risks, *Journal of Political Economy* **127**. doi:https://doi.org/10.1086/701890.

Campiglio, E., Dafermos, Y., Monnin, P., Ryan-Collins, J., Schotten, G., and Tanaka, M. (2018). Climate change challenges for central banks and financial regulators, *Nature Climate Change* **8**, 462–468. doi:https://doi.org/10.1038/s41558-018-0175-0.

Capasso, G., Gianfrate, G., and Spinelli, M. (2020). Climate change and credit risk, *Journal of Cleaner Production* **266**, 121634.

Carbon Tracker (2013). Unburnable carbon 2013: Wasted capital and stranded assets, *Technical Report.*

Carbon Tracker (2015). The $2 trillion stranded assets danger zone: How fossil fuel firms risk destroying investor returns, *Carbon Tracker Initiative.*

Carhart, M. (1997). On persistence in mutual fund performance, *The Journal of Finance* **51**, 1, 57–82.

Carmona, R. and Durrleman, V. (2003). Pricing and hedging spread options in an log-normal model, *SIAM Review* **45**, 627–685.

Carmona, R., Fehr, M., and Hinz, J. (2009). Optimal stochastic control and carbon price formation, *SIAM Journal of Control and Optimization* **48**, 2168–2190.

Carmona, R. and Hinz, J. (2010). Risk-neutral models for emission allowance prices and option valuation.

Carney, M. (2021). *Value(s) – Building a Better World for All* (UK: HarperCollins Publishers).

CDP, CDSB, GRI, and SASB (2020). Reporting on Enterprise Value, *Technical Report.*

Cheema-Fox, A., LaPerla, B. R., Serafeim, G., Turkington, D., and Wang, H. (2019). Decarbonization factors. doi:http://dx.doi.org/10.2139/ssrn.3448637.

Chesney, M., Gheyssens, J., and Taschini, L. (2013). *Environmental Finance and Investments.* (Berlin, Heidelberg: Springer-Verlag). doi:https://doi.org/10.1007/978-3-642-36623-9.

Climate Bonds Initiative (2019). Greening the financial system. *Policy Paper*, https://www.climatebonds.net/resources/reports/greening-financial-system-tilting-playing-field-role-central-banks.

Climate Bonds Initiative (2020). Green bond pricing in the primary market: H2 (Q3–Q4) 2020, *Technical Report.*

Collin-Dufresne, P., Goldstein, R. S., and Spencer, M. J. (2001). The Determinants of Credit Spread Changes, *The Journal of Finance* **56**, 6, 2177–2207.

Croissant, Y. and Millo, G. (2018). *Panel Data Econometrics with r* (Wiley & Sons Ltd.).

Cullenward, D. and Victor, D. G. (2020). *Making Climate Policy Work* (Polity).

Da, Z., Guo, R.-J., and Jagannathan, R. (2012). CAPM for estimating the cost of equity capital: Interpreting the empirical evidence, *Journal of Financial Economics* **103**, 1, 204–220. doi:https://doi.org/10.1016/j.jfineco.2011.08.011.

Dafermos, Y., Nikolaidi, M., and Galanis, G. (2018). Climate change, financial stability and monetary policy, *Ecological Economics* **152**, 219–234. doi:https://doi.org/10.1016/j.ecolecon.2018.05.011.

Daniel, K., Litterman, R. B., and Wagner, G. (2016). Applying asset pricing theory to calibrate the price of climate risk, *NBER Working Paper Series* 22795.

Davino, C., Furno, M., and Vistocco, D. (2014). *Quantile Regression: Theory and Applications* (UK: John Wiley & Sons, Ltd.).

De Angelis, T., Tankov, P., and Zerbib, O. D. (2020). Environmental impact investing. doi:http://dx.doi.org/10.2139/ssrn.3562534.

Deutsche Energie Agentur (2021). Corporate green PPAs: Oekonomische analyse, *Technical Report.*

Dietz, S. (2011). High impact, low probability? An empirical analysis of risk in the economics of climate change, *Climatic Change* **108**, 519–541. doi:https://doi.org/10.1007/s10584-010-9993-4.

Dietz, S., Bowen, A., Dixon, C., and Gradwell, P. (2016). Climate value at risk of global financial assets, *Nature Climate Change* **6**, 676–679.

Dietz, S., Gollier, C., and Kessler, L. (2018). The climate beta, *Journal of Environmental Economics and Management* **87**, 258–274.

Dixon, D., Halperin, I., and Bilokon, P. (2020). *Machine Learning in Finance* (Switzerland: Springer Nature).

Dwork, C. and Roth, A. (2014). The algorithmic foundations of differential privacy, *Foundations and Trends Theoretical Computer Science* **9**, 3–4, 211–407, https://www.cis.upenn.edu/~aaroth/Papers/privacybook.pdf.

Ehlers, T., Mojon, B., and Packer, F. (2020). Green bonds and carbon emissions: Exploring the case for a rating system at the firm level, *BIS Quarterly Review*, September 2020, https://www.bis.org/publ/qtrpdf/r_qt2009c.htm.

Ehlers, T. and Packer, F. (2017). Green bond finance and certification. *BIS Quarterly Review*, September 2017, https://papers.ssrn.com/sol3/papers.cfm?abstract_id=3042378.

Embrechts, P., Klüppelberg, C., and Mikosch, T. (1997). *Modeling Extremal Events for Insurance and Finance*, 1st ed. (Berlin; Heidelberg, Germany: Springer-Verlag).

Endres, A. (2011). *Environmental Economics.* (Cambridge: Cambridge University Press). doi:https://doi.org/10.1017/CBO9780511976650.

Engl, H., Hanke, M. and Neubauer, A. (2000). *Regularization of Inverse Problems* (Dordrecht: Kluwer Academic Publishers).

Engle, R. F., Giglio, S., Kelly, B., Lee, H., and Stroebel, J. (2020). Hedging climate change news, *The Review of Financial Studies* **33**, 1184–1216. doi:https://doi.org/10.1093/rfs/hhz072.

Ericsson, J., Jacobs, K., and Oviedo, R. (2009). The determinants of credit default swap premia, *The Journal of Financial and Quantitative Analysis* **44**, 1, 109–132.

European Commission (2020). Overview of sustainable finance, European commission — Questions and answers.

Faccini, R. and Matin, R. (2021a). Are Climate Change Risks Priced in the U.S. Stock Market? *Danmarks Nationalbank. Analysis No. 3.*

Faccini, R. and Matin, R. (2021b). Are Climate Change Risks Priced in the U.S. Stock Market? *Danmarks Nationalbank. Working Paper No. 169.*

Fama, E. and French, K. (2015). A five-factor asset pricing model, *Journal of Finance Economics* **116**, 1, 1–22.

Fama, E. F. and French, K. R. (1993). Common risk factors in the returns on stocks and bonds, *Journal of Financial Economics* **33**, 1, 3–56. doi:https://doi.org/10.1016/0304-405X(93)90023-5.

Fankhauser, S., Hepburn, C., and Park, J. (2011). Combining multiple climate policy instruments: How not to do it, Centre for Climate Change Economics and Policy, *Working Paper No. 48*; Grantham Research Institute on Climate Change and the Environment, *Working Paper No. 38.*

Fasen, V., Klüppelberg, C., and Menzel, A. (2014). Quantifying extreme risks, in C. Küppelberg, D. Straub, and I. M. Welpe (eds.), *Risk – A Multidisciplinary Introduction* (Switzerland: Springer International Publishing), pp. 151–181.

Fichtner, M. (2018). Carbon risk and cost of equity capital for Germany and Austria. Master thesis. LEF, University of Duisburg-Essen, available on request.

Financial Times (2020). Norway's new oil fund chief seeks more ESG-driven investments, *Financial Times.*

Financial Times (2021). Time to clean up climate reporting standards, *Financial Times.*

Fink, L. (2021). Larry Fink's 2021 letter to CEOs, https://www.blackrock.com.

Fischer, A.-K. (2020). *The Risks of Terrorism, Demographic Change and Climate Change: Analyzing the Dynamics of Public Risk Perception and the Influence of Media Coverage in the USA and Germany from 1990 to 2015*, Ph.D. thesis, University of Duisburg-Essen.

Flammer, C. (2020). Corporate green bonds, *Journal of Financial Economics (JFE), Forthcoming.*

Frankhauser, S. and Hepburn, C. (2009). Carbon markets in space and time, Centre for Climate Change Economics and Policy, *Working Paper No. 4*; Grantham Research Institute on Climate Change and the Environment, *Working Paper No. 3.*

Galil, K., Shapir, O. M., Amiram, D., and Ben-Zion, U. (2014). The determinants of cds spreads, *Journal of Banking & Finance* **41**, 271–282. http://www.sciencedirect.com/science/article/pii/S0378426613004676.

Gates, B. (2021). *How to Avoid a Climate Disaster: The Solutions We Have and the Breakthroughs We Need* (UK: Allen Lane, Penguin Random House).

Goergen, M., Jacob, A., Nerlinger, M., Riordan, R., Rohleder, M., and Wilkens, M. (2020). Carbon risk, *SSRN.*

Gollier, C. (2012). *Pricing the Planet's Future: The Economics of Discounting in an Uncertain World* (USA, UK: Princeton University Press).

Gollier, C. (2020). The cost-efficiency carbon pricing puzzle, TSE Working Paper. 18-952.

Greene, W. H. (2018). *Econometric Analysis*, 8th ed. (New York: Pearson).

Ghussain, A. Al. (2021). The biggest problem with carbon offsetting is that it doesn't really work, *Greenpeace UK.*

Griffin, P. A., Jaffe, A. M., Lont, D. H., and Dominguez-Faus, R. (2015). Science and the stock market: Investors' recognition of unburnable carbon, *Energy Economics* **52**, 1–12.

Gruell, G. and Kiesel, R. (2012). Quantifying the CO_2 permit price sensitivity. *Z Energiewirtschaft* **36**, 101–111.

Gu, S., Kelly, B., and Xiu, D. (2020). Empirical asset pricing via machine learning, *The Review of Financial Studies* **33**, 2223–2273. doi:https://doi.org/10.1093/rfs/hhaa009.

Ha-Duong, M. and Treich, N. (2004). Risk aversion, intergenerational equity and climate change, *Environmental and Resource Economics* **28**, 2, 195–207.

Hambel, C., Kraft, H., and Schwartz, E. (2020). Optimal carbon abatement in a stochastic equilibrium model with climate change, *European Economic Review* **132**, Article 103642.

Haya, B. and Orenstein, K. (2008). Trading in fake carbon credits: Problems with the Clean Development Mechanism. Available at: https://foe.org/blog/2008-10-trading-in-fake-carbon-credits-problems-with-the-cle. Retrieved on April 13, 2021.

Helm, D. (2020). *Net Zero: How We Stop Causing Climate Change* (HarperCollins Publishers Limited).

Hepburn, C. (2009). Carbon taxes, emission trading, and hybrid schemes, in D. Helm and C. Hepburn (eds.), *The Economics and Politics of Climate Change* (Oxford, UK: Oxford University Press), pp. 365–384.

Hook, L. (2020). 2020 ties for hottest year on record, *Financial Times.*

Hull, J. C. (2018). *Risk Management for Financial Institutions*, 5th ed. (John Wiley & Sons, Inc., Wiley Finance).

Huynh, T. D. and Xia, Y. (2020). Climate change news risk and corporate bond returns, *Journal of Financial and Quantitative Analysis* First View, 1–25.

Hwang, I. C., Tol, R. S. J., and Hofkes, M. W. (2016). Fat-tailed risk about climate change and climate policy, *Energy Policy* **89**, 25–35. doi:https://doi.org/10.1016/j.enpol.2015.11.012.

Hyun, S., Park, D., and Tian, S. (2019). Differences between green bonds versus conventional bonds, in J. D. Sachs, W. Woo, N. Yoshino, and F. Taghizadeh-Hesary (eds.), *Handbook of Green Finance* (Singapore: Springer).

Ilhan, E., Sautner, Z., and Vilkov, G. (2020). Carbon Tail Risk, *The Review of Financial Studies.*

In, S. Y., Park, K. Y., Monk, A., *et al.* (2019). Is 'being green' rewarded in the market? An empirical investigation of decarbonization and stock returns. *Stanford Global Project Center Working Paper.*

InfluenceMap (2021). Asset managers and climate change 2021, *Influencemap report.*

International Capital Market Association (2018). Green Bond Principles. Voluntary Process Guidelines for Issuing Green Bonds.

IPBES (2020). Summary for policymakers of the global assessment report on biodiversity and ecosystem services of the intergovernmental science-policy platform on biodiversity and ecosystem services, *Technical Report*, https://www.economist.com/finance-and-economics/2021/02/27/can-chinas-new-carbon-market-take-off.

IPCC (2014). Climate change 2014, *Synthesis report.*, https://www.ipcc.ch/site/assets/uploads/2018/05/SYR_AR5_FINAL_full_wcover.pdf.

IPCC (2019). Global warming of 1.5°c, An IPCC special report on the impacts of global warming of 1.5°c above pre-industrial levels and related global greenhouse gas emission pathways, in the context of strengthening the global response to the threat of climate change, sustainable development, and efforts to eradicate poverty. https://www.ipcc.ch/sr15/.

IPCC (2007). *Fourth Assessment Report: Climate Change 2007.* (Cambridge: Cambridge University Press).

James, G., Witten, D., Hastie, T., and Tibshirani, R. (2017). *An Introduction to Statistical Learning* (New York: Springer).

Jarrow, R. A. (2010). The Economics of Credit Default Swaps (CDS), *SSRN.*

Jung, J., Herbohn, K., and Clarkson, P. (2018). Carbon risk, carbon risk awareness and the cost of debt financing, *Journal of Business Ethics* **150**, 1151–1171. doi:https://doi.org/10.1007/s10551-016-3207-6.

Kapraun, J. and Scheins, C. (2019). (In)-Credibly Green: Which Bonds Trade at a Green Bond Premium? https://papers.ssrn.com/sol3/papers.cfm?abstract_id=3347337, *Proceedings of Paris December 2019 Finance Meeting EUROFIDAI — ESSEC.*

Kiesel, R., Rühlicke, R., Stahl, G., and Zheng, J. (2016). The Wasserstein metric and robustness in risk management, *Risks* **4**, 3. https://www.mdpi.com/2227-9091/4/3/32.

Killick, R., Fearnhead, P., and Eckely, I. (2012). Optimal detection of changepoints with a linear computational cost, *Journal of the American Statistical Association.* **107**, 1590–1598.

Kim, Y.-B., An, H. T., and Kim, J. D. (2015). The effect of carbon risk on the cost of equity capital, *Journal of Cleaner Production* **93**, Supplement C, 279–287.

Kleimeier, S. and Viehs, M. (2018). Carbon disclosure, emission levels, and the cost of debt, *SSRN.*

Klibanoff, P., Marinacci, M., and Mukerji, S. (2005). A smooth model of decision making under ambiguity, *Econometrica* **73**, 6, 1849–1892.

Klibanoff, P., Marinacci, M., and Mukerji, S. (2009). Recursive smooth ambiguity preferences, *Journal of Economic Theory* **144**, 3, 930–976.

Klusak, P., Agarwala, M., M.and Burke, Kraemer, M., and Mohaddes, K. (2021). Rising Temperatures, Falling Ratings: The Effect of Climate Change on Sovereign Creditworthiness, *Bennett Institute working paper.*

Knuth, H. and Fischer, T. (2020). Plant for the Planet: Der Märchenwald, *Die Zeit.*

Koch, N., Grosjean, G., Fuss, S., and Edenhofer, O. (2016). Politics matters: Regulatory events as catalysts for price formation under cap-and-trade, *Journal of Environmental Economics and Management* **78**, 121–139. doi:https://doi.org/10.1016/j.jeem.2016.03.004, http://www.sciencedirect.com/science/article/pii/S0095069616300031.

Kollenberg, S. and Taschini, L. (2019). Dynamic supply adjustment and banking under uncertainty in an emission trading scheme: The market stability reserve, *European Economic Review,* **118**, 213–226. doi:https://doi.org/10.1016/j.euroecorev.2019.05.013.

Koutmos, D. (2019). Asset Pricing Factors and Bank CDS Spreads, *Journal of International Financial Markets, Institutions and Money* **58**, 19–41.

Kunreuther, H., Gupta, S., Bosetti, V., Cooke, R., Dutt, V., Ha-Duong, M., Held, H., Llanes-Regueiro, J., Patt, A., Shittu, E., *et al.* (2014). *Integrated Risk and Uncertainty Assessment of Climate Change Response Policies* (Cambridge: Cambridge University Press).

Kunreuther, H., Heal, G., Allen, M., Edenhofer, O., Field, C. B., and Yohe, G. (2012). Risk management and climate change. *Nature Climate Change.* **3**, 447–450. doi:https://doi.org/10.1038/nclimate1740.

Lemoine, D. (2020). The climate risk premium: How uncertainty affects the social cost of carbon. *University of Arizona Department of Economics Working Paper 15-01.* doi:http://dx.doi.org/10.2139/ssrn.2560031.

Lewellen, J. (2015). The Cross-section of expected stock returns. *Critical Finance Review* **4**, 1–44.

Maltais, A. and Nykvist, B. (2020). Understanding the role of green bonds in advancing sustainability, *Journal of Sustainable Finance & Investment.* doi:https://doi.org/10.1080/20430795.2020.1724864.

Mann, M. E. (2021). *The New Climate War: The Fight to Take Back Our Planet* (New York: PublicAffairs).

Margrabe, W. (1978). The value of an option to exchange one asset for another, *The Journal of Finance* **33**, 1, 177–186.

Matikainen, S., Campiglio, E., and Zenghelis, D. (2017). The climate impact of quantitative easing, *Policy Paper.*

McGlade, C. and Ekins, P. (2015). The geographical distribution of fossil fuels unused when limiting global warming to 2 degree Celsius, *Nature* **517**, 187–190.

Meinshausen, M., Meinshausen, N., Hare, W., Raper, S., and Frieler, K. (2009). Greenhouse-gas emission targets for limiting global warming to 2 degree Celcius, *Nature* 458, 1158–1163.

Merton, R. C. (1974). On the pricing of corporate debt: The risk structure of interest rates, *The Journal of Finance* **29**, 2. http://dx.doi.org/10.1111/j.1540-6261.1974.tb03058.x.

Meyer, G. (2021). Arctic blast triggers power squeeze in energy-rich texas, *Financial Times.*

Millner, A. (2013). On welfare frameworks and catastrophic climate risks, *Journal of Environmental Economics and Management* **65**, 2, 310–325.

Millner, A., Dietz, S., and Heal, G. (2013). Scientific ambiguity and climate policy, *Environmental and Resource Economics* **55**, 21–46.

Munk, C. (2013). *Financial Asset pricing Theory* (Oxford, UK: Oxford University Press).

Network for Greening the Financial System (2019). Annual report 2019.

New York Times (2012). Behind the Libor scandal, *New York Times.*

Nield, K. and Pereira, R. (2011). Fraud on the European Union emissions trading scheme: Effects, vulnerabilities and regulatory reform, *European Energy and Environmental Law Review* **20**, 255–289.

Nordhaus, W. (2008). *A Question of Balance: Economic Modeling of Global Warming* (New Haven: Yale University Press).

Nordhaus, W. D. (2007). A review of the Stern review on the economics of climate change, *Journal of Economic Literature* **45**, 3, 686–702.

Nordhaus, W. D. (2017). Revisiting the social cost of carbon, *Proceedings of the National Academy of Sciences (PNAS)* **114**, 1518–1523.

Oestreich, M. and Tsiakas, I. (2015). Carbon emissions and stock returns: Evidence from the EU Emissions Trading Scheme. *Journal of Banking Finance* **58**, 294–308.

Oliver, J. (2021). Italy raises 8.5 bn EUR in Europe's biggest-ever green bond debut, *Financial Times.*

Painter, M. (2020). An inconvenient cost: The effect of climate change on municipal bonds, *Journal of Financial Economics* **135**, 468–482.

Park, D. J. (2018). United States news media and climate change in the era of US President Trump, *Integrated Environmental Assessment and Management (IEAM)* **14**, 161–309. First published: 29 November 2017.

Pastor, L., Stambaugh, R. F., and Taylor, L. A. (2020). Sustainable investing in equilibrium, *Journal of Financial Economics, Forthcoming.*

Perino, G., Pahle, M., Pause, F., Quemin, S., Scheuing, H., and Willner, M. (2021). EU ETS stability mechanism needs new design. Policy Brief. *University of Hamburg. Center for Earth System Research and Sustainability (CEN).* https://www.cen.uni-hamburg.de/en/research/policy-briefs/eu-ets-perino-page.html.

Pesaran, M. H. (2007). A simple panel unit root test in the presence of cross-section dependence, *Journal of Applied Econometrics* **22**, 2, 265–312.

Philipp, K., Sautner, Z., and Starks, L. T. (2019). The Importance of Climate Risks for Institutional Investors, *Swiss Finance Institute Research Paper Series No. 18-58. European Corporate Governance Institute (ECGI) — Finance Working Paper No. 610/2019.* http://dx.doi.org/10.2139/ssrn.3235190.

Pillutla, K., Kakade, S., and Harchaoui, Z. (2019). Robust aggregation for federated learning. *arXiv.* https://arxiv.org/pdf/1912.13445.pdf.

Pindyck, R. (2012). Uncertain outcomes and climate change policy, *Journal of Environmental Economics and Management* **63**, 289–303.

Pires, P., Pereira, J. A. P., and Martins, L. F. (2015). The empirical determinants of credit default swap spreads: A quantile regression approach, *European Financial Management* **21**, 3, 556–589.

Press, W., Teukolsky, S., Vetterling, W., and Flannery, B. (1992). *Numerical Recipes in c* (Cambridge, New York, Melbourne: Cambridge University Press).

Quiggin, J. (2017). The importance of 'extremely unlikely' events: Tail risk and the cost of climate change, *Australian Journal of Agricultural and Resource Economics* **62**, 4–20.

Rachev, S. T. (1991). *Probability metrics and the stability of Stochastic models* (New York: John Wiley & Sons Ltd.).

RealClimate (2015). What's going on in the north Atlantic? http://www.realclimate.org/index.php/archives/2015/03/whats-going-on-in-the-north-atlantic/.

Riahi, K., van Vuuren, D. P., Kriegler, E. *et al.* (2017). The shared socioeconomic pathways and their energy, land use, and greenhouse gas emissions implications: An overview, *Global Environmental Change* **42**, 153–168.

Santis, R. A. D., Geis, A., Juskaite, A., and Cruz, L. V. (2018). The impact of the corporate sector purchase programme on corporate bond markets and the financing of euro area non-financial corporations, *ECB Economic Bulletin* **3**. https://www.ecb.europa.eu/pub/pdf/other/ecb.ebart201803_02.en.pdf.

Schoenmaker, D. (2019). Greening monetary policy. *Bruegel Working Paper* **2**. https://www.bruegel.org/2019/02/greening-monetary-policy/.

Schulten, A., Bertolotti, A., Hayes, P., and Madaan, A. (2019). Getting physical: Scenario analysis for assessing climate-related risks. *BlackRock Investment Institute. Global Insights.* https://www.blackrock.com/ch/individual/en/insights/physical-climate-risks.

Seifert, J., Uhrig-Homburg, M., and Wagner, M. (2008). Dynamic behavior of CO_2 spot prices, *Journal of Environmental Economics and Management* **56**, 180–194.

Seltzer, L., Starks, L., and Zhu, Q. (2020). Climate regulatory risks and bond returns, *SSRN*.

Semieniuk, G., Campiglio, E., Mercure, J., Volz, U., and Edwards, N. R. (2020). Low-carbon transition risks for finance, *WIREs Climate Change*. doi:https://doi.org/10.1002/wcc.678.

Smith, L. A. and Stern, N. (2011). Uncertainty in science and its role in climate policy, *Philosophical Transactions of the Royal Society of London A: Mathematical, Physical and Engineering Sciences* **369**, 1956, 4818–4841.

Spedding, P., Mehta, K., and Robins, N. (2013). Oil & carbon revisited: Value at risk from unburnable reserves, HSBC Bank plc. https://www.longfinance.net/media/documents/hsbc_oilcarbon_2013.pdf.

Steffen, W., Rockström, J., Richardson, K. *et al.* (2018). Trajectories of the Earth System in the Anthropocene, *Proceedings of the National Academy of Sciences (PNAS)* **115**, 8252–8259. https://doi.org/10.1073/pnas.1810141115.

Stern, N. (2007a). *The Economics of Climate Change: The Stern Review.* (Cambridge: Cambridge University Press). doi:http://dx.doi.org/10.1017/CBO9780511817434

Stern, N. (2010). The economics of climate change, in S. M. Gardiner, S. Caney, D. Jamieson, and H. Shue (eds.), *Climate Ethics* (New York: Oxford University Press), pp. 39–76.

Stern, N. H. (2007b). *The Economics of Climate Change: The Stern Review* (Cambridge University press).

Taleb, N. (2008). *The Black Swan: The Impact of the Highly Improbable* (Penguin Books).

Tantet, A. and Tankov, P. (2019). Climate data for physical risk assessment in finance. doi:http://dx.doi.org/10.2139/ssrn.3480156.

Taskforce on Scaling Voluntary Carbon Markets (2021). Final report. https://www.iif.com/tsvcm.

TCFD (2020a). Task Force on Climate-related Financial Disclosures. Guidance on risk management integration and disclosure.

TCFD (2020b). Task Force on Climate-related Financial Disclosures. 2020 status report.

TCFD (2020c). Task Force on Climate-related Financial Disclosures. Forward-looking financial sector metrics. Consultation.

Technical Expert Group on Sustainable Finance (2020). Taxonomy: Final report of the Technical Expert Group on Sustainable Finance. *Teg Technical Report*, https://knowledge4policy.ec.europa.eu/publication/sustainable-finance-teg-final-report-eu-taxonomy_en.

The Economist (2021a). Telling all, *The Economist*.

The Economist (2021b). Cleaning up: Can china's new carbon market take off? *Technical Report*, https://www.economist.com/finance-and-economics/2021/02/27/can-chinas-new-carbon-market-take-off.

The Institutional Investors Group on Climate Change (IIGCC) (2020). Paris aligned investment initiative: Net zero investment framework for consultation. https://www.iigcc.org/resource/net-zero-investment-framework-for-consultation/.

The World Bank (2020). Blockchain and emerging digital technologies for enhancing post-2020 climate markets, *Technical Report.*

Tian, Y., Akimov, A., Roca, E., and Wong, V. (2016). Does the carbon market help or hurt the stock price of electricity companies? Further evidence from the European context, *Journal of Cleaner Production* **112**, 1619–1626.

Tol, R. S. J. (2019). *Climate Economics: Economic Analysis of Climate, Climate Change and Climate Policy*, 2nd ed. (UK, USA: Edward Elgar Publishing).

Traeger, C. P. (2014). Why uncertainty matters: Discounting under intertemporal risk aversion and ambiguity, *Economic Theory* **56**, 3, 627–664.

Trinks, A. *et al.* (2020). Carbon intensity and the cost of equity capital. *SSRN*. https://papers.ssrn.com/sol3/papers.cfm?abstract_id=3035864.

United in Science (2020). Global climate, *Technical Report.*

Van Vuuren, D. P. *et al.* (2011). The representative concentration pathways: An overview, *Climatic Change* **109**, 1–2, 5.

Vermeulen, R. (2019). The heat is on: A framework measuring financial stress under disruptive energy transition scenarios, *DNB Working Paper, No. 625.*

Volz, U., Beirneand, J., Preudhommeand, N. A., Fentonand, A., Mazzacurati, E., Renzhi, N., and Stampe, J. (2020). Climate Change and Sovereign Risk. *Technical Report.*

von Avenarius, A. (2019). Carbon finance — Evidence of successful carbon credit projects and carbon risk in credit risk, *Technical Report*, University of Duisburg-Essen.

Weitzman, M. (1974). Prices vs. Quantities, *The Review of Economic Studies* **41**, 4, 477–491.

Weitzman, M. (2009). On modeling and interpreting the economics of catastrophic climate change, *Review of Economics and Statistics* **91**, 1–19.

Weitzman, M. (2011). Fat-tailed uncertainty in the economics of catastrophic climate change, *Review of Environmental Economics and Policy* **5**, 2, 275–292. doi:https://doi.org/10.1093/reep/rer006.

Weitzman, M. (2014). Fat tails and the social cost of carbon, *American Economic Review* **104**, 544–546.

Wen, Y. and Kiesel, R. (2016). Pricing options on EU ETS certificates with a time-varying market price of risk model, in F. E. Benth and G. Di Nunno (eds.), *Stochastics of Environmental and Financial Economics* (Switzerland: Springer International Publishing), pp. 341–360.

Wesslen, R. (2018). Computer-assisted text analysis for social science: Topic models and beyond, *CoRR*, arXiv:1803.11045.

Wooldridge, J. M. (2010). *Econometric Analysis of Cross Section and Panel Data* (MIT Press Books, The MIT Press).

World Resources Institute and World Business Council for Sustainable Development (2004). *The Greenhouse Gas Protocol.*, Washington, D.C.

World Economic Forum (2021). The global risks report 2021, *Technical Report.*

Yang, Q., Liu, Y., Cheng, Y., Kang, Y., Chen, T., and Yu, H. (2020). *Federated Learning*, (USA: Morgan & Claypool Publishers).

Ying, W., Xin, Z., Haiyan, L., Minsi, Z., and We, T. (2018). Risk identification and management of carbon finance. *Environmental Defense Fund & National Center for Climate Change Strategy and International Cooperation.*

Yu, K., Lu, Z., and Stander, J. (2003). Quantile regression: Applications and current research areas, *Journal of the Royal Statistical Society: Series D* **52**, 3, 331–350.

Zerbib, O. D. (2018). Is There a Green Bond Premium? The yield differential between green and conventional bonds. https://papers.ssrn.com/sol3/papers.cfm?abstract_id=2889690. In *Journal of Banking and Finance* **98**, 39–60, 2019, as 'The effect of pro-environmental preferences on bond prices: Evidence from green bonds.'

Index

V

W